The Giant Book of Natural Healing Recipes

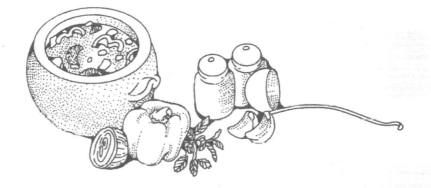

A Wellness Program
for Optimal Health
Bessie Jo Tillman, M.D.

Foreword by
L. Terry Chappell, M.D.
Past President, American College for Advancement in Medicine

Sterling Publishing Co., Inc.
New York

To my staff, patients, friends, and loved ones who through knowledge, motivation, and inspiration have become responsible for their own well-being.

Library of Congress Cataloging-in-Publication Data Available

1 3 5 7 9 10 8 6 4 2

Published by Sterling Publishing Company, Inc.
387 Park Avenue South, New York, N.Y. 10016
© 2000 by Bessie Jo Tillman
Portions of this work were previously published as
The Natural Healing Cookbook by Rudra Press
Distributed in Canada by Sterling Publishing
c/o Canadian Manda Group, One Atlantic Avenue, Suite 105
Toronto, Ontario, Canada M6K 3E7
Distributed in Great Britain and Europe by Cassell PLC
Wellington House, 125 Strand, London WC2R 0BB, England
Distributed in Australia by Capricorn Link (Australia) Pty Ltd.
P.O. Box 6651, Baulkham Hills, Business Centre, NSW 2153, Australia

Manufactured in the United States of America
All rights reserved

Sterling ISBN 0-8069-2955-3

Contents

CHARTS, WORKSHEETS, AND TABLES

Foreword

Most of our chronic illness is related to the food we put into our bodies. The majority of cancers grow more readily with poor nutrition. Heart disease and strokes can be caused by diets high in oxidized fats and other nutritional factors. Arthritis and digestive problems are often aggravated by food allergies and food sensitivities.

The ability of our immune systems to resist infections and maintain a healthy balance of yeast, normal bacteria, and other organisms can be severely hampered by high intakes of sugar, additives, and other anti-nutrients.

How we feel physically and mentally, how we look to others and relate to them, how we feel about ourselves can all depend a great deal upon what we eat. By offering our bodies excellent nutrition, we can usually prolong our lives and, more importantly, dramatically improve the quality of our lives during our visit on Planet Earth.

If we know all this and it makes sense, why then do most of us eat so poorly? Why is it so hard to change and embrace a genuinely healthy nutritional program for ourselves? Why do we place ourselves at risk when we know better?

One reason is that our upbringing and our fast-paced, high-pressured society linked so closely to the advertising industry have taught us the quick rewards of sweets and fast food. Another is that we are prisoners of our habits—the good ones as well as the bad. It is difficult to change them.

If we are enslaved by our habits regardless, then we would be much better off choosing good habits rather than detrimental ones. To accomplish this, we need a comprehensive guide that makes the process easy and answers all the excuses, tricks, and pleas that our minds and bodies throw at us when we try to change.

In this precious cookbook, Dr. Bessie Jo Tillman provides us with all we need. She makes our task simple by giving us a straightforward, step-by-step blueprint to follow.

All of the hard questions and obstacles are answered. Things like: How can we cook delicious, satisfying meals with the foods that are really good for us? What do we eat for breakfast? How can we pack meals to eat on the run when we have to? How do we identify and deal with food allergies? What can we do about those awful food cravings? What if I get constipated? And much more ...

Dr. Jo's *The New Natural Healing Cookbook* is an ideal companion for beginners to nutritional thinking as well as for seasoned veterans who have been trying to get well for a long time. Read it and use it over and over again. You will be very happy that you did.

—L. TERRY CHAPPELL, M.D.
Past President, American College for Advancement in Medicine

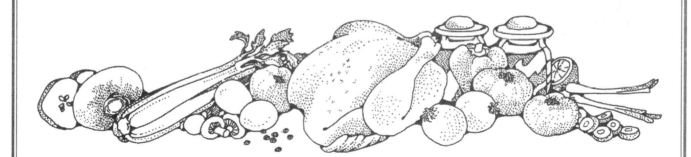

Acknowledgments

Without the cooperation and contributions of many people, this cookbook would have never developed. Big, heartfelt thank-yous to all of you cannot fully express my gratitude for your unselfish sharing for the benefit of others.

Thanks to my staff:

Mary Ball, whose love and bright smile inspires and encourages everyone, and whose "Summer Soup" at cooking classes teaches patients how enjoyable and delicious healthy eating can be.

Cheryl Crabtree, whose keen insight and caring for others led her to develop the first cooking classes.

Joan Tully, who loved us enough to expand our thinking and taught the first "Wellness in Action" groups where we cooked, ate, shared, supported, and set goals together.

Marilyn Carlson, who with a twinkle in her eye and efficiency of effort showered her love on patients and staff—and inspired us to exercise.

Carol Gagnow, whose loving family teaches us how to feed active, healthy children.

Donna Welty, who shows her love by keeping the rest of us organized.

Thanks to my patients

You have taught me, challenged me to learn more, and shared many of your wonderful recipes with us for this book.

Introduction

The New Natural Healing Cookbook is designed to spark your individual creativity in combining nutritious and colorful foods that serve the body well. The goal is optimal health. Therefore, we only use nourishing, beneficial foods that include animal protein, all vegetables including legumes, and whole grains like rice, millet, amaranth, quinoa, teff, and wild rice.

The concepts in this cookbook are based on the research of Weston A. Price, D.D.S.; Francis M. Pottenger, Jr., M.D.; Melvin Page, D.D.S.; and Robert Bruce Pacetti, D.D.S. Tapping into some natural laws of the body, Dr. Page discovered that certain foods serve the body well while others upset body chemistry and lead to the process of disease. Eating only foods that serve the body well allows body chemistry to stabilize. This enables the body to heal itself. This is repeatedly proven by my patients. Those who catch the vision and change their eating habits experience remarkable improvements in their health and sense of well-being. In other words, their new lifestyle eating plan serves their bodies well.

But, first, let me explain how I became interested in nutrition. After graduating from the University of California Medical School, San Francisco, I was an emergency room staff physician for seven and a half years. For two more years I was on the staff of a walk-in medical care facility. After treating severely ill patients for this long, I decided that what I really wanted to do was to stop "putting out fires' and learn how to develop "fire lines" to prevent debilitating disease processes.

To me, preventing medical problems was more logical than treating the symptoms of severe pathology. It also seemed more economical and certainly would prevent a lot of suffering. Seeing a patient for ten or fifteen minutes allows a doctor only enough time to deal with medical problems superficially. The cause of the problem is seldom attacked. I believed that if doctors spent more time with individual patients, they could get to the root cause of their illnesses and help lead them back into optimal health.

Even though my premises seemed right, I lacked the knowledge to implement them. In my quest to learn more about disease prevention and natural healing, I initially studied physical exercise, including some information on nutrition—and was amazed at how much people could do for themselves in the healing process!

Having gotten a taste of the healing power of nutrition, I was sucked into a life-long learning program. At first, absorbing nutritional knowledge was overwhelming and often confusing until I learned the natural laws of balancing body chemistry. Once balanced, the body can heal itself. Nutrition plays a big part in allowing this to happen and the active nutritional concepts are really very simple. However, putting them into practice is not easy because old habits must be broken.

Helping people break old habits involves teaching them about things that serve the body well, evaluating their present state of health, and giving them support in making lifestyle changes. In fact, I tell my patients that my job is to evaluate, educate, and encourage. Whatever results they achieve in getting healthy occur because they are willing to give up "victim consciousness" and become personally responsible for their own health.

While I enjoyed my stint as an emergency room physician and a clinic physician, I am more fulfilled working closely with patients motivated to implement the healing process in their own lives. Watching chronically ill patients who have never been helped by other healing methods achieve their own optimal level of health and well-being is very rewarding. I know that my study of natural healing approaches will continue for the rest of my life.

I wrote *The New Natural Healing Cookbook* to share my experience of the healing aspects of food and an approach that is accurately called the "Get Healthy Eating Plan."

So let's get started!

The Get Healthy Eating Plan

SEEING FOOD IN A NEW WAY

GETTING ORGANIZED

PUTTING THE MEAL TOGETHER

LEARNING TO READ YOUR BODY

INFORMATION ON CERTAIN FOODS

COOKING TIPS

The Get Healthy Eating Plan

The "Get Healthy Eating Plan" can help you get healthy or help you stay that way. The eight-week program allows (1) your body chemistry to balance itself and (2) the gastrointestinal tract and immune system to heal. Its effectiveness lies in the many aspects of the healing process addressed. As a lifelong basis for your meal planning, it is extremely important for the following reasons:

FIRST, it eliminates upsetting foods. This results in a balanced body chemistry that allows your body to heal itself.

SECOND, it eliminates common food sensitizers that disturb body chemistry.

THIRD, it provides all the nutrients you need at each meal. As a result, you will feel more satisfied and not be tempted to snack.

FOURTH, it allows the blood sugar to stabilize. Without the stress of radical highs and lows in blood sugar levels, the pancreas, liver, and adrenal glands can regenerate.

FIFTH, it helps heal the protective layers of the gastrointestinal tract and restores balance in the normal intestinal bacteria.

SIXTH, it feeds the body without stimulating the overgrowth of candida, a yeast that occurs commonly in the gastrointestinal tract,

SEVENTH, the "Get Healthy Eating Plan" is nutritious and colorful with infinite variety. It is adaptable to each person's taste, likes and dislikes, and preference for being a vegetarian or a meat eater.

I want to emphasize that *The New Natural Healing Cookbook* is designed to help people attain optimal good health and become vitally alive. It particularly helps those who are ill regain their health. The appetizing and nutritious recipes are not boring. They are good food and good food combinations developed over the years from cooking classes designed with the individual and the family in mind. Many participants have shared their favorite foods and menus with my staff, adding to the variety.

Since meats, seafood, vegetables, rice, millet, amaranth, teff, wild rice, and quinoa serve the body best, these are the only foods used. However, after eating for eight weeks according to the "Get Healthy

Eating Plan," most people improve sufficiently to add back other foods such as whole fruits, whole grains, nuts, and seeds. Some people find that, to further their healing process, they need to adhere to the plan for longer than eight weeks. Still others maintain it for the rest of their lives simply because they know that they are receiving adequate nourishment and it makes them feel good.

I recommend that the "Get Healthy Eating Plan" be used in conjunction with evaluation and guidance by a professional, nutrition-oriented health practitioner who can answer questions, give support, and provide appropriate treatments in the healing process. Healthy people as well benefit enormously from using *The New Natural Healing Cookbook*. After all, we don't have to be sick to want to feel better.

The following "Food Classification Chart" identifies the foods that I use in my practice; namely, foods that serve the body best, foods that are less beneficial, and items to eliminate altogether from your diet:

CLASS A FOODS serve the body best. Generally well tolerated by people who are ill, they are the only foods used in the "Get Healthy Eating Plan."

CLASS B FOODS are a little more difficult for the body to assimilate and can be reintroduced after following the plan for eight weeks or longer.

CLASS C FOODS are more difficult for the body to handle. They should not be added to the eating plan until Class B foods have proved acceptable to the body. As a rule, I advise against adding milk and milk products to the eating plan. However, some people tolerate cultured dairy products if eaten sparingly and between meals. Always avoid coffee (regular and decaffeinated) and black tea.

CLASS D ITEMS upset the body and should be avoided.

CLASS E ITEMS are chemicals that upset body chemistry and should never be ingested. This list includes tobacco.

See the chart on the next two pages.

FOOD CLASSIFICATION CHART

Class A Foods

Green Leafy Vegetables

artichokes
brussels sprouts
cabbage
chives
collard greens
endive
iceberg lettuce
mustard greens
parsley
romaine lettuce
spinach
Swiss chard
watercress

Green Vegetables

asparagus
broccoli
celery
green bell peppers
leeks
okra
scallions
sprouts, alfalfa
sprouts, mung bean

Yellow or White Vegetables

avocado
cauliflower
corn
cucumber
squash, acorn
squash, yellow
squash, zucchini
yellow wax beans

Red, Orange & Purple Vegetables

beets
carrots
eggplant
pumpkin
sweet potatoes
tomatoes

Root Vegetables

kohlrabi
onions
parsnips
potato, white
radishes
rutabaga
turnips (bottom)

Red Meats & Poultry

beef
chicken
duck
egg white
egg yolk
gelatin—unflavored
lamb
liver, calves'
turkey
veal

Bony Fish, Crustaceans, & Mollusks

anchovy
clam
cod
crab
flounder
grouper
halibut
herring
lobster
mackerel
mullet
mussels
oyster
perch
pompano
red snapper
salmon
sardine
scallops
sea bass
shrimp
sole
swordfish
trout
tuna

Legumes, Dries Beans, & Grains

beans:
adzuki
black beans
black-eyed peas
garbanzo
green peas
kidney
lentils
lima
navy
pinto
string
grains:
amaranth
brown rice
millet
quinoa
teff
wild rice

Fresh Herbs & Spices

basil
bay leaf
caraway
cayenne
chili pepper
dill
dulse /sea lettuce
fennel
garlic
kelp
marjoram
mustard seed
nutmeg
oregano
paprika
pepper, black & white
sage
thyme

Condiments

butter, raw & unsalted
lemon
lime
olive oil
poppyseed
expeller-pressed oils:
flax oil
safflower oil
sesame oil
sunflower oil

Class B Foods

Beans
soy
tofu

Fruits
apple
apricot
banana
blackberry
cantaloupe
cherry
coconut
cranberry
date
fig
grape, raisin
honeydew
nectarine
papaya
peach
pear
pineapple
plum (prune)
strawberry
watermelon

Nuts/Seeds
almond
Brazil nut
filbert
pecan
pistachio
sunflower
walnut

Grains
barley
buckwheat
oats
rye
wheat

Class C Foods

Fruits
grapefruit
mango
orange
tangerine

Dairy
buttermilk
cheese
cottage cheese
cream cheese
milk, cow's & goat's
yogurt

Herbs & Condiments
cinnamon
clove
cottonseed oil
curry
honey
peppermint
vanilla

Miscellaneous
carob
cashew
coffee, decaf & regular
corn gluten
cornstarch
fructose
hops
molasses
white flour
peanut
tea, black

Yeasts
baker's yeast
brewer's yeast
mushroom

Class D Items

Sweeteners & Confections
aspartame
barley malt
cocoa/chocolate
beet sugar
cane sugar
corn sugar
date sugar
maple sugar
saccharin
turbinado sugar

Class E Items

Chemicals & Additives
acetaminophen
alcohol
aspirin
baking powder
BHT/BHA
caffeine
food coloring
formaldehydes
MSG
petroleum by-products
sodium benzoate

SEEING FOOD IN A NEW WAY

Some people prefer to work into the "Get Healthy Eating Plan" gradually. This can be done by eating a "Get Healthy" meal for lunch and dinner for three consecutive days while having your usual breakfast. On the fourth day, try a "Get Healthy" breakfast, which should be very similar to lunch and dinner.

Another way to adjust to the new food plan is to continue eating fruit for the first few weeks—until you have weaned yourself from the desire for refined sugar. Fruit helps satisfy the craving developed for sweets and does not upset body chemistry like refined sugar. Eat whole fruit (not juice) between meals—one hour before or two hours after a meal. This way it will not interfere with the digestion of other foods.

As soon as you can, eliminate fruit from your diet for at least eight weeks. This will allow your blood sugar and metabolism to stabilize. This is important for the following reasons:

◆ If you have candida, fruit will continue to feed it.

◆ If you have highs and lows in blood sugar levels, fruit will stimulate the pancreas to over-secrete insulin, keeping blood sugar swings active.

More than one patient has said that the best side effect of this natural healing program is weight loss. This is because once body chemistry is balanced and appropriate eating habits are learned, body weight will normalize.

Look at the "Create Your Own Worksheet" on pages 19–20, and make plenty of copies to use for your personalized eating plans. Study the seven different food categories. Interestingly, foods that are similar in color have varying amounts of the same nutrients. Choosing one food for each meal from each category will provide all the necessary nutrients your body needs. It is not essential to have all seven foods at each meal. If you feel overwhelmed at first, eat three or four of the foods in one meal and pick up the other three or four at another meal during the day. In fact, some people enjoy better digestion by not eating such a variety of foods at each sitting.

This is a new way to think about eating. And you will discover that it is fun to learn how to combine foods creatively. For example, look at the "Eating Plan Ideas" on page 21. We have made one choice from each of the seven food categories—chicken (or black beans), brown rice, spinach, snow peas, carrots, onions, and jicama. Then we describe seven ways to prepare seven different appetizing meals using condiments and recipes from our recipe section.

It is amazing to see the variety that comes from just seven foods. Think of the possibilities with all the foods on the list! Using the law of probabilities to calculate the potential number of food combinations from the "Get Healthy Eating Plan," one could enjoy 1,876,297,500 different food combinations.

Some Basic Principles

I have highlighted some basic principles to follow as you begin to think about preparing and eating your meals.

1. *Eat a variety of foods.* This will prevent you from developing food sensitivities. Avoid eating the same foods every day. Rotate them every other day. For instance, have carrots for your root vegetable on Monday, choose jicama on Tuesday, and on Wednesday eat carrots again or pick another root vegetable for more variety.

2. *Do not use the same vegetable for more than one category in the same meal.* Some vegetables are listed in two categories. For example, carrots are a root vegetable and also a red vegetable. If carrots are chosen as the red vegetable for the day, pick another vegetable from the root category.

3. *Eat small amounts of a variety of foods.* Foods digest better if a variety is eaten in small amounts. This method also helps prevent food sensitivities. Start with 2 tablespoons of one food from each of the seven

categories for each meal. You now have 14 tablespoons of food for that particular meal. See if that amount satisfies your appetite.

Wait at least two hours before eating again. If you are hungry, eat another meal exactly the same size. Generally, the sicker the person, the smaller their meals should be—and meals can be eaten as frequently as every two hours.

If you are relatively healthy, working, and active, it may be impractical to eat every two hours. Instead you will need to adjust the amount of each food to satisfy your body for those four or five hours between meals. Most healthy people find that ¼ cup to ⅓ cup of the chosen food from each of the seven lists will satisfy them if they eat three meals a day. The idea is to listen to your body and eat only what is needed to satisfy your appetite. Overeating is destructive to the gastrointestinal tract and overwhelms the immune system with toxins.

4. *When increasing the amount of each food, leave the protein serving the same.* For relatively healthy people, the amount of protein served for each meal should be about the size of an egg or ¼ cup. If you are very active and need more calories in a meal, increase the portions of the other six categories rather than the size of the protein serving.

5. *Vegetarians should eat beans and grains together.* In order for vegetarians to have a complete protein at each meal, they should eat a bean and a grain together. The amino acids in beans and grains complement one another and make a complete protein. Quinoa is a complete protein by itself.

6. *Drink purified or distilled water.* While you should drink at least eight 8-ounce glasses of water between meals every day, it is better to drink nothing with meals. This is because beverages may dilute digestive enzymes, slowing down digestion and allowing food to putrefy in the gut. However, you may find that you digest better when ingesting fluids with meals. Experiment to determine what is best for your digestion. If you need to drink something with your meals, drink only small amounts of purified or distilled water.

7. *Chew your food thoroughly.* The sicker you are, the more you need to chew. The busier you are, the more you need to concentrate on actually counting the number of times you chew. Start by chewing each mouthful 28 times. Consciously practice counting the times you chew until it becomes a habit. Chew until the food is pulverized to the consistency of fine particles and mixed well with saliva. If chewing 28 times per mouthful fails to pulverize your food enough, then chew some more! Besides the obvious benefits of preparing the food for your gastrointestinal tract, thorough chewing helps you relax. You enjoy your food more and help keep your intestines from overworking.

8. *Eat only in a peaceful, relaxing environment.* Eliminate discussing business or family matters, reading, watching television, or anything that disturbs the meal's atmosphere. This includes music—unless it is a kind agreeable to every member of the family.

9. *Enjoy your food. Enjoy the texture, feel, taste, and color of every mouthful.* Be thankful for every bite.

10. *Only eat foods from the "Get Healthy Eating Plan."* You may add other vegetables, animal proteins, or legumes (except peanuts), However, do not add any other grains or food categories.

Go ahead, fix a meal. Have fun! It is easier to do than to read about. Make salads or soups. Steam, stir-cook, or sauté your food in a colorful, eye-appealing, body- and soul-satisfying way.

CREATE YOUR OWN WORKSHEET

1	2	3	4
Complete Protein	**Legume & Grain Combo**	**Root Vegetables**	**Yellow or White Vegetables**
beef	beans: adzuki	beets	acorn squash
chicken	black-eyed peas	carrots	avocado
clams	garbanzo	Jerusalem artichokes	banana squash
bean & grain	green peas	jicama	cauliflower
combination	kidney	kohlrabi	crookneck squash
crab	lentils	onions	cucumbers
duck	lima	parsnips	fresh corn
eggs	navy	potatoes	hubbard squash
fish	pinto	rutabagas	jicama
lamb	snap peas	sweet potatoes	onions
lobster	snow peas	turnips	parsnips
oysters	string beans	yams	radishes
shrimp	grains: amaranth		rutabagas
snails	brown rice		spaghetti squash
turkey	millet		turnips
	quinoa		
	teff		
	wild rice		

CREATE YOUR OWN LIST

CREATE YOUR OWN WORKSHEET

5	6	7	Extras
Green Vegetables	**Red, Orange, & Purple Vegetables**	**Green Leafy Vegetables**	**Condiments** (use only as directed)
artichokes	beets	alfalfa sprouts	
asparagus	butternut squash	beet tops	
broccoflower	carrots	bok choy	
celery	eggplant	brussels sprouts	
endive	pumpkin	cabbage	
green bell peppers	purple cabbage	Chinese cabbage	
leeks	red bell peppers	collard greens	
okra	sweet potatoes	endive	
scallions	tomatoes	kale	
snap peas	yams	lettuce:	
snow peas		Bibb, leafy, romaine	
sprouts		mung bean sprouts	
string beans		mustard greens	
zucchini		parsley	
		spinach	
		Swiss chard	
		turnip greens	
		watercress	

CREATE YOUR OWN LIST

EATING PLAN IDEAS

Food List: Chicken, brown rice, spinach, snow peas, carrots, onion, and jicama. Vegetarians substitute black beans for chicken.

1. Thinly slice vegetables and chicken, steam 8 minutes. Add spinach last and steam until just wilted. Serve over brown rice.

2. Stir-cook sliced onion, add chicken and cook until almost done. At the end add jicama, snow peas, spinach, and grated carrots. Cook until heated through. Serve over brown rice with "Oriental Dressing" (page 80).

3. Marinate chicken breasts and broil them separately (vegetarians use "Marinated Black Beans," page 63). Make a salad of spinach, snow peas, julienned carrots, jicama, and onion. Sprinkle salad with tarragon, then drizzle safflower oil and lemon juice (optional) over salad and toss. Serve with hot buttered brown rice.

4. Stir-cook chicken, brown rice, spinach, and onion. Serve with a vegetable plate of raw carrots, jicama, and snow peas.

5. Soup: Simmer chicken and onion in water until chicken is tender. Add rounds of carrots. Simmer 10 minutes. Add snow peas, chunks of jicama, tiny bits of spinach, and cooked rice. Cook until heated through.

6. Make a salad of cold cooked chicken with steamed or sautéed onion. Add spinach, grated carrots, jicama, and snow peas. Serve with "Curry Sauce" (page 88).

7. Chicken Kabobs: Marinate chicken in "Marinade for Chicken and Other Poultry" (page 87). Marinate vegetables in "Sally's Vegetable Marinade" (page 87). Alternate marinated chicken and vegetables on skewers. Barbecue or broil kabobs. Serve over hot brown rice.

GETTING ORGANIZED

It is simple to organize your menu plan. First take a blank copy of the worksheet. Then select two foods from each of the seven food categories listed across the top. Next write them down in the designated space. Presto! You have two sets of foods to rotate. You can buy more variety if you like —but your minimum quantities should give you two sets of meats and vegetables to use.

Let me illustrate with a "Sample Worksheet" (pages 23–24). From the protein list, we have chosen chicken and fish; from the legume and grain list, brown rice and red beans; from the root list, yams and white potatoes; from the yellow/white list, onions and yellow squash; from the green list, broccoli and green beans; from the red list, carrots and red cabbage; from the green leafy list, lettuce and spinach. We now have our shopping list!

When possible, buy your vegetables fresh and organically grown. Avoiding pesticides and other chemicals on food is best for your body. But be practical! If you can't find organically grown produce, use whatever is available.

Cleaning and Storing Your Food

Clean your vegetables so that they will be ready to use at mealtime. To rid them of unwanted parasites, bacteria, insecticides, and other chemicals, use one of the following vegetable soaks:

◆ 1 tablespoon of 3% hydrogen peroxide per gallon of water

◆ ½ teaspoon of bleach per gallon of water

Soak leafy vegetables for five minutes in one of these solutions; rinse them thoroughly and drain. Soak root vegetables for ten minutes; rinse them thoroughly and drain. Wrap each vegetable in paper towels.

SAMPLE WORKSHEET

1	2	3	4
Complete Protein	**Legume & Grain Combo**	**Root Vegetables**	**Yellow or White Vegetables**
beef	beans: adzuki	beets	acorn squash
chicken	black-eyed peas	carrots	avocado
clams	garbanzo	Jerusalem artichokes	banana squash
bean & grain combination	green peas	jicama	cauliflower
crab	kidney	kohlrabi	crookneck squash
duck	lentils	onions	cucumbers
eggs	lima	parsnips	fresh corn
fish	navy	potatoes	hubbard squash
lamb	pinto	rutabagas	jicama
lobster	snap peas	sweet potatoes	onions
oysters	snow peas	turnips	parsnips
shrimp	string beans	yams	radishes
snails	grains: amaranth		rutabagas
turkey	brown rice		spaghetti squash
	millet		turnips
	quinoa		
	teff		
	wild rice		

CREATE YOUR OWN LIST

chicken	*brown rice*	*yams*	*onions*
fish	*red beans*	*white potatoes*	*crookneck squash*

SAMPLE WORKSHEET

5	6	7	Extras
Green Vegetables	**Red, Orange, & Purple Vegetables**	**Green Leafy Vegetables**	**Condiments** (use only as directed)
artichokes	beets	alfalfa sprouts	
asparagus	butternut squash	beet tops	
broccoflower	carrots	bok choy	
celery	eggplant	brussels sprouts	
endive	pumpkin	cabbage	
green bell peppers	purple cabbage	Chinese cabbage	
leeks	red bell peppers	collard greens	
okra	sweet potatoes	endive	
scallions	tomatoes	kale	
snap peas	yams	lettuce:	
snow peas		Bibb, leafy, romaine	
sprouts		mung bean sprouts	
string beans		mustard greens	
zucchini		parsley	
		spinach	
		Swiss chard	
		turnip greens	
		watercress	

CREATE YOUR OWN LIST

broccoli	*carrots*	*lettuce*	
green beans	*red cabbage*	*spinach*	

Separate your two sets of food (now washed and wrapped in paper towels) into two groups. Place them in perforated plastic bags or refrigerator drawers. (If your plastic bags are not perforated, leave them open.) This keeps vegetables moist without causing them to rot. If the paper towels get too soggy, replace them with fresh ones.

To make it easy to rotate your chosen foods, label the two sets "A" and "B." Use the foods from set A on even numbered days of the month and those from set B on uneven numbered days. You can even use several sets of foods and rotate them every three or four days according to your creativity and preference. Soon putting foods together in a rainbow of colors will become easy and automatic—and you will have acquired a new healthy habit.

Practical Tips

People who are busy during the work week can chop vegetables ahead of time and keep them in sealed plastic bags or use frozen vegetables. Be practical. If this is a good way for you to master the natural heating eating plan, then do it! Just remember that some nutritional value is lost by chopping them ahead of time. If you are sensitive to mold, try to prepare your vegetables fresh daily.

Another option for busy people is to cook up a soup, stew, or something that will freeze readily. Freeze it in serving-size portions. When you are in a hurry, pull out one to heat up quickly or take along with you.

The best and most practical approach is to chop vegetables once a day and prepare enough food to last for the next 24 hours. Divide the prepared food into three to six meals—depending on how many you eat during the day. Whether you steam, sauté, or stir-cook your food, eat it hot the first time. For the next meals, try eating it cold and add a homemade sauce, marinade, or dressing that changes the taste of it. This will lend more variety to your diet.

Dried beans take longer to fix than other foods. Prepare them as outlined under "Cooking Tips" (at the end of Part 1) and store them so that they can be prepared quickly. A convenient trick is to freeze them in ice cube trays. Once frozen, the cubes can be popped out of the trays and stored in the freezer in plastic bags. Then you can use one or two "bean cubes" per serving. However, when refrigerating (not freezing) beans, do not store them beyond two days.

To freeze vegetables and beans, remove them individually from the cooking pot, spread them out on cookie sheets, and freeze them. When frozen, store them in plastic bags in the freezer. They are now ready to use in stir-cooking or other dishes.

Because rice and millet take longer to prepare than the rest of the meal, it is helpful to cook a little extra to keep in the refrigerator. Note: They do not freeze well. Refrigerate them for no more than two days, especially if you are sensitive to yeast and molds. In general, the more mold-sensitive you are, the less time you should store leftover foods in the refrigerator. See "Grains" in the recipe section for cooking directions and other exotic grain alternatives.

PUTTING THE MEAL TOGETHER

Living foods supply nutrients for living body cells. Overprocessing and overcooking kills foods by destroying living enzymes. Dead foods impair live cells and produce half-dead people. Therefore, people need to eat living foods for optimal health. This makes sense—doesn't it!

Nutritious Ways to Prepare Food

I want to emphasize that nutritional quality is best preserved in raw foods first and frozen or dried foods second. However, few people choose to live on raw foods alone— and so we cook! But not all cooking is the same as far as preserving the nutritional quality of foods goes. Let's look at the recommended ways to prepare healthy meals.

Raw foods have the greatest food value. However, some people cannot tolerate any raw foods and others can only tolerate certain foods raw. You must learn to listen to your body and see what works for you. One way is to start with all steamed foods, gradually substituting one or two raw vegetables for the steamed ones. Continue adding raw vegetables until you see how much raw food you can handle. As your digestive tract gets stronger, add more raw vegetables to your diet.

With **raw meat**, be realistic. The highest food value is in raw meat—but we cannot overlook the problem of parasites and bacteria. Cook meats until they are heated all the way through. They should stay moist, and tender—but should not be overcooked and tough. Cooked chicken should not be pink—but should be soft and easily chewed. Fish should flake easily and remain moist—it should not be dried out.

Steaming is the next best way to prepare your foods. And it is simple to prepare small meals or big ones. Just plop a steamer basket into a pot, bring the water to a boil, and add the basic seven foods you have chosen in layers. Slice your vegetables very thin so that they cook quickly. Put longer-cooking vegetables in at the beginning of the steaming process, adding ones that take little time at the end. Throw in greens last (like spinach) to wilt. To avoid overcooking, chop or slice all your vegetables before you begin steaming.

Generally, steaming will be done in eight minutes. Vegetables should retain their original bright colors and be slightly crisp.

We have a saying that goes "If you smell them, you've overcooked them."

Stir-cooking retains almost as much food value as steaming. Start the stir-cooking process in a wok or skillet with just a small amount of oil. Don't overheat the oil. As you add foods, also add a little water to prevent sticking. At the end of the cooking process, if desired, add more oil, lemon juice, spices, some dressing, or a sauce for flavor. The secret to stir-cooking is to use thinly sliced vegetables and to stir constantly so that they do not burn or overcook. Keep the heat fairly low but high enough to seal in the juices.

Broiling or **baking** is acceptable. **Barbecuing** is acceptable occasionally—but it is preferable to use an electric starter to avoid charcoal lighter fluid.

Unacceptable Cooking Practices
I consider **frying** and **microwaving** to be unacceptable cooking methods. Complete evidence is not available on the use of microwaves and the method remains controversial. Even in the 1950s and 1960s, health-care practitioners at the Page Clinic in St. Petersburg, Florida, found that ill people did not get well on microwaved food. And it was at this clinic that the "Get Healthy Eating Plan" developed based on Dr. Melvin Page's discoveries in the area of body chemistry and nutrition.

Furthermore, **canned foods** are out! Canned foods have been heated to high temperatures that destroy most of their nutritional value. To achieve optimal health, people should only put into their bodies those foods that are alive with active enzymes—not foods that have been thrashed, beaten, processed, and overheated until thoroughly dead.

HOW TO COMBINE FOODS

Food combining does not have to be intimidating. It just takes a little thought. For instance, look over the sample worksheets included here: Breakfast Combination Ideas, Salad Combination Ideas, Soup Combination Ideas, Steamed Food Combination Ideas, and Stir-Cook Combination Ideas. They show food combinations put together in our clinic kitchen and "Wellness In Action" group meetings. Try them and discover your favorites. You will find that your combinations vary with the availability of seasonal vegetables, providing another food rotation pattern. (See charts on the following pages.)

BREAKFAST COMBINATION IDEAS

1	2	3	4
Complete Protein	**Legume & Grain Combo**	**Root Vegetables**	**Yellow or White Vegetables**
beef	beans: adzuki	beets	acorn squash
chicken	black-eyed peas	carrots	avocado
clams	garbanzo	artichokes	banana squash
bean & grain	green peas	jicama	cauliflower
combination	kidney	kohlrabi	crookneck squash
crab	lentils	onions	cucumbers
duck	lima	parsnips	fresh corn
eggs	navy	potatoes	hubbard squash
fish	pinto	rutabagas	jicama
lamb	snap peas	sweet potatoes	onions
lobster	snow peas	turnips	parsnips
oysters	string beans	yams	radishes
shrimp	grains: amaranth		rutabagas
snails	brown rice		spaghetti squash
turkey	millet		turnips
	quinoa		
	teff		
	wild rice		

1	2	3	4
	cooked amaranth. lima beans	*onions*	*crookneck squash*
	cooked quinoa, green peas	*potatoes*	*acorn squash*
fish or rice	*kidney beans*	*beets*	*cauliflower*
soft-boiled egg	*string beans*	*turnips*	*onions*
beef or quinoa	*green peas*	*rutabaga*	*banana squash*
turkey or lentils	*millet*	*Jerusalem artichokes*	*corn*
shrimp	*rice*	*jicama*	*avocado*

BREAKFAST COMBINATION IDEAS

5	6	7	Extras
Green Vegetables	**Red, Orange, & Purple Vegetables**	**Green Leafy Vegetables**	**Condiments** (use only as directed)
artichokes	beets	alfalfa sprouts	
asparagus	butternut squash	beet tops	
broccoflower	carrots	bok choy	
celery	eggplant	Brussels sprouts	
endive	pumpkin	cabbage	
green bell peppers	purple cabbage	Chinese cabbage	
leeks		collard greens	
okra		endive	
scallions		kale	
snap peas		lettuce:	
snow peas		Bibb, leafy, romaine	
sprouts		mung bean sprouts	
string beans		mustard greens	
zucchini		parsley	
		spinach	
		Swiss chard	
		turnip greens	
		watercress	

okra	purple cabbage	spinach	
asparagus	sweet potatoes	mung bean sprouts	
zucchini	eggplant	brussels sprouts	
broccoli	red bell peppers	swiss chard	
celery	yams	romaine lettuce	
leeks	carrots	leaf lettuce	
green bell peppers	tomatoes	spinach	

NOTE:
For breakfast, steam or stir-cook vegetables and serve with cooked legume, grain, and/or protein.

SALAD COMBINATION IDEAS

1	2	3	4
Complete Protein	**Legume & Grain Combo**	**Root Vegetables**	**Yellow or White Vegetables**
beef	beans: adzuki	beets	acorn squash
chicken	black-eyed peas	carrots	avocado
clams	garbanzo	Jerusalem artichokes	banana squash
bean & grain	green peas	jicama	cauliflower
combination	kidney	kohlrabi	crookneck squash
crab	lentils	onions	cucumbers
duck	lima	parsnips	fresh corn
eggs	navy	potatoes	hubbard squash
fish	pinto	rutabagas	jicama
lamb	snap peas	sweet potatoes	onions
lobster	snow peas	turnips	parsnips
oysters	string beans	yams	radishes
shrimp	grains: amaranth		rutabagas
snails	brown rice		spaghetti squash
turkey	millet		turnips
	quinoa		
	teff		
	wild rice		

chicken or garbanzos	*brown rice*	*carrots*	*avocado*
petite scallops or quinoa	*black-eyed peas*	*kohlrabi*	*cucumbers*
beef strips or brown rice	*pinto beans*	*jicama*	*onions*
fish or millet	*snow peas*	*Jerusalem artichokes*	*radishes*
lamb or quinoa	*kidney beans*	*potatoes cooked and cubed*	*fresh corn*
salad shrimp	*frozen green peas, slightly thawed*	*onions*	*avocado*
egg	*lima beans*	*beets*	*cauliflower*

SALAD COMBINATION IDEAS

5	6	7	Extras
Green Vegetables	**Red, Orange, & Purple Vegetables**	**Green Leafy Vegetables**	**Condiments** (use only as directed)
artichokes	beets	alfalfa sprouts	
asparagus	butternut squash	beet tops	
broccoflower	carrots	bok choy	
celery	eggplant	brussels sprouts	
endive	pumpkin	cabbage	
green bell peppers	purple cabbage	Chinese cabbage	
leeks	red bell peppers	collard greens	
okra	sweet potatoes	endive	
scallions	tomatoes	kale	
snap peas	yams	lettuce:	
snow peas		Bibb, leafy, romaine	
sprouts		mung bean sprouts	
string beans		mustard greens	
zucchini		parsley	
		spinach	
		Swiss chard	
		turnip greens	
		watercress	

celery	tomatoes	leafy lettuce	garbanzo dressing
sprouts (mixed green)	purple cabbage	parsley	herb dressing
green bell peppers	tomatoes	romaine lettuce	taco spice or Juana's salsa
scallions	carrots	Chinese cabbage	Oriental dressing
zucchini	red bell peppers	Bibb lettuce	Italian dressing
celery	carrots	spinach	parsley dressing
artichoke hearts	sweet potatoes	mung bean sprouts	green goddess dressing

SOUP COMBINATION IDEAS

1	2	3	4
Complete Protein	**Legume & Grain Combo**	**Root Vegetables**	**Yellow or White Vegetables**
beef	beans: adzuki	beets	acorn squash
chicken	black-eyed peas	carrots	avocado
clams	garbanzo	Jerusalem artichokes	banana squash
bean & grain	green peas	jicama	cauliflower
combination	kidney	kohlrabi	crookneck squash
crab	lentils	onions	cucumbers
duck	lima	parsnips	fresh corn
eggs	navy	potatoes	hubbard squash
fish	pinto	rutabagas	jicama
lamb	snap peas	sweet potatoes	onions
lobster	snow peas	turnips	parsnips
oysters	string beans	yams	radishes
shrimp	grains: amaranth		rutabagas
snails	brown rice		spaghetti squash
turkey	millet		turnips
	quinoa		
	teff		
	wild rice		

chicken* or green peas	*brown rice*	*potatoes or jicama*	*onions*
turkey or lima beans	*quinoa*	*parsnips*	*cauliflower*
beef or kidney beans	*millet*	*carrots*	*rutabagas*
quinoa or vegetable broth	*green peas*	*onions*	*corn fresh or frozen*

★Boil the chicken first to make a nice broth. (Leftover broth can be frozen and used at a later time.)

While the chicken broth is cooking, cook the brown rice in a separate pot. Steam groups 3 through 7 in a steamer pot and add to the hot chicken broth just before serving. Mix the rice into the soup and presto—a wonderful soup that is not overcooked. Or add thinly sliced, raw vegetables from groups 3 through 7 to the hot chicken broth just before serving.

Important: Do not be afraid to let your imagination run free. There are endless combinations for great soups.

SOUP COMBINATION IDEAS

5	6	7	Extras
Green Vegetables	**Red, Orange, & Purple Vegetables**	**Green Leafy Vegetables**	**Condiments** (use only as directed)
artichokes	beets	alfalfa sprouts	
asparagus	butternut squash	beet tops	
broccoflower	carrots	bok choy	
celery	eggplant	brussels sprouts	
endive	pumpkin	cabbage	
green bell peppers	purple cabbage	Chinese cabbage	
leeks	red bell peppers	collard greens	
okra	sweet potatoes	endive	
scallions	tomatoes	kale	
snap peas	yams	lettuce:	
snow peas		Bibb, leafy, romaine	
sprouts		mung bean sprouts	
string beans		mustard greens	
zucchini		parsley	
		spinach	
		Swiss chard	
		turnip greens	
		watercress	

5	6	7	Extras
celery or broccoflower	*carrots*	*bok choy*	
zucchini	*pumpkin*	*beet tops*	
leeks	*tomatoes*	*parsley*	
asparagus	*purple cabbage*	*spinach*	

STEAMED FOOD COMBINATION IDEAS

1	2	3	4
Complete Protein	**Legume & Grain Combo**	**Root Vegetables**	**Yellow or White Vegetables**
beef	beans: adzuki	beets	acorn squash
chicken	black-eyed peas	carrots	avocado
clams	garbanzo	Jerusalem artichokes	banana squash
bean & grain	green peas	jicama	cauliflower
combination	kidney	kohlrabi	crookneck squash
crab	lentils	onions	cucumbers
duck	lima	parsnips	fresh corn
eggs	navy	potatoes	hubbard squash
fish	pinto	rutabagas	jicama
lamb	snap peas	sweet potatoes	onions
lobster	snow peas	turnips	parsnips
oysters	string beans	yams	radishes
shrimp	grains: amaranth		rutabagas
snails	brown rice		spaghetti squash
turkey	millet		turnips
	quinoa		
	teff		
	wild rice		

scallops or lima beans	*frozen green peas*	*Jerusalem artichokes*	*onions*
tuna or garbanzos	*wild rice*	*jicama*	*avocado*
catfish or adzuki beans	*millet*	*sweet potatoes*	*yellow squash*
lamb or quinoa	*red kidney beans*	*parsnip*	*fresh or frozen corn*
liver or rice	*black beans*	*kohlrabi*	*cauliflower*
chicken or millet	*snow peas*	*potatoes*	*crookneck squash*
fish or lentil beans	*brown rice*	*onions*	*fresh cucumber slices*

STEAMED FOOD COMBINATION IDEAS

5	6	7	Extras
Green Vegetables	**Red, Orange, & Purple Vegetables**	**Green Leafy Vegetables**	**Condiments** (use only as directed)
artichokes	beets	alfalfa sprouts	
asparagus	butternut squash	beet tops	
broccoflower	carrots	bok choy	
celery	eggplant	brussels sprouts	
endive	pumpkin	cabbage	
green bell peppers	purple cabbage	Chinese cabbage	
leeks	red bell peppers	collard greens	
okra	sweet potatoes	endive	
scallions	tomatoes	kale	
snap peas	yams	lettuce:	
snow peas		Bibb, leafy, romaine	
sprouts		mung bean sprouts	
string beans		mustard greens	
zucchini		parsley	
		spinach	
		Swiss chard	
		turnip greens	
		watercress	
celery	*eggplant*	*mustard greens*	
broccoli	*red bell peppers*	*swiss chard*	
okra	*red cabbage*	*brussels sprouts*	
zucchini	*pumpkin*	*cabbage*	
snap peas	*beets*	*spinach*	
green bell peppers	*carrots*	*bok choy*	
asparagus	*eggplant*	*bean sprouts*	

STIR-COOK COMBINATION IDEAS

1	2	3	4
Complete Protein	**Legume & Grain Combo**	**Root Vegetables**	**Yellow or White Vegetables**
beef	beans: adzuki	beets	acorn squash
chicken	black-eyed peas	carrots	avocado
clams	garbanzo	Jerusalem artichokes	banana squash
bean & grain	green peas	jicama	cauliflower
combination	kidney	kohlrabi	crookneck squash
crab	lentils	onions	cucumbers
duck	lima	parsnips	fresh corn
eggs	navy	potatoes	hubbard squash
fish	pinto	rutabagas	jicama
lamb	snap peas	sweet potatoes	onions
lobster	snow peas	turnips	parsnips
oysters	string beans	yams	radishes
shrimp	grains: amaranth		rutabagas
snails	brown rice		spaghetti squash
turkey	millet		turnips
	quinoa		
	teff		
	wild rice		

1	2	3	4
beef strips or millet	frozen green peas	jicama	crookneck squash
salad shrimp or rice	snap peas	Jerusalem artichokes	avocado
turkey or black beans	millet	beets	fresh corn
chicken or millet	snow peas	carrots	cauliflower
egg	kidney beans	onions	cucumbers
scallops or quinoa	marinated black beans	grated carrots	grated rutabaga
ground beef or rice	frozen green peas	onions	crookneck squash

STIR-COOK COMBINATION IDEAS

5	6	7	Extras
Green Vegetables	**Red, Orange, & Purple Vegetables**	**Green Leafy Vegetables**	**Condiments** (use only as directed)
artichokes	beets	alfalfa sprouts	
asparagus	butternut squash	beet tops	
broccoflower	carrots	bok choy	
celery	eggplant	brussels sprouts	
endive	pumpkin	cabbage	
green bell peppers	purple cabbage	Chinese cabbage	
leeks	red bell peppers	collard greens	
okra	sweet potatoes	endive	
scallions	tomatoes	kale	
snap peas	yams	lettuce:	
snow peas		Bibb, leafy, romaine	
sprouts		mung bean sprouts	
string beans		mustard greens	
zucchini		parsley	
		spinach	
		Swiss chard	
		turnip greens	
		watercress	

zucchini	*carrots*	*romaine lettuce*	
celery	*red bell peppers*	*spinach*	
scallions	*pumpkin*	*swiss chard*	
broccoflower	*purple cabbage*	*bok choy*	*oriental dressing*
green bell peppers	*eggplant*	*cabbage*	*taco spice*
zucchini	*sweet potatoes*	*kale*	
snow peas	*red bell peppers*	*spinach*	

LEARNING TO READ YOUR BODY

An essential part of healing and developing healthy eating habits is learning to read your body. It is the body, after all, that will give you the signals needed to fine-tune your eating program so that it serves you in the best possible way.

Elemental to learning to read your body is determining if you have any food sensitivities. The "Get Healthy Eating Plan" automatically removes from your diet the most common food sensitizers (which are dairy products, wheat, soybean products, peanuts, sugar, chocolate, and coffee). However, a person can be sensitized to any food, even ones that generally serve the body well. Common food sensitizers left on the "Get Healthy Eating Plan" are eggs, tomatoes, corn, and beef. Some people may find that they can eat fresh corn but not processed corn products (such as corn chips, tortilla chips, or cornmeal). One reason for this may be that corn syrup or dextrose is used in many of today's processed foods making people who have eaten an overabundance of such foods sensitive to corn.

Testing Foods

If, after seven to ten days on the "Get Healthy Eating Plan," you are still not feeling well, you need to start testing foods. Something may be upsetting your body chemistry. To do this, test one food at a time by eliminating it for five full days. Let's take eggs, for example. For five days, eat no eggs at all—not a smidgen in anything as even a tiny amount will set off a food sensitivity reaction. On the sixth day, eat a soft-boiled egg by itself between meals. Now it is time to listen to your body for the next two hours. If you are sensitive to the egg, you will have stronger reactions because you have been off of it for five days. Reactions will also be more noticeable simply because you are paying more attention to your body.

Food reactions are varied and numerous. Symptoms might be sleepiness, hyperactivity, increased heart rate (by ten to twelve beats per minute), red ears, mental spacing or fatigue, irritability, or headache. If such symptoms occur within the first two hours, it is fairly easy to tell that you are having a food reaction. However, some symptoms may be delayed for as long as 48 hours and are difficult to recognize. Do not test another food within a 48-hour time period. This way, you may be able to detect delayed reactions as well. Delayed reactions can manifest as joint pain, bladder irritation, bowel irritation, gas and bloating, muscle pain, fatigue, or brain symptoms such as difficulty with learning, irritability, depression, and trouble remembering things. Detecting your food sensitivities with the elimination method just described is ideal because it tests the different ways a person can react to foods.

Keep a list of your food reactions and avoid those sensitizers for at least three months. At the end of this time period, try reintroducing the removed foods one at a time. If you have no reaction, you can begin eating them again—but not daily. Eat them no more often than every four days.

Admittedly, this is a very limited discussion of food sensitivities. If food sensitivities are a problem for you, consult a health-care practitioner trained in this field. You should also do more reading on the subject.

Detoxification

Often when starting the "Get Healthy Eating Plan," people find that they don't feel well at first because the body is undergoing a detoxification process to eliminate toxins and similar garbage that have collected over the years. The first five days are usually the most difficult. After that, people start feeling better. Drink lots of pure water and pamper yourself to get through those first five days. Hang in! After this period of time, you will begin feeling better—and your cravings for foods that upset your body chemistry will subside.

Many of you will have strong cravings for foods you have just eliminated from your personalized "Get Healthy Eating Plan." This is a sign that you are reacting to that particular food and experiencing a process just like drug and alcohol addiction withdrawal. Stick it out! Stay off that food for at least five days and the cravings will subside. By eating that food again, you set yourself up to repeat your withdrawal. And once is enough! Have someone to call who will encourage you to hang in for one more hour, just one more hour. If you have to call that friend every hour, do it until the withdrawal phase passes.

People tend to detoxify in the reverse order of ingestion. In other words, if you had a backache ten years ago, bursitis eight years ago, gas and bloating six years ago, and now you are feeling spacey, you will detoxify in the reverse order. First you will feel spacey and then have gas and bloating. Next you might have a recurrence of the bursitis followed by the backache. You will probably detoxify faster than you toxified—if you allow yourself to. However, if you are feeling too miserable, add fruit back into your diet to slow down the detoxification process. Eat one piece of fruit twice daily between meals. And remember to drink lots of pure water to flush the toxins from your system.

Some people give up on the "Get Healthy Eating Plan" because their bowels get sluggish. This condition is understandable if you have gone off fruit or some food that stimulates the bowels. Most people find that their bowels normalize in a short period of time. To help the detoxification process and prevent such a problem, I ask my patients to go on a mild bowel detoxification program when they begin the "Get Healthy Eating Plan." While I recommend the following mild bowel detoxifiers and herbal cleansers (which you can find at your local health food or nutrition store), you should experiment to find the one(s) that suit(s) you best:

◆ **LBX by Nature's Sunshine** is a mild herbal cleanser that cleanses the body and only mildly stimulates the bowel. For better results, some people need to add **slippery elm**. If constipation occurs, **cascara sagrada** may be taken in the evening. By the next day the bowels should move well. Avoid staying on cascara sagrada or other herbal cleansers for long periods of time as dependency on them may develop.

◆ **Psyllium** is a good natural fiber to take if you are not wheat sensitive. (Be sure it is sugar free.) Start with 1 teaspoon daily mixed with 16 ounces of water. It turns into a thick solution, so drink it down quickly! If you do not like the consistency, get psyllium capsules—but always be sure to drink 16 ounces of water with them. As your bowel adjusts to 1 teaspoon of psyllium, increase the amount to 1 teaspoon morning and evening. However, increase the fiber slowly or it may cause some uncomfortable gas and bloating. You eventually may be able to tolerate 2 teaspoons in the morning and 2 teaspoons in the evening.

The best time to take psyllium is when you first get up in the morning (or an hour before breakfast) and again at about 4 PM to allow the fluids to leave your system before bedtime. If you are sensitive to wheat or psyllium, use the alternate fibers gluco-mannan or oat bran.

◆ **Bentonite** bowel cleanser is a clay that has been refined for human consumption and made into a liquid. It adsorbs (in contrast to absorbs) and removes toxins from the body and helps to reestablish normal organisms in the gastrointestinal tract. Start with 1 tablespoon of bentonite daily and gradually increase the amount to 2 tablespoons, one in the morning and one in the evening. Mix it with psyllium and water or take it by itself.

◆ During detoxification, **acidophilus bacteria** should be added to the regime. This will help to establish a healthy bacterial flora in the gastrointestinal tract. Traditionally, most acidophilus has been grown on milk or soy, which are common allergens. In its place, use rice-, carrot-, or other hypoallergenic-based acidophilus. The preferred form is capsules because the good bacterial organisms stay alive better than in liquid. Once adjusted to acidophilus, your body can take a lot without experiencing gas or bloating. However, you may initially experience some discomfort. Start with one capsule daily and gradually increase the number to about six or whatever the bottle recommends. (Note: Refrigerate the bottle of capsules after opening it.) Every brand recommends a different method of taking acidophilus: some say before meals and some say with meals. I recommend that you do what is practical. If you remember to take them a half hour before eating, fine. But if you forget, then take them with your meal.

This bowel cleansing program helps normalize bowel movements whether you have diarrhea, constipation, or normal bowel habits (one to three bowel movements per day). It may be necessary to vary the amount of each ingredient to find the correct dosage for you. Basically, it will not interrupt normal lifestyle. Although some people are afraid it will make them run to the bathroom, in actuality this program encourages regular bowel movements. If constipation occurs, switch from the fiber to an herbal laxative (such as cascara sagrada). When bowels are moving more regularly, gradually reintroduce the fiber. Start with ¼ teaspoon and build to 1 to 2 teaspoons twice daily. You should have at least one bowel movement per day to rid your body of toxins. Most colon hygienists feel three per day is better.

If you have never cleansed your system before, I recommend following the bowel cleansing program for three months. At least do it for two to four weeks and then repeat it at six- to twelve-month intervals for a week or two for maintenance purposes. However, to prevent your colon from becoming dependent on herbal cleansers, taper them off after four to six weeks.

You can safely stay on the psyllium or other fiber indefinitely. If you are sensitive to psyllium or if you become easily sensitized to items you ingest, vary the fibers through rotation. For instance, use oat bran one day and gluco-mannan the next.

INFORMATION ON CERTAIN FOODS

In my practice of nutrition, I use a lot of common and some less common cooking ingredients, As you run across them in *The New Natural Healing Cookbook*, try to think about them or use them as I do. And for a healthy beginning, I urge you to avoid the items outlined in "Foods to Avoid" and consider the advice that follows.

Black olives may be used occasionally as a condiment. However, avoid green olives in vinegar.

Bragg Liquid Aminos is an unfermented soy product found in natural food stores and some fish markets. It is a good soy sauce substitute (if you are not sensitive to soy) and people with yeast sensitivity and/or candida can often tolerate it. But be careful! Test yourself to see if your body can handle it. Use it sparingly on foods.

Broth bouillon and stock should be homemade. (See the recipe section.) Canned broth or bouillon cubes are not permitted on the "Get Healthy Eating Plan" because most contain sugar or yeast. When a recipe calls for chicken, beef, or vegetable broth or stock, make it yourself.

Butter is permissible. Raw (unpasteurized) butter is the most nutritious, but can (although rarely) contain unfriendly bacte-ria. If you do not tolerate butter, substitute oil in recipes.

Canned foods generally should be avoided—although an occasional recipe may call for tomato paste or tomato sauce. Consider these as condiments with essentially no food value. Read the can labels carefully to avoid sugar, sweeteners, or other unwanted additives.

Calcium deficiency is of concern to some people who give up dairy products. However, the foods allowed on this eating plan (especially the green leafy vegetables) supply you with sufficient calcium once your body chemistry is balanced.

Nonetheless, as added insurance, you can take a supplement of chelated calcium such as calcium magnesium aspartate.

Garlic means freshly grated. I find it easiest to "press" using a ceramic ginger grater with fine teeth that stick up.

Herbal mixes and seasonings, if store bought, should be free of sugar, yeast, citric acid, and other food items that upset body chemistry.

Lettuce refers to leaf lettuce—not head (or iceberg) lettuce. The latter is hard to digest and very low in nutrient content.

Mayonnaise means homemade. (See the recipes in this cookbook.) Other mayonnaise has honey, sugar, vinegar, or

FOODS TO AVOID

Foods that upset the body chemistry:

1. Refined carbohydrates: sugar and white flour

2. Caffeine

3. Alcohol

4. Dairy products

Foods to avoid because they commonly cause food sensitivity reactions:

1. Wheat

2. Soy

3. Chocolate

Foods to avoid due to yeast overgrowth (candidiasis):

1. High-gluten grains (wheat, oats, barley, rye)
   Small amounts of oat bran may be eaten.

2. Fruit (feeds yeast) Fruit is avoided because many people have overeaten concentrated sweets. This causes high blood sugar levels which stimulate the pancreas to oversecrete insulin. Staying off fruit for eight weeks allows insulin reactions to normalize.

3. Nuts (hard to digest and feed yeast)

4. Fermented substances (vinegar, soy sauce)

5. Any other yeast or mold by-products (citric acid, autolyzed yeast)

6. Vitamins derived from yeast

something that is not used on the "Get Healthy Eating Plan."

Meats should be natural beef, chicken, and turkey raised free of hormones, antibiotics, etc. In other words, don't buy turkey that is injected with sugar, phosphates, or butter after it is butchered. Also, ground meat loses its food value quickly and should be freshly ground (by you if possible) and eaten immediately. Otherwise, freeze what you buy at the store until you are ready to use it.

Oil should only be cold pressed or expeller pressed. Brand names like Hain and Spectrum are available in natural food stores or your grocery's natural food section. The Omega Nutrition Company processes oils excellently.

Pepper should be freshly ground only.

Permissible foods are dried herbs and spices (unless you are sensitive to mold), spices, black olives, lemon juice, vegetables, meats, beans, and the following grains—brown rice, millet, amaranth, quinoa, teff, and wild rice. If you have weak digestion, avoid spices and herbs for the first eight weeks.

Rice always means whole grain brown rice. There are several varieties you can choose from: short grain, medium grain, long grain, basmati, and new blends and hybrids. (Rice does not have to be boring!)

Rice cakes and rice crackers are allowed— but not recommended since they are dead foods (following the processing used in their preparation). Eat them no more than two days a week, and only one or two on those days.

Salt refers to "sea salt" (available in natural food stores and some grocery stores). Other salts contain dextrose (refined sugar from corn), synthetic iodine, or other added chemicals. Sea salt is evaporated in the sun, kiln dried, and contains essential trace minerals. If you have been advised to limit the salt in your diet, simply omit it from each recipe. Salt is optional. As less salt is used, the taste buds will regenerate and a little salt will taste as salty as a larger amount did previously. When people eat in a way that serves the body well, salt is not a big culprit in the disease-producing process. For instance, fluid retention may be due to allergies, toxins, nutrient deficiencies, or impaired organs. Even though limiting dietary salt may help to reduce fluid retention, it does not treat the underlying problem. Therefore, salt in moderation will be tolerated once the problem is identified and eliminated, the body cleansed, nutrients supplemented, and the organs strengthened.

Sugar hides behind many names: dextrose (from corn syrup), maltose, sucrose, fructose (fruit sugar), maltodextrin, malted barley, molasses, lactose, levulose, and sorbitol.

None are allowed on the "Get Healthy Eating Plan."

Fats and Oils

Most Americans eat too much of the detrimental kind of fats and not enough of the beneficial kind. The detrimental kinds are overheated, overprocessed fats and oils. Examples of overheated oils are margarines and oils used to fry foods at high temperatures. Margarines start out as good oils, but the high temperatures used to solidify them create abnormal fats that the human body cannot metabolize properly.

Good unsaturated fats are extracted from nuts, seeds, and grains with as little heat as possible. They are labeled "expeller pressed" or "cold pressed." Brand names commonly available are Hain and Spectrum.

Oils are classified into three types: omega-3, omega-6, and omega-9. Omega-3 oils are flaxseed, walnut, fish oil, and canola. Although advertised as a healthy omega-3 oil, more recent evidence indicates canola oil has a long chain fatty acid that accumulates and is detrimental to the liver. Therefore canola oil products are not recommended. Pumpkin seeds and walnuts are foods high in omega-3 oil. Most Americans do not eat enough omega-3 oil. This leads to dry skin, hang nails, weak nails that flake off easily, and "chicken skin" (fine flesh-colored bumps on arms and legs). If you have symptoms of omega-3 deficiency, ingest two tablespoons of omega-3 oil daily for a while. Omega-6 oils are safflower, corn, sunflower, sesame, and evening primrose oil. Omega-9 oil is olive oil. Some nutritionists feel it is the best oil to use since it can be extracted with the least amount of processing due to the nature of its soft fruit.

Be sure to refrigerate oils after opening to prevent rancidity.

I recommend keeping a bottle of omega-3 oil and one of omega-6 oil in your refrigerator and using 1 or 2 tablespoons a day from each. While it takes about three months for the body to experience a complete "oil change," you will start to see beneficial results earlier.

Most dairy products upset body chemistry. However, Dr. Page found that butter did not—it actually contained some nutrients needed by the body especially if it is not pasteurized (raw). Of course, the possibility of bacterial contamination in raw butter exists and you will have to weigh the possibility of contamination with your desire to have the nutrients raw butter provides. Arguments aside, moderation is still best—so keep your daily consumption under a tablespoon.

Note: A good way to balance saturated and unsaturated fats is to combine 2 cups of softened butter with 1¾ cups of oil in a blender. Process until mixed thoroughly.

Pour into food containers and store in the refrigerator. When chilled, the mixture makes a soft spread.

The very best sources of essential fats are olive oil, butter, safflower oil, and flaxseeds. (Grind flaxseeds in a spice grinder and eat immediately sprinkled over other foods.)

Beef

Are you surprised to see red meats and other high fat meats included in the "Get Healthy Eating Plan"? Don't be! Remember—when your body chemistry is in balance, you will metabolize natural fats that have not been overheated in a normal and beneficial way. However, if you continue to upset your body chemistry with sugar, white flour, caffeine, alcohol, dairy products, and overheated, rancid fats, then you will certainly not metabolize these beneficial fats properly. Upsets in fat metabolism lead to the adverse effects on the body that are discussed frequently in the media. Also, on this eating plan you will be eating smaller meat portions to allow more beneficial digestion and assimilation. Test yourself to see if you tolerate these meats. (Refer to the earlier section entitled "Learning to Read Your Body.") For instance, people with arthritis often have to eliminate red meats completely.

To allow your body to efficiently utilize red meats and other high fat meats, keep these recommendations in mind:

◆ Eat small servings of beef or high fat meats—¼ cup or less per meal. (This is about the size of an egg.)

◆ Eat these meats only once or twice a week.

◆ Buy naturally raised beef, free of hormones and antibiotics.

◆ Avoid overcooking meats.

◆ Test yourself to determine your tolerance to them.

◆ When using ground meat (ground beef, for example), grind it yourself immediately before preparing it.

◆ Make small portions of beef more exciting by preparing stir-cook dishes with lots of colorful vegetables and a tasty dressing (see "Sukiyaki" and "Chop Suey") in the beef recipes. To help you through the transition of eating less beef and more vegetables, I include some traditional beef recipes. Since traditional cooking tends to overcook foods, I urge you to gradually use them less frequently and to eat them in smaller amounts than usual.

◆ Always serve beef and high fat meats with a raw salad.

COOKING TIPS

Before you read through the recipes in this cookbook, I want to add a few personal cooking tips. I hope that they will help you in your quest to eat well and feel better.

Dried Beans

Method 1: Sort through 2 cups of dried beans and remove debris (like bean-sized pebbles that may escape the sorting process). Rinse the beans thoroughly in cold water. Drain them, put them in a pot, and cover them with fresh water. Add 1 teaspoon of baking soda and let them soak overnight. Drain the water, rinse them well, and again cover with water. To help reduce gas formation during digestion and to increase the mineral content, add 1 tablespoon of crushed dried arame seaweed or a strip of kombu seaweed. Bring the ingredients to a boil, reduce the heat, and simmer the beans until they are tender. Add sea salt to taste at the end of cooking time.

Method 2: Sort, rinse, and drain the dried beans as in method 1. Place them in a pot and add 3 to 4 times their volume in water. Bring the ingredients to a boil, reduce the heat, and let them simmer for 5 minutes. Remove the pot from the heat, cover it tightly, and let it stand for 2 hours. Proceed as if the beans had soaked overnight (method 1).

Brown Rice

Partially cooked: Measure 1 cup of uncooked brown rice and rinse it well in cold water. Place the rice in a 2-quart saucepan, add ¾ teaspoon of sea salt, and cover with water until the water level is an inch above the rice. Cover the pot and bring to a boil; reduce the heat to simmer and cook for 25 minutes. Drain the rice in a colander or with a slotted spoon. The rice will still be hard but will finish cooking when added to a recipe during the last 15 to 20 minutes of cooking.

Crunchy: Sauté 1 cup of uncooked brown rice in hot oil until the kernels are coated with oil and begin to pop. Add enough liquid (water or broth as desired) and cover to finish cooking. Cook until crisp-tender (about 25 minutes). Vegetables and meat can be steamed on top of the rice as it cooks. Add sea salt and freshly ground pepper to taste.

Chicken

To reduce fat content in your diet, skin chicken before you cook it. This is done easily by holding the chicken under warm running water and pulling off the skin.

Flavor Tips

To add flavor to otherwise plain meals, use dips, salad dressings, or marinades on vegetables (steamed or raw), on baked potatoes, and to bind stir-cooked or steamed dishes. See recipes.

Grains

Cooking directions for amaranth, rice, millet, quinoa, teff, and wild rice are found in the recipe section under "Grains." To reduce cooking time by half, soak the grains overnight and cook them in the soaking water.

Spaghetti Squash

Spaghetti squash is also known as calabash and sussa melon. It is actually not a true squash but an edible gourd. After cooking, the pulp assumes a stringy, spaghetti-like appearance and is delicious in combination with various sauces.

Method 1: Pierce the squash in several places with the prongs of a fork. Place the whole squash in an oiled baking pan and bake at 350 degrees for 1 hour. Remove it from the oven and set it aside to cool. When cool enough to handle, cut the squash in half, discard its seeds, and scoop out the pulp after scoring it with a fork (which turns the pulp into spaghetti-like strings). Serve with a sauce, Italian vegetables, or the recipe for "Chilled Squash and Chickpea Salad."

Method 2: Cut the raw squash in half (around its smallest diameter). Remove its seeds. Turn the hollow end down and slit the top of each piece. Place both ends (hollow end down) in a pot holding 1 to 2 inches of boiling water. Turn down the heat and simmer until a fork can barely pierce the end. Remove the squash and let it cool slightly. Scoop out the pulp (after scoring it with a fork) and serve it with a sauce or Italian vegetables.

Crisp-tender Vegetables

The secret to crisp-tender sautéed or stir-cooked vegetables lies in their preparation. Slice them thinly and cook them briefly. To stir-cook vegetables, sauté them in a minimal amount of oil until they are coated. Then add a little water to finish the cooking. Cook only until crisp-tender.

When trying out new or exotic vegetables (or when preparing your least favorite ones), mix them with other vegetables. This changes the taste.

TIPS FOR WEIGHT LOSS

Many patients have commented that the best side effect of the Get Healthy Eating Plan is weight loss. Holding onto extra pounds is a symptom of upset body chemistry. Since the Get Healthy Eating Plan allows your body chemistry to balance, weight loss (or gain if you are too thin) naturally follows. The following are some extra tips to aid you in achieving optimal weight.

Drink at least two quarts of water per day. Fill a bottle that you can carry with you all day. If you have not drained 2 quarts worth by bedtime, try harder the next day until you have developed the habit of drinking at least 2 quarts per day. Good times to drink water:

◆ As soon as you get out of bed in the morning, drink 2 glasses.

◆ Drink 1 to 2 glasses ½ hour before each meal. This helps your stomach prepare for digestion. If you forget to drink ½ hour before the meal, drink the 1 to 2 glasses with your meal. At one time we thought drinking water with the meal diluted your digestive enzymes and made it more difficult to digest the food. New evidence suggests that water acts as a lubricant and facilitator in the digestive process. Experiment with drinking water with meals or avoiding water with meals to determine which way agrees with your digestion.

◆ Drink another glass of water about 2 hours after meals to complete the digestive process.

◆ If you wait until you are thirsty to drink water, then you have waited too long.

◆ Always drink more water in the heat.

When you feel hungry, you may actually be thirsty. If drinking 1 or 2 glasses of water satisfies your hunger, then you can wait to eat.

Exercise aids digestion and helps you burn fat. It activates the fat burners in the muscles, which are the primary fat burners of the body. Since exercise increases muscle mass, you will increase your ability to burn fat even in your sleep. Pick something you enjoy for your exercise program such as biking, dancing, Yoga, martial arts, walking, swimming, etc. Try this easy program. Walk 5 minutes before and after breakfast and lunch. Do stretching and relaxation exercises before dinner. Walk another 10 to 15 minutes after dinner. Wait 15 to 20 minutes after each meal to start your walk.

More muscle increases the amount of fat burning tissue in the body. Add weight training to your optimal health program to increase muscle mass. You can simply lift cans of food initially (that's the best use of canned food anyway since the nutrition is so depleted in canned foods). Also, look for a good book on weight training or seek instruction from a trainer at a gym in order to develop muscle safely and appropriately. You do not need to look like a body builder to improve your muscle mass by replacing fat with muscle.

The Get Healthy Eating Plan allows the overactive insulin response to normalize. The Standard American Diet (SAD) usually involves eating a sweetened cereal and orange juice for breakfast (lots of sugar in that meal), or a doughnut and coffee. By mid-morning the sugar craving kicks in again for a snack of a soft drink, doughnut, or piece of fruit. Lunch brings a quick sandwich and soft drink, then the midafternoon candy bar, hopefully a fairly well balanced dinner and then dessert. Each of these meals and snacks are a major stress to the pancreas because they cause glucose (sugar) to surge into the bloodstream. These high glucose levels are a state of emergency to the pancreas. The pancreas's sirens and bells start going off as it has to respond by pouring lots of insulin into the blood stream to reduce the high sugar level. Then suddenly there is no more glucose entering the blood stream because these refined carbohydrates are absorbed so quickly. At that point when the blood insulin levels are

high and no more sugar is entering the blood stream, the blood sugar levels drop abnormally low. This is a state of emergency for the adrenal glands, which secrete cortisol to find glucose wherever it can to bring the blood sugar level back up to protect the brain (which only burns sugar, not fat). The cortisol will break down body proteins (including muscles, your major fat burning organs) if necessary. The liver is also stressed with these daily major abnormal swings in blood glucose. The Get Healthy Eating Plan automatically removes the concentrated sweets (sugars, pastries, ice cream, fruit juices) from your diet **and automatically provides you with a balance of complex carbohydrates, protein and fats at each meal.** When you eat this food combination the glucose drips into the blood stream slowly and steadily and allows the over reactive insulin and adrenal responses to return to normal.

Avoid eating fruit the first eight weeks of the Get Healthy Eating Plan since fruit is naturally sweet enough to perpetuate the over secretion of insulin. After eight weeks gradually add small amounts of whole fruit into your diet. Always avoid fruit juices just as you will want to always avoid other refined carbohydrates since they upset body chemistry and contribute to ill health.

BLOOD GLUCOSE–INSULIN RESPONSE

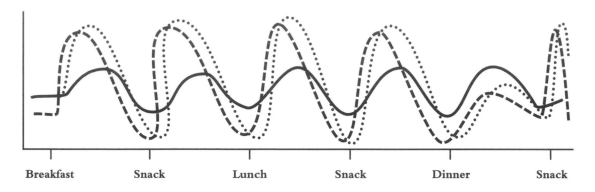

| Breakfast | Snack | Lunch | Snack | Dinner | Snack |

—— Normal glucose (blood sugar) response after a meal with a balanced ratio of carbohydrates, protein, and fat

--- Blood sugar swings when meals and snacks contain refined carbohydrates or too much carbohydrate in proportion to proteins and fat.

······ Insulin over-secretion in response to high blood glucose levels.

High insulin levels force the carbohydrates you eat into storage as fat, thus weight gain. Eating a balance of protein, carbohydrate, and fat at each meal stimulates your body to secrete glucagon, which enables the body to burn fat for energy, thus normalizing weight. This balance of protein, fat and carbohydrate at each meal or snack also normalizes adrenal response. Now the adrenals can stop cannibalizing important structural and muscle proteins, and the body can utilize the dietary proteins for much needed repair work. Your body heals. You normalize your weight and become optimally healthy. The popular concept that a low fat, high carbohydrate diet promotes weight loss has lost its appeal since people have found that it is simply not effective. They have gained weight on this high carbohydrate, low fat plan. Also this eating approach did not usually distinguish between simple carbohydrates and complex carbohydrates. Anything with refined sugar (sucrose, fructose, dextrose, brown sugar, etc.) or refined flour (white flour, potato chips, corn chips, etc.) in it is a simple carbohydrate. Fruit juices are also refined carbohydrates. Complex carbohydrates are whole foods, properly prepared with nothing removed from them. They include whole grains, root vegetables, beans, and whole fruit. Although refined carbohydrates promote marked over secretion of insulin and suppression of glucagon, eating complex carbohydrates in the wrong proportion to proteins and fats also promotes enough over secretion of insulin to cause weight gain.

Find the proper ratio of protein, carbohydrate and fat that your body requires to aid weight loss. The most popular books on weight loss and diets are now mostly promoting the 40–30–30 plan, which means eating 40% of your total calories per meal as carbohydrate, 30% as protein, and 30% as fat, at each meal or snack. This approach may work well for many people, but you may need to vary these percentages of the macronutrients (protein, fats, and carbohydrates) in your diet. Take the metabolic profiling quiz to determine your metabolic type, then experiment with the food combinations in the examples for your metabolic type to see if it works for you.

Artificial sweeteners stimulate over-secretion of insulin. Therefore, they will also encourage fat storage and retention. The only safe sweetener may be the natural herb Stevia, available at health food stores. As you avoid sweeteners, your taste buds will regenerate and you will savor the differences in tastes of the various foods. Also, vine ripened, organically grown foods are naturally much sweeter and tastier.

IMBALANCED & BALANCED DIETS

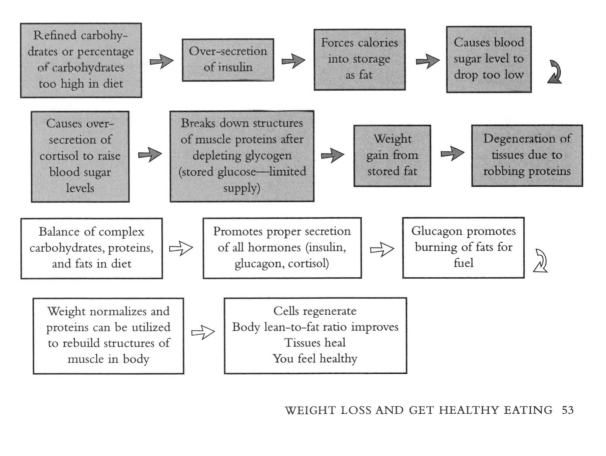

Eat regularly spaced meals and snacks.
Your blood sugar will remain at a normal steady state when you eat regularly. With stabilization of blood sugar hunger and sugar cravings will subside and your body and mind will be happier. You will also be much less likely to grab something to eat that does not serve your body well. If you are fairly healthy and have good digestion, eat 3 meals per day. Always be sure to eat breakfast since breakfast sets your metabolism for the day. Include the proper ratio of proteins, fats and carbohydrates in your breakfast meal. If your health is compromised, or you are not digesting well, then eat six meals per day. Also, some people lose weight better on six small meals per day rather than 3 larger ones. Fix enough food at one time to last for the next 24 hours and divide it into six meals. Then you will not have to be in the kitchen all the time. Invest in a cool pack lunch bag so you will have your meal with you when it is time to eat.

Eat a snack at bedtime? A small snack containing a balance of the macronutrients at bedtime may serve you well. Try it. If you do not sleep well or you tend to gain weight when you eat a bedtime snack, then stop eating it.

MORE WEIGHT LOSS HELP

Most people lose weight by simply following the Get Healthy Eating Plan because it automatically eliminates many of the foods that promote weight gain such as refined carbohydrates, abnormal fats and the most common food allergens. For some people determining and eliminating their hidden food allergens causes rapid weight loss. Also the Get Healthy Eating Plan automatically balances the carbohydrate, protein, and fat in each meal. By paying attention to how my body and digestive tract responded to the amounts of carbohydrate, protein and fats in my meals, I had determined the proper ratios for me by following the Get Healthy Eating Plan. If you have been unable to determine the proper ratios for you or if you have not lost weight after following the Get Healthy Eating Plan for 2 to 3 weeks, then take the following steps.

Take the Metabolic Profile Survey and score it according to the instructions at the bottom of the second page to determine your metabolic profile. This survey was developed based on the research of several prominent and well-known nutritional researchers. Dr. Frances Pottenger, M.D. whose book, *Symptoms of Visceral Disease*, published in 1919 demonstrated the effect nutrients have on the autonomic nervous system (ANS) and that the ANS is the basis of metabolic individuality. In the 1950's Dr. Melvin Page, DDS, and Dr. Henry Bieler, M.D., determined that the genetically inherited balance in our endocrine glands affected which foods were best for each body type. Also, in the 1950's Dr. George Watson noted that some people burned foods faster than others, dubbing them "fast oxidizers" or "slow oxidizers." These three factors (the autonomic nervous system, the balance in the endocrine glands, and slow or fast oxidation) were utilized to determine the first three metabolic profiles (1, 2, and 3). Dr. William Kelley, DDS, further researched and developed the metabolic profiling in the 1980's. Profile 4 is a more recent development in response to the ineffectiveness of the low fat, high carbohydrate diet for many people.

You are metabolically unique. One eating plan does not work for everyone. After you determine your profile from the Metabolic Profiling Survey, turn to the "Recommended Foods and Eating Plan" chart in the following pages that correlates with your Profile. Use the amounts of food from each of the 7 food categories for each meal for 2 weeks. If you are not losing weight nor feeling alert, energetic, and comfortable in your digestive tract, you may need to experiment with the other profiles. Since only the first three profiles were utilized in developing the Metabolic Survey, you will have to listen to your body to determine if Profile 4 is right for you. You may want to try Profile 4 if you feel you need more good fats in your diet. Obvious

signs of inadequate ingestion of the essential omega 3-oils include dry skin, hang nails, flaky soft nails, and fine rough flesh colored bumps on the back of the arms (chicken skin). Since all cells require the essential oils for proper functioning of the cell membranes, many other symptoms may be due to fatty acid deficiency. I feel you may not be eating the necessary amounts of essential fatty acids if you adhere strictly to the amounts of fats recommended in Profiles 1, 2, and 3. Therefore, if one of those Profiles seems to be working well for you, but you seem to need more essential fats, increase the added fats to 1 tablespoon of the omega-3 oils and 1 tablespoon of the omega-6 oils daily, especially if you have not been eating good fats for a long time. It takes 3 months for a complete oil change in the human body. Essential fatty acids are necessary for proper functioning of the brown fat that cushions our inner organs. According to current research essential fatty acids provide the prostaglandin precursors that stimulate the mitochondria in the brown fat to burn better and faster, thus increasing our metabolism. So, eating essential fats aids weight loss.

USING THE METABOLIC PROFILE CHARTS

Take the Metabolic Profile Survey to determine your profile.

Turn to the Recommended Foods and Eating Plan for your profile.

Select the calorie level appropriate for you. Most people should not eat less than 1200 calories per day. If you are physically active (everyone should be), select a mid-range calorie level for starters and adjust as needed for weight loss and signs of hunger. The larger your frame, the higher your metabolism and the more active you are, the greater the number of calories you may consume.

Each calorie level has 4 to 5 examples of the way to combine foods for one meal. To prepare one meal, select and measure the amount of food listed in each category horizontally across the page. In some categories you may choose from the low, **OR** medium, **OR** high carbohydrates of that food list. In the chart the symbol "/" means **OR**. For instance, in selecting a root vegetable the chart may read "½C lo/¼C me/⅛C Hi". So you would choose ½ cup of beets, **OR** ¼ cup of potatoes, **OR** ⅛ cup of yam. Refer to the Carbohydrate–Protein–Fat Classification of Foods for the listing of the food by category and low, medium, or high carbohydrate level.

The following is an example of a meal for Profile 4. From the top line of the 1600 calorie level select:

◆ ⅜ cup medium fat raw protein (dark chicken, no skin)

◆ 3 tablespoons cooked grain (brown rice)

◆ 6½ tablespoons medium carbohydrate raw root vegetable (carrot)

◆ ⅜ cup low carbohydrate raw yellow/white vegetable (cucumbers)

◆ ⅜ cup medium carbohydrate raw green vegetable (snap peas)

◆ ⅜ cup low carbohydrate raw red/orange/purple vegetable (red pepper)

◆ 1⅝ cup low carbohydrate raw green leafy vegetable (red or green leafy lettuce)

◆ 4¾ teaspoon of a fat

Now get creative. Broil the chicken and make a hearty salad of the rest of the ingredients. Or stir cook all of the ingredients into a tasty dish, perhaps substituting spinach for the lettuce. Or make soup or a stew. Remember to eat some raw foods at every meal. Use the allotted amount of fat for stir cooking or for salad dressings or marinades.

To speed meal preparation, make enough at one time to last the next 24 hours.

All this measuring is a pain. I agree. Meal preparation is much more fun when it is spontaneous and occurs without much thought. Any task becomes much easier when you do not have to consciously think about it. Since it only takes 21 days to develop a new habit, you may be able to create a delicious, beautiful, satisfying meal that is right for your metabolic type after carefully measuring for only 3 weeks. Then this new habit is automatic and you will know how to estimate the amounts of each food you need without a lot of conscious effort. Remember your body will tell you if you go astray of your eating plan, especially if your body feels better than it ever has in your life once you start feeding it appropriately. I have never wanted anyone to have to calculate calories or grams in preparing their meals. That is why I have already done the calculations for you. Follow the charts until you have mastered the feel of the right foods and carbohydrate–protein–fat percentages for your body.

Measure the foods raw since the calculations were all based on raw food except for grains. Measure grains after cooking them.

Making measuring easier: Each Recommended Foods and Eating Plan has a chart for converting the number of tablespoons to the amount of a cup on the upper left side. Where possible in the charts I listed the measuring cup amounts. At times I had to list the number of tablespoons for keeping accuracy in the carbo-hydrate–protein–fat ratios. For a short cut to measuring 13 tablespoons of a food, measure ¾ cup and add 1 tablespoon. Or to measure 11 tablespoons of a food, measure ¾ cup and remove 1 tablespoon.

Abbreviations used in the Profile Recommended Foods and Eating Plan charts:

> **C = cup**
> **T = tablespoon**
> **tsp = teaspoon**
> **lo = low**
> **me or med = medium**
> **Hi = high**

Some amounts called for may be ridiculous. For instance, at the 2000 caloric level you could choose 2 cups of a low carbohydrate green vegetable. Since it may not be good for digestion to eat 2 cups of celery at one meal, cut down on the amount to a reasonable level like ¼ to ½ cup. I included those high amounts of low carbohydrate foods on the charts because those amounts made the calculated ratios of carbohydrate–protein–fat perfect for that meal. But in actuality, the amount of carbohydrates in the low carbohydrate category are so low that they will have little effect on the ratio of carbohydrate to protein and fat if you decrease them. For instance, 1 cup of low carbohydrate green vegetables only contain four grams of carbohydrates and one cup of green leafy vegetables only contains one gram of carbohydrates.

Note that Profiles 1 and 2 list the foods that are ideal for that body type. Eating primarily from the foods listed may help you feel the best and lose weight more efficiently. However, you may add foods from the main list periodically for variety, always paying attention to how your body responds. Profiles 3 and 4 may select from all the foods on the food classification chart.

Please note on the Carbohydrate–Protein–Fat Classification of Foods chart: The 3 numbers separated by a dash at the bottom of the list of foods represents the average amount of carbohydrate–pro-tein–fat in ½ cup of those foods. For example, ½ cup of a medium fat protein has 0 grams carbohydrate, 32 grams of protein and 9.5 grams of fat. I included these numbers for informational purposes only. You will not need to use them unless you like to do your own calculations.

The grams of fat in the meats listed on the charts are based on the amount of fat in lean red meats and skinless poultry prepared by broiling, baking or boiling. If you use fat to sauté or marinate the meat, or in a sauce, the amount of fat you use must be selected from the fat category.

Note that quinoa and teff are denser than the other grains, so use ½ as much of quinoa or teff as noted on the charts.

METABOLIC PROFILE SURVEY

Instructions:

◆ Place a check ❑ in the square to the left of each choice that best applies to you.

◆ Make only one selection per category.

◆ If no choice applies to you, leave that category unchecked.

◆ Important: The choices as written may not describe you exactly. So, it is very important that you choose the answer that best describes your tendencies. The answer doesn't need to be a perfect description, just an indication of your trend.

◆ Consider letting a close friend or family member check your answers for accuracy.

◆ Be as honest and accurate as you can. After all, you want to be sure to obtain the right product for your kind of metabolism.

◆ Some choices in some columns are purposefully left blank.

CHARACTERISTIC	❏ COLUMN 1	❏ COLUMN 2	❏ COLUMN 3
Aging	❏ Look older than others my age	❏ Look younger than others my age	▬▬▬▬▬
Aloofness	❏ Cool, distant, aloof, loner, slow to make friends, hard to get to know	❏ Warm, open, expressive, easily make friends, approachable	▬▬▬▬▬
Appetite	❏ Weak, lacking, diminished	❏ Strong, excessive, enhanced	❏ Average appetite
Chest Pressure	▬▬▬▬▬	❏ Tend to get	▬▬▬▬▬
Climate	❏ Love warm, hot weather	❏ Do well in cold, poor in hot	❏ Doesn't matter
Cold Sores and/or Fever Blisters	▬▬▬▬▬	❏ Tend to get	▬▬▬▬▬
Coughing	▬▬▬▬▬	❏ Tend to cough most every day	▬▬▬▬▬
Cracking Skin (any weather)	▬▬▬▬▬	❏ Tend to get	▬▬▬▬▬
Dandruff	▬▬▬▬▬	❏ Tend to get	▬▬▬▬▬
Desserts	❏ Love sweets, need something sweet with meal to feel satisfied	❏ Don't really care for sweet desserts, but like something fatty or salty (like cheese, chips or popcorn) for snacks after meals	❏ Can take them or leave them
Digestion	❏ Poor, weak, slow	❏ Good, strong, rapid	❏ Average digestion
Eating Before Bed	❏ Usually worsens sleep, especially if heavy food	❏ Usually improves sleep	❏ Doesn't matter, but heavy snacks are not the best
Eating Habits	❏ Eat to live—unconcerned with food and eating	❏ Live to eat—need to eat often to feel good, be at best	❏ Average eating habits and need for food, meal times, etc.
TOTALS	❏ COLUMN 1	❏ COLUMN 2	❏ COLUMN 3

CHARACTERISTIC	❑ COLUMN 1	❑ COLUMN 2	❑ COLUMN 3
Emotional Expression	❑ Hard to express feelings, not naturally demonstrative	❑ Easily express feelings	
Emotions	❑ Beneath surface, under control, non-emotional type, tend to hold feelings inside	❑ Wear heart on sleeve, others always know how I feel	
Eye Moisture	❑ Tend toward dry eyes	❑ Tend toward moist or tearing eyes	
Facial Coloring	❑ Tend toward pale, chalky	❑ Tend toward ruddy, rosy, flushed	
Facial Complexion	❑ Tend toward dull, unclear	❑ Tend toward bright, clear	
Fatty Food (if you like or dislike, not what you think is good for you)	❑ Don't care for it	❑ Love it, crave it, would like it often	❑ Take it or leave it
Fatty Food Reaction	❑ Decreases energy and well-being	❑ Increases well-being	❑ Average reaction
Fingernails	❑ Tend to be thick, hard, strong	❑ Tend to be thin, soft, weak	
4 Hours Without Eating	❑ Doesn't bother	❑ Makes irritable, jittery, weak, famished or depressed	❑ Feel normal hunger
Gooseflesh	❑ Tend to form easily		
Gum Bleeding		❑ Tend to get after brushing	
Gum Color	❑ Light, pale	❑ Dark, pink, red	
Hunger Feelings	❑ Rarely get, passes quickly, can go long periods w/o eating easily	❑ Often hungry, need to eat regularly and often	❑ When late for meals only, not between meals usually
TOTALS	❑ COLUMN 1	❑ COLUMN 2	❑ COLUMN 3

CHARACTERISTIC	❑ COLUMN 1	❑ COLUMN 2	❑ COLUMN 3
Insect Bite/Sting	Weak reaction, disappears fast	❑ Strong, lasting reaction	▓▓▓▓▓▓▓▓▓
Itching Eyes	▓▓▓▓▓▓▓▓▓	❑ Tend to get	▓▓▓▓▓▓▓▓▓
Itching Skin	▓▓▓▓▓▓▓▓▓	❑ Tend to get	❑ Average reaction
Juice or Water Fasting	❑ Can handle very well, feels good	❑ Fasting makes me feel awful	❑ React O.K., can fast if necessary
Meal Portions	❑ Prefer small	❑ Prefer large, or if not large, need it often	❑ Average
Orange Juice Alone	❑ Energizes, satisfies me	❑ Can make me light-headed, hungry, jittery, shaky, or nauseated	❑ No ill effects
Potatoes	❑ Not real fond of them	❑ Could eat them almost everyday, love them	❑ Take them or leave them
Red Meat, like a steak or roast beef meal	❑ Decreases energy and well-being	❑ Increases well-being, energy	❑ Average reaction
Saliva Amount	❑ Tend toward dry mouth	❑ Excessive saliva	▓▓▓▓▓▓▓▓▓
Saliva Texture	❑ Tends to be thick, ropy	❑ Tends to be thin, watery	▓▓▓▓▓▓▓▓▓
Salty Foods	❑ Foods often taste too salty	❑ Really love or crave salt on foods	❑ Average like for
Skin Healing	❑ Cuts heal slowly	❑ Cuts heal quickly	❑ Average healing time
Skin Moisture	❑ Tend toward dry skin	❑ Tend toward oily/moist skin	❑ Average skin moisture
Skipping Meals	❑ Can skip with no ill effects	❑ Must eat regularly (or often)	❑ Can get by w/o eating but really feel best eating 3 meals per day
TOTALS	❑ COLUMN 1	❑ COLUMN 2	❑ COLUMN 3

CHARACTERISTIC	❏ COLUMN 1	❏ COLUMN 2	❏ COLUMN 3
Snacking	❏ Rarely or never want snacks	❏ Want to eat between meals	▬▬▬▬▬
Sneezing (any time)	▬▬▬▬▬	❏ Tend to sneeze every day	▬▬▬▬▬
Sour Foods (vinegar or pickles or lemons or sauerkraut or yogurt)	❏ Don't care for, want or crave	❏ Really like	❏ Sometimes like
Sweets	❏ Can do fairly well on	❏ Don't do well on, sweet foods can seem too sweet	❏ No noticeable bad effect
Vegetarian Meal	❏ Is satisfying	❏ Not satisfying, or bad result, become hungry soon after or feel unsatisfied	❏ O.K., but not really satisfying
Wheezing	▬▬▬▬▬	❏ Tend to get	▬▬▬▬▬
If I eat MEAT for BREAKFAST like ham, bacon, sausage, steak, or salmon…	❏ I get tired, sleepy, lethargic and/or very thirsty by midmorning	❏ I feel great, energetic, have good stamina, keeps me going without getting hungry before lunch	❏ It's o.k., but not in large proportions
If I eat MEAT for LUNCH like hamburger, steak, roast beef or salmon…	❏ I get tired, sleepy, lethargic, and/or lose my energy in the afternoon	❏ I feel great, energetic, have good stamina, keeps me going without getting hungry before dinner	❏ It's o.k., but not in large proportions
If I feel low on energy…	❏ Fruit, pastry, or candy restores and gives me lasting energy; meat or fatty food makes me more tired	❏ Meat or fatty food restores my energy, fruit, pastry, or candy makes me worse…quick lift followed by a crash	❏ Pretty much any food restores my energy
TOTALS	❏ COLUMN 1	❏ COLUMN 2	❏ COLUMN 3

CHARACTERISTIC	❏ COLUMN 1	❏ COLUMN 2	❏ COLUMN 3
In a social setting I'm...	❏ Introverted, shy, quiet, non-talkative	❏ Extroverted, social, expressive, easily make conversation	❏ Extroverted, social, expressive, easily make conversation
TOTALS	❏ COLUMN 1	❏ COLUMN 2	❏ COLUMN 3

Steps for Profile Selection

Great. That was easy, right? Now, on to finding out which profile you are. Just follow these steps:

1. Add up the total choices made in each column and enter your total score in the spaces provided at the end of the survey.

2. If your highest score in one column is 5 points or more higher than both of the other two columns, and

> ... if you made the most choices in column 1, Profile 1 is your metabolic type.
> ... if you made the most choices in column 2, Profile 2 is your metabolic type.
> ... if you made the most choices in column 3, Profile 3 is your metabolic type.

If the column with your highest score is not 6 points higher than both of the other two columns, find your results below:

3. If columns 1 and 2 are tied or have less than 5 points difference, Profile 3 is your metabolic type.

4. If columns 1 and 3 are tied or have less than 5 points difference, Profile 1 is your metabolic type.

5. If columns 2 and 3 are tied or have less than 5 points difference, Profile 2 is your metabolic type.

6. If all three columns are tied or have scores with 5 points or less difference (e.g., 13, 18, 16), Profile 3 is your metabolic type.

It's quite possible that due to such factors as time, age, stress and activity levels, etc., your nutritional needs could change. Whenever you feel that a change may have taken place, answer again the questions above and re-do the steps for your metabolic type. Good luck and enjoy.

CARBOHYDRATE–PROTEIN–FAT CLASSIFICATION OF FOODS

Protein

Med Fat Protein
lean beef
dark chicken (no skin)
dark turkey (no skin)
lean lamb
salmon
½ cup
0–32–9.5

Low Fat Fowl
light meat chicken
light meat turkey
½ cup
0–35–5

Low Fat Fish
bass
clams
cod
crab
crayfish
flounder
haddock
halibut
lobster
monkfish
perch, ocean
scallops (12 large)
sea bass
shrimp
snapper
sole
tuna
½ cup
.75–24–1

Egg
large, whole 0–6–5
egg white 0–4–0
egg yolk 0–3–5

Beans And Grains

Dry Beans
adzuki
black-eyed peas
garbanzos
green peas
kidney
lentils
lima
navy
pinto
½ cup cooked
24–8–1

Grains
amaranth
brown rice
millet
wild rice
½ cup cooked
22–3–1
*quinoa
*teff
*¼ cup cooked
*20–3.5–2.5

*Note: when using quinoa or teff, decrease the amount of grain listed on the charts by ½.

Root Vegetables

Low Carbohydrate
beets
jicama
kohlrabi
onions
rutabagas
turnips
½ cup
6–1–1

Med Carbohydrate
carrots
jerusalem artichokes
parsnips
potatoes
½ cup
13–1–0

High Carbohydrate
sweet potatoes
yam
½ cup
24–1–0

Yellow, White Veg.

Low Carbohydrate
crookneck squash
cucumbers
jicama
onions
radish
rutabagas
spaghetti squash
turnips
½ cup
5–.5–0

Med Carbohydrate
banana squash
cauliflower
corn
hubbard squash
parsnips
½ cup
12–2–0
½ cup

---

2 T = ⅛ cup   **4 T = ¼ cup**   **6 T = ⅜ cup**   **8 T = ½ cup**

Green Vegetables

Low Carbohydrate
celery
endive
green pepper
green sprouts
zucchini
½ cup
2–0–0
Med Carbohydrate
artichoke, ½ med.
asparagus
broccoli
broccoflower
leeks
okra
scallions
snap peas
snow peas
string beans
½ cup
7-2–0

Red, Orange, Purple

Low Carbohydrate
beets
eggplant
pumpkin
purple cabbage
red peppers
tomatoes
½ cup
6–1-0
Med Carbohydrate
butternut squash
carrots
½ cup
12–1–0
High Carbohydrate
sweet potatoes
yams
½ cup
24–1–0

Green Leafy

Low Carbohydrate
alfalfa sprouts
beet tops
bok choy
cabbage
Chinese cabbage
collard greens
endive
kale
lettuce
mustard greens
parsley
spinach
turnip greens
water cress
1 cup
1–0–0
Med Carbohydrate
brussels sprouts
romaine lettuce
mung sprouts
1 cup
6–3–0

Fats

Approximately
1 tablespoon oil =
1 tablespoon butter =
1 tbsp. mayonnaise =
6 large olives
Any Oil
flax seed oil
olive oil
safflower oil
sesame oil
sunflower oil
and others
1 tablespoon
0–0–14
Butter
1 tablespoon
0–0–11
Mayonnaise
1 tablespoon
0–0–11
olives
2 large
0–0–4
Class B Fats
almonds
cashews
pine nuts
pumpkin seeds
sesame seeds
sunflower seeds
walnuts
1 tablespoon raw
3–3–8
nut butters
1 tablespoon
4–4–9

10 T = ⅝ cup   **12 T = ¾ cup**   **14 T = ⅞ cup**   **16 T = 1 cup**

PROFILE 1 CALORIE–GRAM PORTIONS

TOTAL DAILY CALORIE–GRAM PORTIONS

Total Grams	70% CHO		20% Protein		10% Fat		Total Cals
	Cals	Grams	Cals	Grams	Cals	Grams	
222	622	155	178	44	200	22	999
267	748	187	214	53	240	27	1202
311	871	218	249	62	280	31	1400
356	997	249	285	71	320	36	1602
400	1120	280	320	80	360	40	1800
444	1243	319	355	89	400	44	1998
489	1369	342	391	98	440	49	2201
534	1495	374	427	107	481	53	2403

CALORIE–GRAM PORTIONS PER MEAL

74	207	52	59	15	67	7	333
89	249	62	71	18	80	9	401
104	290	73	83	21	93	10	467
119	332	83	95	24	107	12	534
133	373	93	107	27	120	13	600
148	414	104	118	30	133	15	666
163	456	114	130	33	147	16	734
178	498	125	142	36	160	18	801

PROFILE 1 RECOMMENDED FOODS AND EATING PLAN
70% CHO–20% PROTEIN–10% FAT

Calories	Protein	Beans & Grains	Root Vegetables	Yellow, White Veg.
2 T = ⅛ cup	light poultry	all beans	**Low carbohydrate**	**Low carbohydrate**
4 T = ¼ cup	cod	all grains	beets jicama	cucumber
6 T = ⅜ cup	turbot		rutabagas	onion
8 T = ½ cup	egg		**Med carbohydrate**	spaghetti squash
10 T = ⅝ cup	white tuna		carrots	
12 T = ¾ cup	flounder		potatoes	
14 T = ⅞ cup	haddock		**High carbohydrate**	
16 T = 1 cup	perch		sweet potatoes	
	scrod		yams	
	sole			

1000 calories	⅛ C low fat fish	⅜ C grain ⅜ C bean	½C lo/¼/C me/⅛C Hi	¼ C low/⅛ C med
	⅛ cup low fat fowl	⅜ C grain ⅜ C bean	½C lo/¼/C me/⅛C Hi	¼ C low/⅛ C med
	1 egg	⅜ C grain ⅜ C bean	½C lo/¼/C me/⅛C Hi	¼ C low/⅛ C med
	⅛ C med fat protein	⅜ C grain ⅜ C bean	½C lo/¼/C me/⅛C Hi	¼ C low/⅛ C med
1200 calories	⅛ C low fat fish	7 T grain 7 T bean	⅝C lo/5T me/2.5T Hi	5T low/⅛ C med
	⅛ C low fat fowl	7 T grain 7 T bean	⅝C lo/5T me/2.5T Hi	5T low/⅛ C med
	1 egg	7 T grain 7 T bean	⅝C lo/5T me/2.5T Hi	5T low/⅛ C med
	⅛ C med fat protein	7 T grain 7 T bean	⅝C lo/5T me/2.5T Hi	5T low/⅛ C med
1400 calories	3T low fat fish	½ C grain ½ C bean	¾C lo/⅜C me/3T high	⅜ C low/3 T med
	3 T low fat fowl	½ C grain ½ C bean	¾C lo/⅜C me/3T high	⅜ C low/3 T med
	1 egg	½ C grain ½ C bean	¾C lo/⅜C me/3T high	⅜ C low/3 T med
	3 T med fat protein	½ C grain ½ C bean	¾C lo/⅜C me/3T high	⅜ C low/3 T med
1600 calories	3 T low fat fish	⅝ C grain ⅝ C bean	¾C low/⅜C me/3T Hi	⅜ C low/3 T med
	3 T low fat fowl	⅝ C grain ⅝ C bean	¾C low/⅜C me/3T Hi	⅜ C low/3 T med
	1 egg	⅝ C grain ⅝ C bean	¾C low/⅜C me/3T Hi	⅜ C low/3 T med
	3 T med fat protein	⅝ C grain ⅝ C bean	¾C low/⅜C me/3T Hi	⅜ C low/3 T med
1800 calories	¼ C low fat fish	11 T grain 11 T bean	⅞C lo/7T me/3.5T Hi	7T low/3 T med
	¼ C low fat fowl	11 T grain 11 T bean	⅞C lo/7T me/3.5T Hi	7T low/3 T med
	2 eggs	11 T grain 11 T bean	⅞C lo/7T me/3.5T Hi	7T low/3 T med
	3 T med fat protein	11 T grain 11 T bean	⅞C lo/7T me/3.5T Hi	7T low/3 T med
2000 calories	¼ C low fat fish	¾ C grain ¾ C bean	1C lo/½C me/¼C Hi	½ C low/¼ C med
	¼ C low fat fowl	¾ C grain ¾ C bean	1C lo/½C me/¼C Hi	½ C low/¼ C med
	2 eggs	¾ C grain ¾ C bean	1C lo/½C me/¼C Hi	½ C low/¼ C med
	¼ C med fat protein	¾ C grain ¾ C bean	1C lo/½C me/¼C Hi	½ C low/¼ C med
2200 calories	¼ C low fat fish	13 T grain 13 T bean	1⅛C lo/9 T me/4.5THi	9 T low/¼ C med
	¼ C low fat fowl	13 T grain 13 T bean	1⅛C lo/9 T me/4.5THi	9 T low/¼ C med
	2 eggs	13 T grain 13 T bean	1⅛C lo/9 T me/4.5THi	9 T low/¼ C med
	¼ C med fat protein	13 T grain 13 T bean	1⅛C lo/9 T me/4.5THi	9 T low/¼ C med
2400 calories	5 T low fat fish	⅞ C grain ⅞C bean	1¼C lo/⅝C me/5T Hi	⅝ C low/5 T med
	5 T low fat fowl	⅞ C grain ⅞C bean	1¼C lo/⅝C me/5T Hi	⅝ C low/5 T med
	2 eggs	⅞ C grain ⅞C bean	1¼C lo/⅝C me/5T Hi	⅝ C low/5 T med
	5 T med fat protein	⅞ C grain ⅞C bean	1¼C lo/⅝C me/5T Hi	⅝ C low/5 T med

PROFILE 1 RECOMMENDED FOODS AND EATING PLAN
70% CHO–20% PROTEIN–10% FAT continued

Calories	Green Vegetables	Red, Orange, Purple	Green Leafy	Fats
2 T = ⅛ cup	**Low carbohydrate**	**Low carbohydrate**	**Low carbohydrate**	All fats sparingly
4 T = ¼ cup	celery green pepper	beets eggplant	kale mustard greens	1 teaspoon any oil =
6 T = ⅜ cup	green sprouts	purple cabbage	Lettuce—Bibb, leafy,	1 teaspoon butter =
8 T = ½ cup	zucchini	red peppers	romaine	1 tsp. mayonnaise =
10 T = ⅝ cup	**Med carbohydrate**	tomatoes	**Med carbohydrate**	2 large olives
12 T = ¾ cup	broccoli	**Med carbo**—carrot	mung sprouts	
14 T = ⅞ cup	leeks	**High carbo**—yam		
16 T = 1 cup	scallions	sweet potatoes		
1000 calories	½ C low/⅛ C med	½C lo/¼C me/⅛C Hi	1 C low/¼ C med	1 teaspoon
	½ C low/⅛ C med	½C lo/¼C me/⅛C Hi	1 C low/¼ C med	1 teaspoon
	½ C low/⅛ C med	½C lo/¼C me/⅛C Hi	1 C low/¼ C med	¼ teaspoon
	½ C low/⅛ C med	½C lo/¼C me/⅛C Hi	1 C low/¼ C med	½ teaspoon
1200 calories	⅝ C low/⅛ C med	⅝C lo/5T me/2.5T Hi	1 C 3 T low/5 T med	1¼ teaspoon
	⅝ C low/⅛ C med	⅝C lo/5T me/2.5T Hi	1 C 3 T low/5 T med	1¼ teaspoon
	⅝ C low/⅛ C med	⅝C lo/5T me/2.5T Hi	1 C 3 T low/5 T med	¼ teaspoon
	⅝ C low/⅛ C med	⅝C lo/5T me/2.5T Hi	1 C 3 T low/5 T med	⅝ teaspoon
1400 calories	11 T low/3T med	¾C lo/⅜C me/3T Hi	1⅜ C low/⅜ C med	1⅜ teaspoon
	11 T low/3T med	¾C lo/⅜C me/3T Hi	1⅜ C low/⅜ C med	1⅜ teaspoon
	11 T low/3T med	¾C lo/⅜C me/3T Hi	1⅜ C low/⅜ C med	½ teaspoon
	11 T low/3T med	¾C lo/⅜C me/3T Hi	1⅜ C low/⅜ C med	¾ teaspoon
1600 calories	13 T low/3 T med	¾C lo/⅜C me/3 T Hi	1⅝ C low/⅜ C med	⅝ teaspoon
	13 T low/3 T med	¾C lo/⅜C me/3 T Hi	1⅝ C low/⅜ C med	⅝ teaspoon
	13 T low/3 T med	¾C lo/⅜C me/3 T Hi	1⅝ C low/⅜ C med	½ teaspoon
	13 T low/3 T med	¾C lo/⅜C me/3 T Hi	1⅝ C low/⅜ C med	¾ teaspoon
1800 calories	⅞ C low/¼ C med	⅞C lo/7T me/3.5T Hi	1¾ C low/7T med	1¾ teaspoon
	⅞ C low/¼ C med	⅞C lo/7T me/3.5T Hi	1¾ C low/7T med	1¾ teaspoon
	⅞ C low/¼ C med	⅞C lo/7T me/3.5T Hi	1¾ C low/7T med	½ teaspoon
	⅞ C low/¼ C med	⅞C lo/7T me/3.5T Hi	1¾ C low/7T med	1 teaspoon
2000 calories	1 C low/¼ C med	1C lo/½C me/¼C Hi	2 C low/½ C med	2 teaspoon
	1 C low/¼ C med	1C lo/½C me/¼C Hi	2 C low/½ C med	2 teaspoon
	1 C low/¼ C med	1C lo/½C me/¼C Hi	2 C low/½ C med	½ teaspoon
	1 C low/¼ C med	1C lo/½C me/¼C Hi	2 C low/½ C med	1 teaspoon
2200 calories	1⅛ C low¼ C med	1⅛C lo/9T me/4.5T Hi	2¼ C low/9 T med	2 ¼ teaspoon
	1⅛ C low¼ C med	1⅛C lo/9T me/4.5T Hi	2¼ C low/9 T med	2 ¼ teaspoon
	1⅛ C low¼ C med	1⅛C lo/9T me/4.5T Hi	2¼ C low/9 T med	½ teaspoon
	1⅛ C low¼ C med	1⅛C lo/9T me/4.5T Hi	2¼ C low/9 T med	1⅛ teaspoon
2400 calories	1 C 3 T low/5 T med	1¼C lo/⅝C me/5 T Hi	2⅜ C low/⅝ C med	2⅜ teaspoon
	1 C 3 T low/5 T med	1¼C lo/⅝C me/5 T Hi	2⅜ C low/⅝ C med	2⅜ teaspoon
	1 C 3 T low/5 T med	1¼C lo/⅝C me/5 T Hi	2⅜ C low/⅝ C med	⅝ teaspoon
	1 C 3 T low/5 T med	1¼C lo/⅝C me/5 T Hi	2⅜ C iow/⅝ C med	1¼ teaspoon

NOTE / means "OR". Choose 2 cups low or ½ cup medium or ¼ cup high

PROFILE 2 CALORIE–GRAM PORTIONS

TOTAL DAILY CALORIE–GRAM PORTIONS

Total Grams	45% CHO		55% Protein		20% Fat		Total Cals
	Cals	Grams	Cals	Grams	Cals	Grams	
173	311	78	381	95	311	35	1003
207	375	93	455	114	375	41	1201
242	435	109	532	133	436	48	1404
276	497	124	607	152	497	55	1601
311	560	140	684	171	560	62	1800
345	621	155	759	190	621	69	2001
380	684	171	836	209	684	76	2204
415	747	187	913	228	747	83	2407

CALORIE–GRAM PORTIONS PER MEAL

58	104	26	127	32	104	12	334
69	124	31	152	38	124	14	400
81	145	36	177	44	145	16	468
92	166	41	202	51	166	18	534
104	187	47	228	57	187	21	600
115	207	52	253	63	207	23	667
127	228	57	279	70	228	25	735
138	249	62	304	76	249	28	802

PROFILE 2 RECOMMENDED FOODS AND EATING PLAN
45% CHO–55% PROTEIN–20% FAT

Calories	Med, Fat Protein		Beans & Grains	Root Vegetables	Yellow, White Veg.
2 T = ⅛ cup	beef	dark fowl	all beans	**High carbohydrate**	**Low carbohydrate**
4 T = ¼ cup	organs	herring	all grains	carrots	crookneck squash
6 T = ⅜ cup	duck	red meat		potatoes	**Med carbohydrate**
8 T = ½ cup	salmon	mackerel			cauliflower
10 T = ⅝ cup	goose	veal			**High carbohydrate**
12 T = ¾ cup	abalone	octopus			acorn, banana,
14 T = ⅞ cup	lamb	venison			hubbard squash
16 T = 1 cup	clam	sardine			fresh corn
1000 calories	7 T med fat		⅛ C grain	⅛ C high	½C low or ¼C med
	7 T med fat		⅛ C bean	⅛ C high	½C low or ¼C med
	⅜C low fat chicken		⅛ C bean	⅛ C high	½C low or ¼C med
	9 T low fat fish		⅛ C bean	⅛ C high	½C low or ¼C med
1200 calories	½ cup med fat		⅛ C grain	⅛ C high	⅝C low or ¼C med
	8 T med fat		⅛ C bean	⅛ C high	⅝C low or ¼C med
	7 T low fat chicken		⅛ C bean	⅛ C high	⅝C low or ¼C med
	11 T low fat fish		⅛ C bean	⅛ C high	⅝C low or ¼C med
1400 calories	10 T med fat		3 T grain	3 T high	11T low or ⅜C med
	10 T med fat		3 T bean	3 T high	11T low or ⅜C med
	½C low fat chicken		3 T bean	3 T high	11T low or ⅜C med
	13 T low fat fish		3 T bean	3 T high	11T low or ⅜C med
1600 calories	11 T med fat		3 T grain	3 T high	13T low or ⅜C med
	11 T med fat		3 T bean	3 T high	13T low or ⅜C med
	10 T low fat chicken		3 T bean	3 T high	13T low or ⅜C med
	14 T low fat fish		3 T bean	3 T high	13T low or ⅜C med
1800 calories	13 T med fat		¼ C grain	¼ C high	⅞C low or 7T med
	13 T med fat		¼ C bean	¼ C high	⅞C low or 7T med
	11 T low fat chicken		¼ C bean	¼ C high	⅞C low or 7T med
	1 cup low fat fish		¼ C bean	¼ C high	⅞C low or 7T med
2000 calories	14 T med fat		¼ C grain	¼ C high	1C low or ½C med
	14 T med fat		¼ C grain	¼ C high	1C low or ½C med
	¾C low fat chicken		¼ C grain	¼ C high	1C low or ½C med
	1⅛ C low fat fish		¼ C grain	¼ C high	1C low or ½C med
2200 calories	15 T med fat		¼ C grain	¼ C high	1⅛C lo or 9T med
	15 T med fat		¼ C bean	¼ C high	1⅛C lo or 9T med
	13 T low fat chicken		¼ C bean	¼ C high	1⅛C lo or 9T med
	1¼ C low fat fish		¼ C bean	¼ C high	1⅛C lo or 9T med
2400 calories	1C + 1T med fat		5 T grain	5 T high	1C 3T lo/ ⅝C med
	1C + 1T med fat		5 T bean	5 T high	1C 3T lo/ ⅝C med
	14 T low fat chicken		5T bean	5 T high	1C 3T lo/ ⅝C med
	1⅜ C low fat fish		5T bean	5 T high	1C 3T lo/ ⅝C med

PROFILE 2 RECOMMENDED FOODS AND EATING PLAN
45% CHO–55% PROTEIN–20% FAT continued

Calories	Green Vegetables	Red, Orange, Purple	Green Leafy	Fats
2 T = ⅛ cup	**Low carbohydrate**	**Med Carbohydrate**	**Low carbohydrate**	**All fats**
4 T = ¼ cup	celery	butternut squash	spinach	1 teaspoon any oil =
6 T = ⅜ cup	**Med carbohydrate**	carrot		1 teaspoon butter=
8 T = ½ cup	asparagus			1 tsp. mayonnaise =
10 T = ⅝ cup	snap, snow peas			2 large olives
12 T = ¾ cup	**High Carbohydrate**			
14 T = ⅞ cup	artichoke			
16 T = 1 cup				
1000 calories	1C low or ¼C med	¼ C med	1 cup low/¼C med	¾ tsp
	½C low or ⅛C med	¼ C med	1 cup low/¼C med	¾ tsp
	½C low or ⅛C med	¼ C med	1 cup low/¼C med	1½ tsp
	½C low or ⅛C med	¼ C med	1 cup low/¼C med	2 tsp
1200 calories	1C 3T low or 5T med	5 T med	1¼C low/5T med	1 tsp
	⅝C lo or ⅛C med	5 T med	1¼C low/5T med	1 tsp
	⅝C lo or ⅛C med	5 T med	1¼C low/5T med	1¾ tsp
	⅝C lo or ⅛C med	5 T med	1¼C low/5T med	2⅜ tsp
1400 calories	1⅜C low or ⅜C med	6 T med	1⅜C low/⅜C med	1 tsp
	11T low or 3T med	6 T med	1⅜C low/⅜C med	1 tsp
	11T low or 3T med	6 T med	1⅜C low/⅜C med	2⅛ tsp
	11T low or 3T med	6 T med	1⅜C low/⅜C med	2¾ tsp
1600 calories	1⅝ C lo or ⅜C med	6 T med	1⅝C low/7T med	1¼ tsp
	13T low or 3T med	6 T med	1⅝C low/7T med	1¼ tsp
	13T low or 3T med	6 T med	1⅝C low/7T med	2⅜ tsp
	13T low or 3T med	6 T med	1⅝C low/7T med	3⅛ tsp
1800 calories	1C 13T lo or 7T med	7 T med	1¾C low/ ½C med	1⅜ tsp
	⅞C lo or ¼C med	7 T med	1¾C low/ ½C med	1⅜ tsp
	⅞C lo or ¼C med	7 T med	1¾C low/ ½C med	3 tsp
	⅞C lo or ¼C med	7 T med	1¾C low/ ½C med	3¾ tsp
2000 calories	2C low or ½C med	½ C med	2C low/½C med	1½ tsp
	1C low or ¼C med	½ C med	2C low/½C med	1½ tsp
	1C low or ¼C med	½ C med	2C low/½C med	3¼ tsp
	1C low or ¼C med	½ C med	2C low/½C med	4 tsp
2200 calories	2C 3T lo/9T med	9 T med	2¼C low/ ½C med	1¾ tsp
	1⅛C lo/¼C med	9 T med	2¼C low/ ½C med	1¾ tsp
	1⅛C lo/¼C med	9 T med	2¼C low/ ½C med	3½ tsp
	1⅛C lo/¼C med	9 T med	2¼C low/ ½C med	4½ tsp
2400 calories	2 ⅜C lo or ⅝C med	10 T med	2⅜C low/¾C med	1¾ tsp
	1C 3T lo/5T med	10 T med	2⅜C low/¾C med	1¾ tsp
	1C 3T lo/5T med	10 T med	2⅜C low/¾C med	3¾ tsp
	1C 3T lo/5T med	10 T med	2⅜C low/¾C med	4¾ tsp

NOTE / means "OR". Choose 2 cups low or ½ cup medium or ¼ cup high.

PROFILE 3 CALORIE–GRAM PORTIONS

TOTAL DAILY CALORIE–GRAM PORTIONS

Total Grams	50% CHO		40% Protein		10% Fat		Total Cals
	Cals	Grams	Cals	Grams	Cals	Grams	
222	444	111	355	89	200	22	999
267	534	134	427	107	240	27	1202
312	624	156	499	125	281	31	1404
356	712	178	570	142	320	36	1602
400	800	200	640	160	360	40	1800
445	890	223	712	178	401	45	2003
489	978	245	782	196	440	49	2201
534	1068	267	854	214	481	53	2403

CALORIE–GRAM PORTIONS PER MEAL

74	148	37	118	30	67	7	333
89	178	45	142	36	80	9	401
104	208	52	166	42	94	10	468
119	237	59	190	47	107	12	534
133	267	67	213	53	120	13	600
148	297	74	237	59	134	15	668
163	326	82	261	65	147	16	734
178	356	89	285	71	160	18	801

PROFILE 3 RECOMMENDED FOODS AND EATING PLAN
50% CHO–40% PROTEIN–10% FAT

Calories	Protein	Beans & Grains	Root Vegetables	Yellow, White Veg.
2 T = ⅛ cup 4 T = ¼ cup 6 T = ⅜ cup 8 T = ½ cup 10 T = ⅝ cup 12 T = ¾ cup 14 T = ⅞ cup 16 T = 1 cup	all foods ok	all foods ok	all foods ok	all foods ok
1000 calories	7 T med fat protein ⅜ C low fat chicken ½ C low fat fish 1egg+⅜C low fat fish	¼ C grain ⅛C grain/⅛C bean ⅛C grain/⅛C bean ⅜ C beans	1C lo/½C me/¼C Hi 1C lo/½C me/¼C Hi 1C lo/½C me/¼C Hi ½C lo/¼C me/⅛C Hi	¼C low/⅛C med ¼C low/⅛C med ¼C low/⅛C med ¼C low/⅛C med
1200 calories	½ C med fat protein 7 T low fat chicken ⅝ C low fat fish 1 egg+7T low fat fish	5 T grain ⅛C grain/⅛C bean ⅛C grain/⅛C bean 7 T beans	1¼C lo/⅝C me/5T Hi 1¼C lo/⅝C me/5T Hi 1¼C lo/⅝C me/5T Hi ⅝C lo/5T me/2.5T Hi	5T low/3T med 5T low/3T med 5T low/3T med 5T low/3T med
1400 calories	⅝ C med fat protein ½ C low fat chicken 11 T low fat fish 1 egg+½C low fat fish	⅜ C grain 3 T grain/3 T bean 3T grain/3T bean ½ C beans	1.5C lo/¾C me/⅜C Hi 1.5C lo/¾C me/⅜C Hi 1.5C lo/¾C me/⅜C Hi ¾C lo/⅜C me/3T Hi	⅜C low/3T med ⅜C low/3T med ⅜C low/3T med ⅜C low/3T med
1600 calories	11 T med fat protein ⅝ C low fat chicken 13 T low fat fish 1 egg+⅝C low fat fish	⅜ C grain 3 T grain/3 T bean 3 T grain/3 T bean ⅝ C beans	1.5C lo/¾C me⅜C lo 1.5C lo/¾C me⅜C lo 1.5C lo/¾C me⅜C lo ¾C lo/⅜C me/3T Hi	⅜C low/3T med ⅜C low/3T med ⅜C low/3T med ⅜C low/3T med
1800 calories	13 T med fat protein 11 T low fat chicken 1 C low fat fish 2eggs+11T low fat fish	7 T grain ¼C grain/¼C bean ¼C grain/¼C bean 11 T beans	1¾C lo/⅞C me/7T Hi 1¾C lo/⅞C me/7T Hi 1¾C lo/⅞C me/7T Hi 1C lo/½C me/¼C Hi	7T low/3T med 7T low/3T med 7T low/3T med 7T low/3T med
2000 calories	⅞ C med fat protein ¾ C low fat chicken ⅞ C low fat fish 2eggs+¾C low fat fish	½ C grain ¼C grain/¼C bean ¼C grain/¼C bean ¾ C beans	2C lo/1C me/½C Hi 2C lo/1C me/½C Hi 2C lo/1C me/½C Hi 1C lo/½C me/¼C Hi	½C low/¼C med ½C low/¼C med ½C low/¼C med ½C low/¼C med
2200 calories	15 T med fat protein 13 T low fat chicken 1⅛ C low fat fish 2eggs+13T low fat fish	9 T grain ¼C grain/¼C bean ¼C grain/¼C bean 13 T beans	2C lo/1C me/⅝C HI 2C lo/1C me/⅝C HI 2C lo/1C me/⅝C HI 1C lo/½C me/¼C Hi	9T low/¼C med 9T low/¼C med 9T low/¼C med 9T low/¼C med
2400 calories	1 C 1T med fat protein ⅞ C low fat chicken 1 C 3 T low fat fish 2eggs+⅞C low fat fish	⅝ C grain 5 T grain/5 T bean 5 T grain/5 T bean ⅞ C beans	2C lo/1C me/⅝C Hi 2C lo/1C me/⅝C Hi 2C lo/1C me/⅝C Hi 1¼C lo/⅝C me/5T Hi	⅝C lo/5T med ⅝C lo/5T med ⅝C lo/5T med ⅝C lo/5T med

PROFILE 3 RECOMMENDED FOODS AND EATING PLAN
50% CHO–40% PROTEIN–10% FAT continued

Calories	Green Vegetables	Red, Orange, Purple	Green Leafy	Fats
2 T = ⅛ cup 4 T = ¼ cup 6 T = ⅜ cup 8 T = ½ cup 10 T = ⅝ cup 12 T = ¾ cup 14 T = ⅞ cup 16 T = 1 cup	all foods ok	all foods ok	all foods ok	all foods ok 1 teaspoon any oil = 1 teaspoon butter = 1 tsp. mayonnaise = 2 large olives
1000 calories	1C lo/¼C med	½C lo/¼C me/⅛C Hi	1C low / ¼C med	0
	1C lo/¼C med	½C lo/¼C me/⅛C Hi	1C low / ¼C med	½ tsp
	1C lo/¼C med	½C lo/¼C me/⅛C Hi	1C low / ¼C med	1 tsp
	1C lo/¼C med	½C lo/¼C me/⅛C Hi	1C low / ¼C med	0
1200 calories	1¼C lo/5T med	⅝C lo/¼C me/⅛C Hi	1C 3T lo/5T med	0
	1¼C lo/5T med	⅝C lo/¼C me/⅛C Hi	1C 3T lo/5T med	⅝ tsp
	1¼C lo/5T med	⅝C lo/¼C me/⅛C Hi	1C 3T lo/5T med	1¼ tsp
	1¼C lo/5T med	⅝C lo/¼C me/⅛C Hi	1C 3T lo/5T med	0
1400 calories	1⅜C lo/⅜C med	¾C lo/⅜C med/3T Hi	1⅜C lo / 5T med	0
	1⅜C lo/⅜C med	¾C lo/⅜C med/3T Hi	1⅜C lo / 5T med	¾ tsp
	1⅜C lo/⅜C med	¾C lo/⅜C med/3T Hi	1⅜C lo / 5T med	1⅜ tsp
	1⅜C lo/⅜C med	¾C lo/⅜C med/3T Hi	1⅜C lo / 5T med	0
1600 calories	1⅝C lo/⅜C med	¾C lo/⅜C med/3T Hi	1⅝C lo / ⅜ C med	0
	1⅝C lo/⅜C med	¾C lo/⅜C med/3T Hi	1⅝C lo / ⅜ C med	¾ tsp
	1⅝C lo/⅜C med	¾C lo/⅜C med/3T Hi	1⅝C lo / ⅜ C med	1 ⅝ tsp
	1⅝C lo/⅜C med	¾C lo/⅜C med/3T Hi	1⅝C lo / ⅜ C med	0
1800 calories	1¾C lo/7T med	⅞C lo/7T med/3.5T Hi	1⅞C lo / 7T med	0
	1¾C lo/7T med	⅞C lo/7T med/3.5T Hi	1⅞C lo / 7T med	⅞ tsp
	1¾C lo/7T med	⅞C lo/7T med/3.5T Hi	1⅞C lo / 7T med	1⅞ tsp
	1¾C lo/7T med	⅞C lo/7T med/3.5T Hi	1⅞C lo / 7T med	0
2000 calories	2C lo/½C med	1C lo/½C med/¼C Hi	2C lo / ½C med	0
	2C lo/½C med	1C lo/½C med/¼C Hi	2C lo / ½C med	⅞ tsp
	2C lo/½C med	1C lo/½C med/¼C Hi	2C lo / ½C med	2 tsp
	2C lo/½C med	1C lo/½C med/¼C Hi	2C lo / ½C med	0
2200 calories	2¼C lo/9T med	1⅛C lo/9T me/¼C Hi	2¼C lo / 9T med	0
	2¼C lo/9T med	1⅛C lo/9T me/¼C Hi	2¼C lo / 9T med	1 tsp
	2¼C lo/9T med	1⅛C lo/9T me/¼C Hi	2¼C lo / 9T med	2¼ tsp
	2¼C lo/9T med	1⅛C lo/9T me/¼C Hi	2¼C lo / 9T med	0
2400 calories	2½C lo/⅝C med	1¼C lo/⅝C me/5T Hi	2⅜C lo / ⅝C med	0
	2½C lo/⅝C med	1¼C lo/⅝C me/5T Hi	2⅜C lo / ⅝C med	1⅛ tsp
	2½C lo/⅝C med	1¼C lo/⅝C me/5T Hi	2⅜C lo / ⅝C med	2⅜ tsp
	2½C lo/⅝C med	1¼C lo/⅝C me/5T Hi	2⅜C lo / ⅝C med	0

NOTE / means "OR". Choose 2 cups low or ½ cup medium or¼ cup high.

PROFILE 4 CALORIE–GRAM PORTIONS

TOTAL DAILY CALORIE–GRAM PORTIONS

Total Grams	40% CHO		30% Protein		30% Fat		Total Cals
	Cals	Grams	Cals	Grams	Cals	Grams	
182	291	73	218	55	491	55	1001
218	349	87	262	65	587	65	1199
255	408	102	306	77	689	77	1403
291	466	116	349	87	786	87	1601
328	525	131	394	98	886	98	1804
364	582	146	437	109	983	109	2002
400	640	160	480	120	1080	120	2200
437	699	178	524	131	1180	131	2404

CALORIE–GRAM PORTIONS PER MEAL

61	97	24	73	18	164	18	334
73	116	29	87	22	196	22	400
85	136	34	102	26	230	26	468
97	155	39	116	29	262	29	534
109	175	44	131	33	295	33	601
121	194	49	146	36	328	36	667
133	213	53	160	40	360	40	733
146	233	58	175	44	393	44	801

PROFILE 4 RECOMMENDED FOODS AND EATING PLAN
40% CHO–30% PROTEIN–30% FAT

Calories	Protein	Beans & Grains	Root Vegetables	Yellow, White Veg.
2 T = ⅛ cup 4 T = ¼ cup 6 T = ⅜ cup 8 T = ½ cup 10 T = ⅝ cup 12 T = ¾ cup 14 T = ⅞ cup 16 T = 1 cup	all foods ok	all foods ok	all foods ok	all foods ok
1000 calories	¼ C med fat protein ¼ C med fat protein ¼C med fat protein ¼ C low fat chicken 5 T low fat fish	⅛ C grain ¼ C grain ¼ C bean ⅛ C bean ⅛ C bean	½C lo/¼C me/⅛C Hi ¼C lo/⅛C me/1T Hi ¼C lo/⅛C me/1T Hi ½C lo/¼C me/⅛C Hi ½C lo/¼C me/⅛C Hi	¼C low/⅛C med ¼C low/⅛C med ¼C low/⅛C med ½C low/¼C med ½C low/¼C med
1200 calories	5T med fat protein 5T med fat protein 5T med fat protein 5 T low fat chicken ⅜C low fat fish	⅛ C grain 5T grain 5T bean ⅛ C bean ⅛ C bean	⅝C lo/5T me/2.5 Hi 5T lo/2.5T me/1.5T Hi 5T lo/2.5T me/1.5T Hi ⅝C lo/5T me/2.5 Hi ⅝C lo/5T me/2.5 Hi	5T low/⅛C med 5T low/⅛C med 5T low/⅛C med ⅝C low/5T med ⅝C low/5T med
1400 calories	⅜ C med fat protein ⅜ C med fat protein ⅜ C med fat protein ⅜ C low fat chicken 7 T low fat fish	3 T grain ⅜ C grain ⅜ C bean 3 T bean 3 T bean	11T lo/5.5T mw/3T Hi ⅜C lo/3T me/1.5T Hi ⅜C lo/3T me/1.5T Hi 11T lo/5.5T mw/3T Hi 11T lo/5.5T mw/3T Hi	⅜C low/3T med ⅜C low/3T med ⅜C low/3T med 11T low/⅜C med 11T low/⅜C med
1600 calories	⅜ C med fat protein ⅜ C med fat protein ⅜ C med fat protein ⅜ C low fat chicken ½ C low fat fish	3 T grain ⅜ C grain ⅜ C bean 3 T bean 3 T bean	13T lo/6.5T me/3T Hi 3/C lo/3T me/1.5T Hi 3/C lo/3T me/1.5T Hi 13T lo/6.5T me/3T Hi 13T lo/6.5T me/3T Hi	⅜C low/3T med ⅜C low/3T med ⅜C low/3T med 13T low/⅜C med 13T low/⅜C med
1800 calories	7 T med fat protein 7 T med fat protein 7 T med fat protein 7 T low fat chicken 9 T low fat fish	¼ C grain 7 T grain 7 T bean ¼ C bean ¼ C bean	⅞C lo/7T me/3.5 T Hi 7T lo/3.5T me/⅛C Hi 7T lo/3.5T me/⅛C Hi ⅞C lo/7T me/3.5 T Hi ⅞C lo/7T me/3.5 T Hi	7T low/¼C med 7T low/¼C med 7T low/¼C med ⅞C low/7T med ⅞C low/7T med
2000 calories	½ C med fat protein ½ C med fat protein ½ C med fat protein ½ C low fat chicken ⅝ C low fat fish	¼ C grain ½ C grain ½ C bean ¼ C bean ¼ C bean	1C lo/½C me/¼C Hi ½C lo/¼C me/⅛C Hi ½C lo/¼C me/⅛C Hi 1C lo/½C me/¼C Hi 1C lo/½C me/¼C Hi	½C low/¼C med ½C low/¼C med ½C low/¼C med 1C low/½C med 1C low/½C med
2200 calories	9T med fat protein 9T med fat protein 9 T med fat protein 9 T low fat chicken 11 T low fat fish	¼ C grain 9 T grain 9 T bean ¼ C bean ¼ C bean	1 ⅛C lo/9T me/¼C Hi 9T lo/¼C me/⅛C Hi 9T lo/¼C me/⅛C Hi 1 ⅛C lo/9T me/¼C Hi 1⅛C lo/9T me/¼C Hi	9T low/¼C med 9T low/¼C med 9T low/¼C med 1⅛C low/9T med 1⅛C low/9T med
2400 calories	⅝ C med fat protein ⅝ C med fat protein ⅝ C med fat protein ⅝ C low fat chicken ¾ C low fat fish	5 T grain ⅝ C grain ⅝ C bean 5 T bean 5 T bean	1¼C lo/ ⅝C me/5T Hi ⅝C lo/5T me/⅛C Hi ⅝C lo/5T me/⅛C Hi 1¼C lo/ ⅝C me/5T Hi 1¼C lo/ ⅝C me/5T Hi	⅝C low/5T med ⅝C low/5T med ⅝C low/5T med 1C 3T low/⅝C med 1C 3T low/⅝C med

PROFILE 4 RECOMMENDED FOODS AND EATING PLAN
40% CHO–30% PROTEIN–30% FAT continued

Calories	Green Vegetables	Red, Orange, Purple	Green Leafy	Fats
2 T = ⅛ cup 4 T = ¼ cup 6 T = ⅜ cup 8 T = ½ cup 10 T = ⅝ cup 12 T = ¾ cup 14 T = ⅞ cup 16 T = 1 cup	all foods ok	all foods ok	all foods ok	all foods ok 1 teaspoon any oil = 1 teaspoon butter = 1 tsp. mayonnaise = 2 large olives
1000 calories	1C low/¼C med	¼C lo/⅛C me/1T Hi	1C lo/¼C med	3 tsp
	1C low/¼C med	¼C lo/⅛C me/1T Hi	1C lo/¼C med	3 tsp
	1C low/¼C med	¼C lo/⅛C me/1T Hi	1C lo/¼C med	3 tsp
	¼C low/1T med	½C lo/¼C me/⅛C Hi	1C lo/¼C med	3 tsp
	¼C low/1T med	½C lo/¼C me/⅛C Hi	1C lo/¼C med	3 ½ tsp
1200 calories	1¼C lo/5T med	5T lo/⅛C me/1T Hi	1C 3T lo/5T med	3 ½ tsp
	1¼C lo/5T med	5T lo/⅛C me/1T Hi	1C 3T lo/5T med	3 ½ tsp
	1¼C lo/5T med	5T lo/⅛C me/1T Hi	1C 3T lo/5T med	3 ½ tsp
	5T low/1T med	⅝C lo/5T me/⅛C H	1C 3T lo/5T med	3 ½ tsp
	5T low/1T med	⅝C lo/5T me/⅛C H	1C 3T lo/5T med	4 ¼ tsp
1400 calories	1⅜C lo/⅜C med	⅜C lo/3T me/1.5T Hi	1⅜C lo/⅜C med	4 ¼ tsp
	1⅜C lo/⅜C med	⅜C lo/3T me/1.5T Hi	1⅜C lo/⅜C med	4 ¼ tsp
	1⅜C lo/⅜C med	⅜C lo/3T me/1.5T Hi	1⅜C lo/⅜C med	4 ¼ tsp
	⅜C low/1T med	¾C lo/⅜C me/3T Hi	1⅜C lo/⅜C med	4 ¼ tsp
	⅜C low/1T med	¾C lo/⅜C me/3T Hi	1⅜C lo/⅜C med	5 tsp
1600 calories	1⅝C lo/⅜C med	⅜C lo/3T me/1.5T Hi	1⅝C lo/⅜C med	4 ¾ tsp
	1⅝C lo/⅜C med	⅜C lo/3T me/1.5T Hi	1⅝C lo/⅜C med	4 ¾ tsp
	1⅝C lo/⅜C med	⅜C lo/3T me/1.5T Hi	1⅝C lo/⅜C med	4 ¾ tsp
	⅜C low/⅛C med	13T lo/⅜C me/3T H	1⅝C lo/⅜C med	4 ¾ tsp
	⅜C low/⅛C med	13T lo/⅜C me/3T H	⅝C lo/⅜C med	5 ¾ tsp
1800 calories	1¾C lo/7T med	7T lo/¼C me/⅛C Hi	1¾C lo/7T med	5 ¼ tsp
	1¾C lo/7T med	7T lo/¼C me/⅛C Hi	1¾C lo/7T med	5 ¼ tsp
	1¾C lo/7T med	7T lo/¼C me/⅛C Hi	1¾C lo/7T med	5 ¼ tsp
	7T low/⅛C med	⅞C lo/7T me/3T Hi	1¾C lo/7T med	5 ¼ tsp
	7T low/⅛C med	⅞C lo/7T me/3T Hi	1¾C lo/7T med	6 ½ tsp
2000 calories	2C lo/½C med	½C lo/¼C me/⅛C Hi	2C lo/½C med	5 ¾ tsp
	2C lo/½C med	½C lo/¼C me/⅛C Hi	2C lo/½C med	5 ¾ tsp
	2C lo/½C med	½C lo/¼C me/⅛C Hi	2C lo/½C med	5 ¾ tsp
	½C low/⅛C med	1C lo/½C me/¼C Hi	2C lo/½C med	5 ¾ tsp
	½C low/⅛C med	1C lo/½C me/¼C Hi	2C lo/½C med	7 ¼ tsp
2200 calories	2¼C lo/9T med	9T lo/¼C me/⅛C Hi	2¼C lo/9T med	6 ¼ tsp
	2¼C lo/9T med	9T lo/¼C me/⅛C Hi	2¼C lo/9T med	6 ¼ tsp
	2¼C lo/9T med	9T lo/¼C me/⅛C Hi	2¼C lo/9T med	6 ¼ tsp
	9T low/⅛C med	1⅛C lo/9T me/¼C Hi	2¼C lo/9T med	6 ¼ tsp
	9T low/⅛C med	1⅛C lo/9T me/¼C Hi	2¼C lo/9T med	8 tsp
2400 calories	2⅜C lo/⅝C med	⅝C lo/5T med/2.5T Hi	2⅜C lo/⅝C med	7 ¼ tsp
	2⅜C lo/⅝C med	⅝C lo/5T med/2.5T Hi	2⅜C lo/⅝C med	7 ¼ tsp
	2⅜C lo/⅝C med	⅝C lo/5T med/2.5T Hi	2⅜C lo/⅝C med	7 ¼ tsp
	⅝C low/⅛C med	1¼C lo/⅝C me/5T Hi	2⅜C lo/⅝C med	7 ¼ tsp
	⅝C low/⅛C med	1¼C lo/⅝C me/5T Hi	2⅜C lo/⅝C med	8 ½ tsp

NOTE / means "OR". Choose 2 cups low or ½ cup medium or ¼ cup high.

REINTRODUCING CLASS B FOODS INTO YOUR DIET

After eight weeks of eating only Class A foods, you may be ready to add some Class B foods to your diet. Most people are especially ready to eat fruit again. Add fruits in this order: start with the lower carbohydrate fruits (berries, peaches, and apricots), then add medium carbohydrate fruit (melons), and last add high carbohydrate fruit (apples, pears, and bananas). Pay attention to how you feel at each addition. If your digestive tract is upset, you may be sensitive to that fruit and will need to avoid it for four more months before you try it again. If you experience gas and bloat after eating fruit, you may still harbor unfriendly organisms in your digestive tract that are fermenting the fruit, creating gas and discomfort as well as toxic by-products of their metabolism that can cause your body to be toxic. You will need more treatment from your health practitioner to replace the unfriendly organisms with friendly organisms before trying fruit again.

When you are able to eat fruit comfortably, experiment to determine if you need to eat it all by itself away from other foods or if you can eat it with meals. Since digestion of fruit occurs mainly in the intestine, it moves through the stomach quickly. However, the initial digestion of proteins occurs in the stomach requiring proteins to stay in the stomach longer. If fruit gets detained in the stomach when proteins are eaten at the same time, the fruit may ferment creating gas and bloat. If you feel the symptoms of fruit fermentation, then eat fruit away from other foods. However, fruit eaten alone may initiate blood sugar swings as described previously. If you tend to have low blood sugar, try eating fruit with meals to slow the absorption of the fruit sugar. Also eat your fruit with meals if you need to incorporate the appropriate balance of carbohydrate, protein, and fat in each meal for weight control purposes and for optimal metabolism. After learning the skill of listening to your body for eight weeks on the Get Healthy Eating Plan, you should be able to determine which method of eating fruit is best for you by paying attention to the signals from your body now.

Eat only two servings of fruit per day to avoid overloading on fruit sugar. One serving of a fruit includes one small apple, ½ banana, or ten grapes.

Nuts and seeds are a healthy addition to your diet because of the beneficial fats they contain. To be sure the fats in nuts are in their most health building form, always eat them freshly shelled and raw (not roasted and salted). If you buy them shelled, freeze them to preserve the fats. The oils in nuts and seeds are called essential because we have to eat them; our bodies cannot manufacture them. These oils are metabolized in our bodies to short acting hormones called prostaglandins. They are also used in construction of cell membranes. When our cell membranes contain abnormal fats, nutrients do not move into the cell efficiently and toxins do not move out efficiently, creating toxic, nutritionally deficient cells. Therefore, be sure to eat adequate amounts of beneficial fats daily and avoid detrimental fats (see previous section on fats and oils).

When you were eating only Class A food, you had to choose your daily essential fats from the best-processed oils available. Since consuming your fats from whole foods is always best, start replacing the oils in your diet with nuts and seeds as much as possible. Eat one tablespoon of an omega-3 nut (flaxseeds, pumpkinseeds, and walnuts) and 1 tablespoon of an omega-6 nut (almonds, pecans, sunflower seeds, and sesame seeds) daily. Soaking nuts and seeds over night in water increases their nutritional value by activating the sprouting process, which increases their nutrient content. It also inactivates the enzyme inhibitors in the nuts making them more digestible. Unless you can chew flaxseeds extremely well, grind them in a blender or spice mill before eating them. Since the fats in nuts and seed oxidize quickly and become rancid when they are ground,

grind them just before eating or soaking them. Recipes for nut milk and a power drink follow.

REINTRODUCING ALLERGENIC FOODS INTO YOUR DIET

Since people are commonly allergic or sensitized to soy and the high gluten grains (also Class B foods), treat them as a food allergen when reintroducing them to your diet.

Continue to avoid any of your major food allergens for a total of at least six to 18 months.

When you are ready to test a food to determine if you can tolerate it once again, eat only that food. For instance, if you want to test wheat, do not eat bread as it contains yeast and other ingredients that you might be allergic to. To test wheat, eat a whole-wheat tortilla, which only contains wheat and oil. Better yet, soak bulgar or soft wheat berries for 12 hours, and then pour off the water. Put the soaked berries in a thermos, pour hot water over them, and steep them overnight. This is the healthiest way to eat any grain. Eat only ¼ to ½ cup of the food that you are testing all by itself, at least two hours after your last meal and two hours before your next meal. Listen to your body. Because you have not eaten that food for several weeks you will probably have obvious reactions to it if you are still allergic. If the reactions occur in the first few hours, they are usually easily recognizable. However, food reactions can be delayed up to 48 hours after ingesting the food. Continue to listen to your body for the 48 hours and wait at least two days before testing another food. Review the section "Learning to Read Your Body" and "Testing Foods" on page 38.

If you have no symptoms after eating a newly reintroduced food the first time, test it again in four to five days. When you stop eating an allergenic food, your body may stop making antibodies to that food. Therefore, after eating the food the first time, there are no antibodies circulating to bind with the food and cause an allergic reaction. If you are still allergic to the food, eating it triggers the production of antibodies again and the second time you eat the food the symptoms of food allergies manifest. If you do not react to the food after the second test, you may include it in your eating plan. However, always eat it in small amounts so you digest it well and wait four days before eating it again so that your body can maintain its ability to handle that food beneficially.

Other causes of food reactions include a degenerated digestive tract that does not digest the food well and a leaky gut that allows larger particles of food to enter the blood stream. The body then mistakes these larger food particles as foreign substances and starts producing antibodies to them. If your digestive tract has not healed in eight weeks on the Get Healthy Eating Plan, be sure to see a health practitioner skilled in guiding you through detoxification and rebuilding of the tissues.

Most of my patients have accumulations of toxic metals (mercury, lead, cadmium, nickel, or aluminum) and chemicals in their tissues. The body does not function well until those are detoxified. Toxicity seems to underlie most allergy problems and most degenerative diseases. This toxicity then fosters the growth of unfriendly organisms like Candida and chronic virus conditions (Epstein-Barr virus, herpes virus, etc.). These organisms cannot be brought under control until the body is detoxified. Therefore, you will need a practitioner skilled in detoxification and rebuilding of the body if you continue to have food allergies and ill health.

If you start gaining weight after adding a food back to your menu, eliminate it again and see what happens. Remember food allergies can be one of the causes of unwanted weight gain. If you start eating bread and the pounds start piling up again, what are you going to do? That's right. Stop eating bread or at least limit it to one piece per day and see if the weight comes under control.

POWER DRINK

To start your day in a healthy, invigorating way, drink this power drink in the morning. It provides your body its daily requirement of essential fatty acids and protein building blocks. This combination sustains your blood sugar at an optimal level, preventing the high to low blood sugar swings that occur after a high carbohydrate diet such as cereal, fruit or doughnuts, etc. If you add a complex carbohydrate to the mixture, you will also create the balance of carbohydrate, protein, and fat in your meal that promotes the optimal insulin-glucagon response for weight control.

1. Grind 1 tablespoon of fresh raw flaxseeds, pumpkinseeds, or walnuts in a blender or spice mill. (These seeds contain omega-3 oils, which have to be eaten, the body cannot make them, for proper cell membrane and prostaglandin formation. Most Americans are very deficient in these essential oils. Be sure you eat 1 2 tablespoons of them daily.)

2. Grind 1 tablespoon of one of the nuts containing omega-6 oils such as fresh raw almonds, pecans, sunflower, or sesame seeds. Eat both omega-3 and omega-6 nuts/seeds daily but choose a different nut/seed from each category each day.

3. Blend these omega-3 and omega-6 nuts/seeds with water.

4. Let stand at room temperature overnight (6–10 hours). This allows the nut to start sprouting, which inactivates the enzyme inhibitors that protect the nut's freshness but make them more difficult to digest because they also inhibit your digestive enzymes.

5. Blend protein into the nut/seed mixture in the morning. 1 egg (I use a raw egg after soaking the egg in the shell in the hydrogen peroxide solution for 20 minutes to eliminate the bacteria on the outside of the shell. Eating raw eggs is controversial. Decide for yourself.) OR

Chicken OR

Fish OR

2 tablespoons cottage cheese (if you tolerate dairy products) OR

2 to 3 tablespoons ion exchange whey protein (processed in a special way to preserve the immune building factors. Do not use blender to mix this whey into the drink. Stir the whey into the drink after blending in everything else. This is an extra precaution for preserving the immune globulins natural to the whey.) OR

Your choice of protein

6. Add spice to taste (cinnamon, vanilla extract, frozen fruit, broth, etc.)

Some of My Favorite Power Drink Combinations

1 T (tablespoon) flaxseed, 1 T almonds soaked in ½ cup water, blend in ⅓ cup crockpot chicken and ½ to 1 cup warm chicken broth.

1 T flaxseed, 1 T pecan soaked in ½ cup water, blend in 1 egg, ½ frozen sliced banana, and 6-8 frozen strawberries.

1 T flaxseed, 1 T almonds soaked in ½ cup water, blend in 1 egg and 1 frozen peach.

1 T pumpkinseeds, 1 T almonds soaked in ½ cup water, blend in ⅓ cup turkey, ⅓ cup cooked pumpkin, and a pinch each of cinnamon, nutmeg, and cloves.

1 T flaxseeds, 1 T sesame seeds soaked in ½ cup water, blend in 1 egg, and ⅓ to ½ cup frozen or fresh blueberries.

Nut Milks

Make nut milks by first grinding ¼ cup of any nut or seed in a blender or spice mill. Add one cup of water.

To allow for easier digestion of the nut milk, leave it at room temperature for 6–10 hours before refrigerating.

Nut milks can be used the same way cow's milk is used. If you want smoother milk, strain the mixture after blending it. For a thicker, creamy consistency, increase the amount of the nut or seed per 1 cup of water.

For a sweeter nut milk taste, add a few drops of the herb Stevia, a small amount of a fruit, or vanilla, cinnamon, or other spice.

*T*he recipes in *The New Natural Healing Cookbook* are here to spark your creativity. In accordance with the "Get Healthy Eating Plan," suggested serving sizes are purposely omitted. This is because you must determine the serving size that best suits your individual digestion. I am of the opinion that, to feel better, people should eat smaller amounts of a variety of foods. (See "Some Basic Principles" in Part One.)

Apply to these recipes the same principles used to create your "Get Healthy" meals. For instance, if a recipe has items from only four of the food groups, then add a salad or some raw vegetable sticks from the other three groups to complete a colorful meal.

Wishing you and your families healthy and happy meals!

Breakfast Foods

These recipes correspond to more traditional concepts of breakfast foods. They will help your transition to eating vegetables for breakfast. Remember that on the "Get Healthy Eating Plan," you can eat the same foods for breakfast that you eat for lunch and dinner.

OMELETTE OF SEVEN #1

chopped onion
green beans, cut in ¼-inch pieces
diced rutabaga
chopped red bell pepper

grated zucchini
spinach
1 tablespoon raw butter
2 eggs

Steam-cook small but equal amounts of the preceding vegetables; set aside. Melt butter in a warm omelette pan. Whisk eggs thoroughly, pour them into the pan, and cook over low heat until set. Spread the steamed vegetables over half of the omelette and flip the other half over to cover. Slide onto a warmed plate and serve at once.

Variation 1

Scramble eggs and add to steamed vegetables.

Variation 2

Use different vegetables and add herbs. For example, steam equal amounts of diced green bell pepper, rutabaga, and grated zucchini. At the end of steaming, add diced tomatoes and chopped spinach.

ॐ ॐ ॐ

OMELETTE OF SEVEN #2

1 tablespoon each
fresh spinach, torn small
diced broccoli
grated carrot
diced yellow squash

minced onion
diced kohlrabi (or another root vegetable)
1 egg
1 teaspoon water
1 tablespoon cooked brown rice, millet, or beans

In an oiled omelette pan, stir-cook the vegetables, adding spinach last. Add 1 tablespoon cooked rice, millet, or beans. Beat egg with water and pour over vegetable mixture. Cook over low heat until barely set. Turn omelette once to heat other side. Slide onto a warmed plate and serve.

ᘓ ᘓ ᘓ

OMELETTE OF SEVEN #3

2 tablespoons or equivalent amounts of each
thinly sliced onion
thinly sliced carrot
asparagus, cut in ¼-inch pieces

chopped purple cabbage
torn spinach leaves
1 egg
1 teaspoon water

Heat an oiled omelette pan and stir-cook onion, carrot, and asparagus. Add purple cabbage and spinach. Beat egg with water and pour over vegetables; cook until just set. Turn omelette once to heat the other side. Serve on a warmed plate with cooked millet.

ᘓ ᘓ ᘓ

STEW WITH EGGS

4 cups eggplant, peeled and cut in cubes

4 cups zucchini, cut in cubes

¼ cup oil

1 cup chopped green bell pepper

1 cup chopped onion

1 tablespoon minced garlic

2 cups chopped tomatoes

3 tablespoons sugar-free tomato paste

1 bay leaf

½ teaspoon dried thyme

sea salt (optional)

freshly ground pepper to taste

8 eggs

Preheat over to 400°.

Sauté eggplant and zucchini in hot oil for 2 minutes, stirring often. Add green bell pepper, onion, and garlic; stir-cook for 6 minutes. Add tomatoes, tomato paste, and seasonings and gently boil while mixture reduces. Transfer stew to a baking dish and, with the bottom of a teacup, make eight indentations on top. Break an egg into each hollow. Bake for 10 minutes.

ॐ ॐ ॐ

CURRIED VEGETABLE OMELETTE

1 tablespoon olive oil

1 small garlic clove, minced

¼ cup sliced leeks

¼ cup carrots, coarsely grated

¼ cup chopped asparagus

¼ cup chopped beet greens

3 tablespoons "Turkey Stock"

¼ teaspoon powdered ginger

½ teaspoon curry powder

1 egg, beaten with a teaspoon of water

In an Omelette pan, heat oil and stir-cook garlic and vegetables, adding beet greens last. Cook until crisp-tender. Add turkey stock and spices; simmer a few more minutes. Pour beaten egg over the mixture and cook until egg barely sets. Turn once to heat other side and slide onto a warmed serving plate.

ॐ ॐ ॐ

RAINBOW EGG FOO YONG

2 minced green onions (tops included)

1/4 cup diced bell pepper (green, red, or yellow)

1/4 cup diced celery

1/4 cup grated carrot

1 1/2 cup grated zucchini

2 cups chopped mung bean sprouts

4 eggs

1/4 cup rice flour

1 tablespoon Bragg Liquid Aminos

1/4 teaspoon grated gingerroot (or 1/2 teaspoon powdered ginger)

1 garlic clove, pressed (or 1/4 teaspoon garlic powder)

Combine all of the vegetables in a mixing bowl; set aside. In a separate bowl, beat eggs lightly and whisk in rice flour, Bragg Liquid Aminos, ginger, and garlic. Pour over vegetables and mix well. Drop by 1/4 cup measures into a hot oiled (or nonstick) skillet and brown on both sides.

ॐ ॐ ॐ

ZUCCHINI EGG FOO YONG

8 eggs

2 cups finely grated zucchini

1/4 cup minced green onions (tops included)

1/4 cup rice flour

1/4 cup arrowroot flour

1 tablespoon Bragg Liquid Aminos

sea salt (optional)

freshly ground pepper to taste

oil for skillet

Beat eggs lightly and stir in zucchini and green onions. Sprinkle rice flour and arrowroot flour over the mixture; mix well. Add seasonings. Drop by 1/4 cup measures into a hot oiled skillet. Brown on both sides.

ॐ ॐ ॐ

POACHED GARDEN EGGS

¾ cup cooked millet or brown rice
(see "Grains")
¾ cup diced green beans
¾ cup grated carrots

¼ cup minced onions
½ cup mung bean sprouts
5 beaten eggs
¼ teaspoon sea salt (optional)

Combine all of the ingredients together in a bowl and mix well. Divide mixture among oiled egg-poaching cups and steam-cook for 9 to 10 minutes or until eggs have set. (This recipe makes about 10 individual servings.)

༄ ༄ ༄

POTATO PANCAKES

3 cups raw potatoes, freshly grated
1 cup grated onion
3 beaten eggs

½ teaspoon sea salt (optional)
2 tablespoons millet flour
2 tablespoons oil

Mix all of the ingredients together. Drop by ¼ cup measures onto a hot oiled skillet. Lower the heat slightly and brown for 8 to 10 minutes. Turn once and brown the other side.

༄ ༄ ༄

EGGLESS POTATO PANCAKES

4 large potatoes, freshly grated   ½ cup grated onion   3 tablespoons potato meal

Combine potatoes, onion, and potato meal; mix well. Drop mixture by spoonfuls onto a hot oiled skillet. Lower heat and cook for 7 to 10 minutes or until brown. Turn pancakes once to brown other side.

Variation

Place mixture in an oiled cake pan and bake at 275° until browned and cooked through.

༄ ༄ ༄

TWO MASHED POTATO PANCAKES

½ cup warm mashed potatoes   ¼ cup grated zucchini
2 beaten eggs   sea salt (optional)
2 tablespoons minced onions   freshly ground pepper

Sauté onions in a hot oiled skillet; reserve. Combine mashed potatoes with eggs and mix well. Stir in sautéed onion, zucchini, and salt. In same hot oiled skillet, form two pancakes. Lower heat and cook for 7 to 10 minutes, or until brown and cooked through. Flip pancakes and brown other side. Sprinkle with pepper and serve at once.

చ చ చ

JERUSALEM ARTICHOKE PANCAKES

½ pound Jerusalem artichokes, scrubbed and   minced fresh herbs to taste (basil, parsley,
   peeled   thyme, etc.)
2 tablespoons fresh lemon juice   raw butter
2 eggs   oil
½ teaspoon sea salt (optional)   freshly ground pepper

Soak Jerusalem artichokes for a few minutes in lemon juice and water to cover. Drain, dry, and finely grate artichokes using a food processor. Mix at once with beaten eggs, salt, and herbs.

   In a nonstick skillet, heat equal amounts of butter and oil over medium-high heat. Drop ¼ cup measures of pancake mixture (enough to spread 3 inches) in the skillet. Brown on each side for 8 to 10 minutes and serve immediately.

Variations

Grate a small onion into the batter, add some minced celery, or substitute some artichoke for another grated vegetable such as carrot, potato, or yam.

చ చ చ

SWEET POTATO PANCAKES

1 grated sweet potato (or yam)

1 grated potato (about the same size as the
    sweet potato)

1 medium onion, minced

1 small carrot, grated

freshly ground pepper to taste

nutmeg, freshly grated to taste

2 eggs, slightly beaten

3 tablespoons rice flour

sesame oil for skillet

Grate sweet potato, potato, onion, and carrot. Mix together and let drain in a colander for 1 hour. Transfer to a bowl and add the remaining ingredients; mix well. Add more flour if necessary to bind the mixture. Drop by ¼ cup measures into a hot oiled skillet for 7 to 10 minutes. Brown other side and serve.

ॐ ॐ ॐ

BROWN RICE PANCAKES

ZUCCHINI MILK

2 cups fresh zucchini, peeled and cubed

dash of sea salt (optional)

water as needed

PANCAKE INGREDIENTS

1 cup brown rice flour

1 beaten egg

1¼ cup zucchini milk

2 tablespoons oil

1 teaspoon baking soda

⅛ teaspoon sea salt

Prepare zucchini milk by puréeing zucchini and salt in a blender until smooth. If the mixture is too thick, add water a teaspoon at a time.

In a mixing bowl, slowly stir the pancake ingredients together with a wooden spoon. Drop batter by ¼ cup measures into a heated oiled skillet. Lower heat and cook for 7 to 10 minutes or until brown. Turn once and brown the other side.

ॐ ॐ ॐ

VEGETABLE "CEREAL"

¼ cup butternut squash, cut in cubes

¼ cup rutabaga, cut in cubes

¼ cup chopped red cabbage

¼ cup crookneck squash, cut in cubes

¼ cup chopped broccoli

1 soft-boiled egg

alfalfa sprouts for garnish

Steam-cook the vegetables and remove from heat; cool slightly. Serve vegetables in a bowl with the egg on top and garnish with alfalfa sprouts.

ᔓ ᔓ ᔓ

Appetizers, Spreads, and Dips

GARBANZO BEAN APPETIZER

2 cups cooked garbanzo beans (see
"Cooking Tips" in Part 1)
¼ cup canola oil
¼ cup fresh lemon juice
6 garlic cloves, pressed

¼ teaspoon sea salt (optional)
2 tablespoons minced green onions
2 tablespoons snipped fresh chives
fresh mint leaves for garnish

In a food processor or blender, purée beans, oil, lemon juice, garlic, and salt until smooth. Transfer to a bowl and mix in green onions and chives. Chill for 1 hour and serve garnished with a few freshly chopped mint leaves.

ॐ ॐ ॐ

SALMON AND CUCUMBER CANAPES

1 cup cooked salmon, flaked
¼ cup "Blender Mayonnaise" or
"Eggless Mayonnaise"
1 teaspoon powdered horseradish

2 teaspoons minced fresh dill (or ¼
teaspoon dried dill)
fresh cucumber
rounds (or slices of peeled jicama)

In a bowl, combine mayonnaise, horseradish, and dill. Add salmon and stir until moistened. Place a spoonful of mixture on cucumber rounds or jicama slices. Arrange on a chilled platter and serve.

ॐ ॐ ॐ

GARLIC POTATO DIP

2 cups potatoes, cubed and cooked

¼ cup cooking water from the potatoes

4 garlic cloves, pressed

3 tablespoons fresh lemon juice

2 tablespoons oil

¼ teaspoon nutmeg

¼ teaspoon sea salt (optional)

¼ teaspoon freshly ground pepper

In a food processor or blender, purée the ingredients until smooth. Serve warm with raw vegetables.

ॐ ॐ ॐ

MARINATED BLACK BEANS

BEANS

1 cup dried black beans (see "Cooking Tips" in Part 1)

1 small onion, peeled

1 whole clove

MARINADE

2½ tablespoons fresh lemon juice

⅓ cup olive oil

1¼ teaspoon Bragg Liquid Aminos (or ½ teaspoon sea salt)

1 garlic Clove, pressed

3 tablespoons minced fresh parsley

3 tablespoons minced green onion

3 tablespoons minced sun-dried tomato

After soaking beans overnight, rinse them thoroughly. Put beans, water, and small onion studded with a whole clove in a pot. Cover, bring to a boil, and simmer for 1½ hours or until beans are tender but not mushy. Remove onion. Drain beans and keep them warm while preparing the marinade.

Whisk marinade ingredients together and pour them over warm beans. Place beans in a container that seals tightly and refrigerate for at least 12 hours. Turn container several times (or stir) while beans marinate. Serve over tossed salad or brown rice.

ॐ ॐ ॐ

ARTICHOKES STUFFED WITH SALMON AND ZUCCHINI

1 cup zucchini, cut in cubes

¼ cup chopped onion

¼ cup chopped green bell pepper

2 tablespoons butter or oil

1 cup salmon, cooked until tender and chunked

1 teaspoon fresh lime or lemon juice

½ cup sliced water chestnuts (optional)

2 medium-sized cooked artichokes

Sauté zucchini, onion, and green bell pepper in butter or oil until crisp-tender. Stir in salmon, lime or lemon juice, and water chestnuts; set aside.

Cook artichokes and cool them enough to handle. Spread their leaves outward and, with a teaspoon, scrape out the center fuzzy choke. Fill the artichoke cavities with warm salmon mixture and serve.

᠀ ᠀ ᠀

GARLIC-ZUCCHINI APPETIZER

1 garlic clove, peeled and sliced

2 tablespoons olive oil

1½ pounds zucchini, cut into ¼-inch rounds

4 tablespoons fresh lemon juice

2 tablespoons minced green onions

2 tablespoons fresh celery leaves, minced

½ teaspoon sea salt (optional)

½ teaspoon freshly ground pepper

a pinch of cayenne

In a large skillet, sauté garlic in olive oil until golden; remove from pan and reserve. In same oil, sauté zucchini until golden, turning only once. Remove to a layer of paper towels. Combine remaining ingredients in a separate bowl and set aside. Arrange zucchini on a platter and drizzle with lemon-herb mixture and garlic. For fuller flavor, let stand at least 4 hours before serving.

Alternate method

To use less oil, instead of sautéing,
bake zucchini on a lightly oiled cookie sheet in a
preheated 350° oven for 30 minutes.

᠀ ᠀ ᠀

LIMED SHRIMP

6 tablespoons canola oil

1½ pounds shelled, deveined raw shrimp

1 garlic clove, pressed

2 tablespoons fresh lime juice

2 teaspoons minced fresh dill (or

¼ teaspoon dried dill)

1 teaspoon freshly ground pepper

½ teaspoon sea salt (optional)

In a large skillet, heat oil. Add shrimp and garlic, stirring constantly until shrimp are pink and tender. Stir in remaining ingredients. Serve immediately with toothpicks.

LEMONY ASPARAGUS SPEARS

2 dozen asparagus spears

¼ cup fresh lemon juice

2 tablespoons chopped fresh parsley

Trim bottoms off asparagus and wash well. Tie loosely together and stand them upright in 2 inches of water in a deep pot. Cover and steam them until crisp-tender (tips steam as stalks boil). Quickly run asparagus under cool water to stop the cooking process and arrange on a platter. Drizzle spears with fresh lemon juice and parsley and serve.

You can grow your own chives in a flowerpot at home to use in soups. (See page 156)

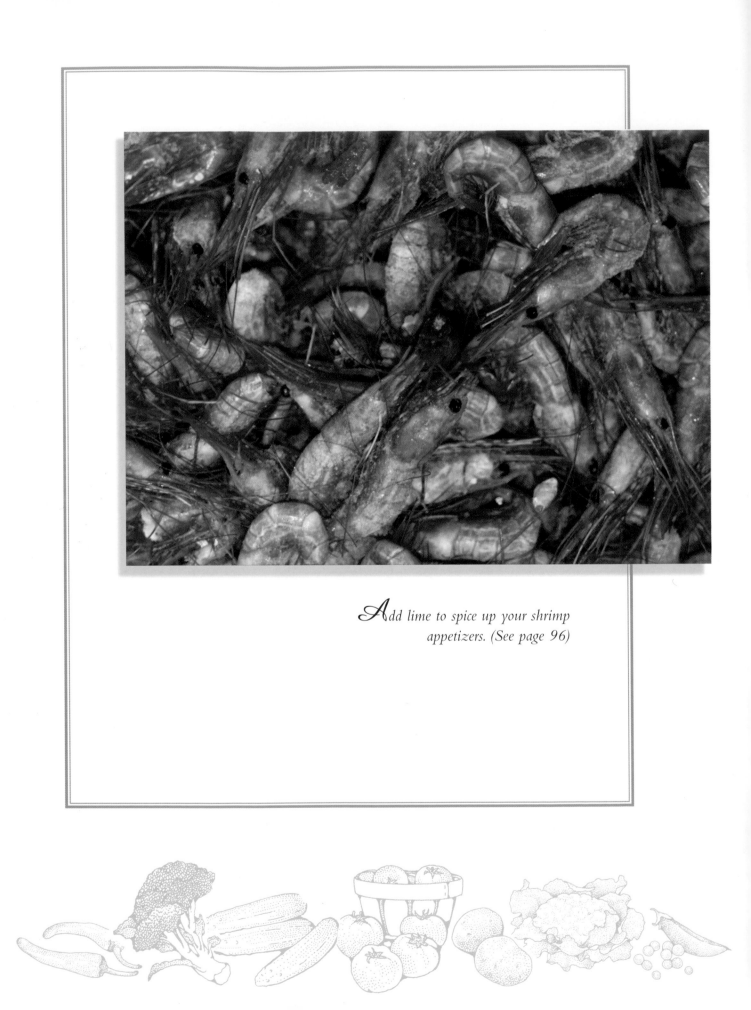

Add lime to spice up your shrimp appetizers. (See page 96)

*A*dd onions to your
omlet for a healthy start to
your day. (See page 85)

*S*almon is a rich source of calcium.
It's good for your bones and your teeth.
(See page 97)

Potatoes provide you with the energy of a Class A food. (See page 178)

Organically grown vegetables retain the most nutrients. (See page 139)

Attention vegetarians!
Grains and beans together
make a complete protein.
(See page 47)

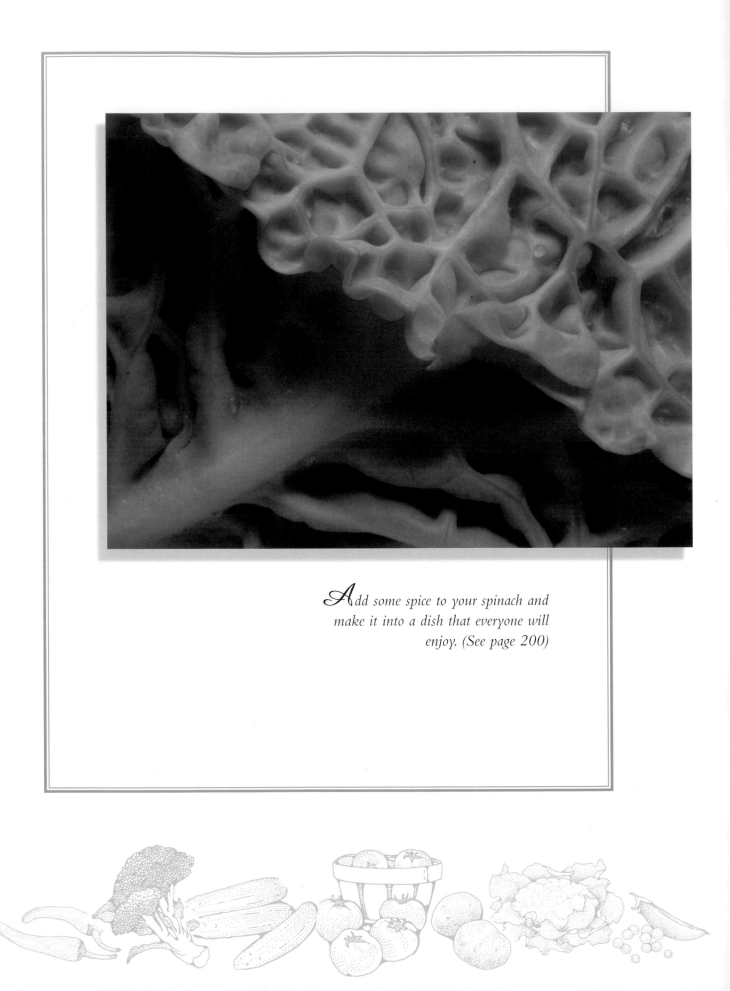

*A*dd some spice to your spinach and make it into a dish that everyone will enjoy. (See page 200)

COLD SALMON WITH CURRIED MAYONNAISE

3 pounds fresh salmon
1 quart "Vegetable Broth"
1 cup "Blender Mayonnaise" or

"Eggless Mayonnaise"
½ teaspoon curry powder
cucumber rounds and jicama slices

Place salmon in kettle with vegetable broth and cover. Bring to a boil, lower heat, and simmer for 10 to 15 minutes, or until flesh is firm but pulls away from the bone. Transfer salmon to a platter, bone it carefully, and refrigerate for 2 hours covered with plastic wrap or a clean damp towel.

To serve, place a chunk of salmon on each cucumber round and jicama slice. Garnish with a small dollop of homemade mayonnaise mixed with curry powder. Arrange on a chilled platter.

ॐ ॐ ॐ

MARINATED JERUSALEM ARTICHOKES

1 pound Jerusalem artichokes
1 leek, thinly sliced
1 garlic clove, peeled and crushed
1¼ cups non-olive oil
¼ cup olive oil

¾ cup fresh lemon juice
½ teaspoon basil
¼ teaspoon sea salt (optional)
a sprinkle of freshly ground pepper

Scrub Jerusalem artichokes, cut them into slices, and set them aside in a bowl. Whisk together the remaining ingredients and pour them over artichokes. Cover and refrigerate at least 12 hours before serving.

ॐ ॐ ॐ

BRUSSELS SPROUTS HORS D'OEUVRES

4 cups small brussels sprouts, trimmed and washed (or cauliflower or broccoli florets)
1 cup water
½ cup fresh lemon juice
2 garlic cloves, peeled and crushed
1 bay leaf

1 tablespoon chopped fresh parsley
½ teaspoon each of dried oregano, basil, and thyme
½ teaspoon sea salt (optional)
¼ teaspoon freshly ground pepper
¼ cup olive oil

With a paring knife, score the base of each brussels sprout with an "X" before steaming. This facilitates cooking and allows the marinade to penetrate the cooked sprouts. Steam until crisp-tender. Run sprouts quickly under cool water to halt the cooking process, drain, and set aside in a bowl.

Bring remaining ingredients (except olive oil) to a boil in a small saucepan and remove from heat. When mixture cools slightly, add olive oil. Pour marinade over sprouts and refrigerate for 2 hours.

Remove from refrigerator 30 minutes before serving to take off the chill. Arrange on a platter and serve with toothpicks.

ॐ ॐ ॐ

BRAISED LEMON-DILL CUCUMBERS

2 medium cucumbers
1 tablespoon unsalted butter
¼ teaspoon fresh lemon juice a dash of freshly ground white pepper

1 tablespoon chopped fresh dill (or ½ teaspoon dried dill)

Peel cucumbers and cut in half lengthwise. Remove seeds (by scraping with a spoon) and cut into ½-inch slices. Place in a small pan with the melted butter, fresh lemon juice, and white pepper. Press a piece of wax paper over cucumbers and cover pan with a lid. Cook over low heat for 7 to 8 minutes until crisp-tender. Remove to a shallow bowl and toss with dill. Serve warm.

Variation 1

Substitute chopped fresh mint leaves (or dried) for the dill.

Variation 2

Cut 3 medium-size ripe tomatoes into wedges or slices. Sauté briefly in a little butter. Season with freshly ground white pepper and Bragg Liquid Aminos. Add the braised cucumbers and serve warm.

ॐ ॐ ॐ

GUACAMOLE GELATIN MOLD

2 envelopes plain gelatin
½ cup cold water
¼ cup "Savory Italian Dressing"
2 dashes hot pepper sauce
1 teaspoon chili powder

1 teaspoon sea salt (optional)
4 medium ripe avocados
1 medium tomato, chopped
1¼ cup combination of minced celery, green
*   pepper, and onion*

In a small saucepan, sprinkle unflavored gelatin over cold water; let stand 1 minute. Stir over low heat for about 5 minutes or until gelatin dissolves completely. Add Italian dressing, hot pepper sauce, chili powder, and sea salt; mix well.

Prepare celery, green pepper, and onion; set aside. Peel and mash avocados and combine with the gelatin mixture. Add the reserved minced vegetables and mix well. Pour into a 5-cup mold or bowl and chill until firm.

ॐ ॐ ॐ

GREEN CHILI BEAN DIP

1 cup cooked pinto beans, drained (see
    "Cooking Tips" in Part 1)
1 cup cooked kidney beans, drained
½ cup reserved cooking water from beans
2 tablespoons oil (optional)
a 4-ounce can of "Ortega" green chilies, drained

1 garlic clove, minced
2 teaspoons fresh lemon juice
¼ teaspoon dry mustard
sea salt to taste (optional)
¼ cup green onions, thinly sliced for garnish

Blend all ingredients (except the green onion garnish) in a food processor or blender. If the mixture is too thick, add some reserved cooking water a few tablespoons at a time. Transfer to a serving bowl and chill for 24 hours. Serve chilled or warmed sprinkled with green onions.

Variation

Substitute 1 tablespoon chili powder for green chilies.

⁊ ⁊ ⁊

BLACK BEAN AND AVOCADO DIP

1 ripe avocado
½ cup cooked black beans, drained (see
    "Cooking Tips" in Part 1)
½ cup cooked brown rice or cooked millet (see
    "Grains")

OPTIONAL

1 garlic clove, minced
¼ cup chopped tomato
1–2 tablespoons minced onion
sea salt to taste
freshly ground pepper to taste

Place cooked black beans in a bowl. Chop the peeled avocado and, with a wooden spoon, mash it into the beans. Mix in the brown rice or millet and any optional ingredients. Serve chilled or at room temperature.

Variation

Substitute another type of bean.

⁊ ⁊ ⁊

EGGPLANT DIP

1 medium eggplant
2 medium tomatoes, chopped
4 tablespoons minced fresh parsley
1 garlic clove, peeled and crushed
¼ cup fresh lemon juice
1 small onion, minced
1 teaspoon red chili powder
1 teaspoon ground cumin
½ teaspoon freshly ground pepper

Bake the whole eggplant at 350° for 45 to 60 minutes, or until soft to the touch. Cool, peel, and cut eggplant in cubes. In a food processor or blender, purée eggplant and ½ of the tomatoes until smooth. Transfer to a bowl and mix in the remaining ingredients thoroughly with a wooden spoon. Chill for at least 1 hour before serving.

ॐ ॐ ॐ

GUACAMOLE

1 ripe avocado
2–3 tablespoons "Blender Mayonnaise" or
    "Eggless Mayonnaise"

1 teaspoon fresh lemon juice
sea salt to taste (optional)

Peel a ripe avocado and, in a bowl, mash it with a fork or wooden spoon. Mix in mayonnaise, lemon juice, and salt; serve.

Variation

Add a pressed garlic clove and 1 or 2 tablespoons of minced onion.

ॐ ॐ ॐ

DR. JO'S GARBANZO DIP

4 cups cooked garbanzo beans, drained
    (see "Cooking Tips" in Part 1)
1 cup reserved cooking water
3 tablespoons oil (optional)
3 tablespoons fresh lemon juice (or to taste)
4 tablespoons chopped onion (or ¼ teaspoon
    onion powder)

1 large garlic clove, chopped (or ¼ teaspoon gar-
    lic powder)
2 tablespoons chopped fresh parsley
1 teaspoon oregano
1 teaspoon basil
½ teaspoon sea salt (optional)

Blend all ingredients in a food processor or blender, adding enough reserved cooking water from the beans (a few tablespoons at a time) to make a smooth paste. Serve chilled or at room temperature.

Variation 1

Substitute 2 teaspoons chili powder for basil and oregano.

Variation 2

Substitute 4 teaspoons powdered horseradish for garlic, onion, basil, and oregano.

෨ ෨ ෨

HOP-N-JOHN DIP

1 cup cooked millet (see "Grains")
1 cup cooked black-eyed peas, drained (see
    "Cooking Tips" in Part 1)
½ cup reserved cooking water from beans
½ cup onion, diced and steam-cooked

½ cup mustard greens, chopped and steam-
    cooked
2 tablespoons fresh lemon juice
2 teaspoons "Sally's Vegetable Marinade"
¾ teaspoon sea salt (optional)

In a food processor or blender, purée millet and black-eyed peas together. If mixture is too think, add some reserved cooking water a tablespoon at a time. Add the remaining ingredients and continue blending until smooth. Serve chilled or at room temperature.

෨ ෨ ෨

ANOTHER HOP-N-JOHN DIP

1 cup cooked millet (see "Grains")

1 cup cooked black-eyed peas, drained (see "Cooking Tips" in Part 1)

1 garlic clove, pressed

6 tablespoons fresh lemon juice

½ cup chopped fresh parsley (or 1 tablespoon dried parsley)

2 tablespoons chopped fresh mint (or 1 teaspoon dried mint)

½ teaspoon basil

¼ cup olive oil

¾ teaspoon sea salt (optional)

freshly ground pepper to taste

In a food processor or blender, purée the millet and black-eyed peas together. Add the other ingredients and continue blending until smooth. Serve chilled or at room temperature.

Variation

Substitute 1¼ teaspoon onion powder and a dash of cayenne for the mint and basil.

ॐ ॐ ॐ

NON-DAIRY CHEEZY SPREAD

2 cups potatoes (peeled, cut in cubes, and steam-cooked)

⅓–½ cup cooking water from the potatoes

2 tablespoons butter or oil (optional)

1 teaspoon fresh lemon juice

1 teaspoon dried minced onion (or

¼ teaspoon onion powder)

⅛ teaspoon garlic powder

a pinch of ground thyme

¼ teaspoon sea salt (optional)

1 tablespoon pimento, drained and minced

Whip the cooked potatoes until smooth with the cooking water, butter, and seasonings; add the pimento last. Use this versatile spread to stuff celery, spread on crackers, as a vegetable dip, or in place of cheese topping.

ॐ ॐ ॐ

Dressings, Marinades, Sauces, and Seasonings

Dressings

BLENDER MAYONNAISE

1 egg
1 cup oil

2 tablespoons fresh lemon juice (or to taste)
¼ teaspoon sea salt (optional)

Have the egg and oil at room temperature. Break egg into a cup first (to avoid eggshell particles) and then slide it into the blender; mix. Add lemon juice and salt; mix. With the blender on low, slowly add oil in a small stream as the mixture thickens. Chill and serve.
Note: Use blender mayonnaise within 2 to 3 days because it spoils quickly.

❧ ❧ ❧

EGGLESS MAYONNAISE

*¼–1 cup mashed potatoes (freshly made
    and still warm)*
3¼ cup oil
2–4 tablespoons fresh lemon juice

¼–½ teaspoon sea salt (optional)
a pinch of favorite herb or spice (optional)

With a mixer or in a blender, combine the ingredients well. Refrigerate until mixture thickens.

❧ ❧ ❧

HERBED MAYONNAISE

1 cup "Blender Mayonnaise"

1 tablespoon each of snipped fresh parsley, fresh
chives, and fresh dill

(or ½ teaspoon dried dill)

1–2 teaspoons fresh lemon juice (optional)

1–2 teaspoons oil (optional)

In a bowl, fold herbs into the mayonnaise. Thin it with a little lemon juice or oil if desired.
Let stand for a few minutes.

శ్రీ శ్రీ శ్రీ

BLENDER GREEN BEAN TOPPING

4 cups fresh green or yellow beans, cut in 1-inch
pieces

1 tablespoon oil

1 medium onion or leek, sliced thin

2–3 tablespoons minced fresh dill or savory

2 soft-boiled eggs, peeled and chopped

fresh lemon juice to taste

1–4 tablespoons "Blender Mayonnaise" or
"Eggless Mayonnaise"

sea salt to taste (optional)

Steam-cook washed and trimmed beans; cool. Sauté onion in hot oil until golden; cool. In
a food processor or blender, coarsely blend the beans, onion, dill, eggs, and fresh lemon
juice. Transfer mixture to a mixing bowl and add enough mayonnaise to bind it together.
Add salt to taste. Chill. Serve on salads or vegetables.

శ్రీ శ్రీ శ్రీ

LEMON DRESSING

2 tablespoons grated lemon peel
½ cup fresh lemon juice
2 garlic cloves, pressed
¼ cup oil

½ teaspoon each of ground coriander, ground
    cumin, mustard seed, and paprika
¼ teaspoon ground ginger
1 teaspoon sea salt (optional)
a dash of cayenne

Blend or whisk all of the ingredients together and let stand for 1 hour to allow flavors to blend. Use this dressing over grains, greens, or seafood.

ও ও ও

HERB DRESSING

1 small garlic clove, peeled and chopped
1 chopped green onion (white part only)
¼ cup water
3 tablespoons fresh lemon juice
1 tablespoon oil

½ teaspoon paprika
¼ teaspoon each of dry mustard and oregano
a dash of cayenne
a pinch of thyme sea salt (optional)
freshly ground pepper to taste

Place the ingredients in a blender and run at high speed for 1 minute. For fuller flavor, let stand for 1 hour before using.

ও ও ও

PARSLEY DRESSING

1 cup chopped fresh parsley, firmly packed
¼ cup non-olive oil
¼ cup olive oil
½ cup chopped cucumber
2 tablespoons fresh lemon juice

2 tablespoons minced fresh dill (or 1 teaspoon
    dried dill)
¼ teaspoon sea salt (optional)
freshly ground pepper to taste

Purée ingredients in a blender for 1 minute (or until parsley appears as tiny specks). Chill before serving over greens or vegetables.

ↀ ↀ ↀ

SPICED GARBANZO DRESSING

1 cup cooked garbanzo beans (see "Cooking Tips" in Part 1)
¼ cup chopped fresh parsley (or 1 tablespoon dried parsley)
2 tablespoons chopped fresh chives

2 tablespoons chopped fresh basil (or 1 teaspoon dried basil)
½ cup water
½ cup safflower oil
1–2 tablespoons fresh lemon juice
sea salt to taste (optional)

Blend the ingredients together in a blender for 1 minute. Chill before serving.

ↀ ↀ ↀ

ORIENTAL DRESSING

¼ cup cold-pressed sesame oil
½ cup fresh lemon juice

4 teaspoons grated gingerroot
4 garlic cloves, pressed

Blend all of the ingredients in a blender for 1 minute. Let stand for 5 minutes to enhance flavor.

This dressing gives steamed vegetables—hot or cold—an oriental flare. It is also delicious on salads.

ↀ ↀ ↀ

EASY ITALIAN DRESSING FOR ONE

1 garlic clove, pressed
1 teaspoon dry mustard
1 tablespoon fresh lemon juice

2 tablespoons oil
fresh chopped chives to taste

With a wooden spoon, mash garlic and mustard together in a small saucepan. Stirring, add lemon juice drop by drop and turn on the heat. Add oil gradually and then chives. Chill before serving over greens or vegetables.

ॐ ॐ ॐ

SAVORY ITALIAN DRESSING

½ cup tomato juice
½ cup fresh lemon juice
¼ cup oil (safflower or olive oil gives best taste)
2 garlic cloves, peeled and crushed
¼ teaspoon dry mustard

2 teaspoons dried oregano
2 teaspoons dried basil
¼ teaspoon freshly ground pepper
a pinch of cayenne

In a jar with a tight lid, shake the ingredients together vigorously. Chill for several hours to bring out the flavors.

ॐ ॐ ॐ

GREEN GODDESS DRESSING

1 cup "Blender Mayonnaise" or "Eggless
   Mayonnaise"
2 tablespoons fresh lemon juice
1 green onion, minced
2 garlic cloves, minced

3 anchovy fillets, minced (or 1 tablespoon
   anchovy paste)
3 tablespoons chopped fresh parsley
1 teaspoon dried tarragon

Whisk the ingredients together in a bowl. Refrigerate until ready to use.

ॐ ॐ ॐ

AVOCADO DRESSING

1 ripe avocado
¾ cup oil
¼ cup fresh lemon juice

¼ teaspoon dry mustard (optional)
¼ teaspoon sea salt (optional)
a pinch of freshly ground pepper

Peel and chop the avocado. Combine with the remaining ingredients in a blender or food processor, mixing until smooth. Serve chilled.

ॐ ॐ ॐ

PARSLEY GARLIC DRESSING

½ bunch fresh parsley
2 garlic cloves, chopped
½ cup oil

¼ cup fresh lemon juice
1 teaspoon sea salt (optional)

Coarsely chop the parsley and put it in a blender or food processor with the other ingredients. Process the mixture until smooth. Chill.

ॐ ॐ ॐ

DILL DRESSING

2 egg yolks
3 tablespoons chopped fresh dill (or 1 teaspoon dried dill)
¼ teaspoon sea salt (optional)

a pinch of white pepper
3 tablespoons fresh lemon juice
½ cup oil

In a bowl, whisk together egg yolks, dill, sea salt, and pepper. Slowly add the lemon juice and oil and continue whisking until mixture thickens. Chill and serve.

ॐ ॐ ॐ

COOL CUCUMBER DRESSING

MAYONNAISE

1 egg

4 tablespoons fresh lemon juice

¼ teaspoon sea salt (optional)

1 ¼ cup oil

MIX-INS

1 medium cucumber (peeled, seeded, and chopped)

1 garlic clove, minced

1 tablespoon snipped fresh dill (or ½ teaspoon dried dill)

2 teaspoons chopped fresh chives

½ teaspoon white pepper

Following the directions for "Blender Mayonnaise," prepare a mayonnaise base using the designated ingredients. Transfer mixture to a bowl.

Mix in the remaining ingredients, stirring until smooth. Chill and serve.

৯ ৯ ৯

TOMATO DRESSING

2 tomatoes, chopped

1 cup oil

½ small onion, chopped

2 tablespoons fresh lemon juice

½ teaspoon dried oregano

½ teaspoon dried basil

½ teaspoon sea salt

In a blender or food processor, purée all of the ingredients until smooth. Chill and serve.

৯ ৯ ৯

THOUSAND ISLAND DRESSING

MAYONNAISE
1 egg
¼ teaspoon oil
1 teaspoon dry mustard
1 teaspoon sea salt (optional)
a dash of cayenne

MIX-INS
1 cup oil
2 tomatoes, finely chopped
3 tablespoons fresh lemon juice
2 teaspoons minced fresh parsley
1 tablespoon diced soft-boiled egg
1 tablespoon minced onion
1 tablespoon minced green bell pepper

Following the directions for "Blender Mayonnaise," use the designated ingredients to make a mayonnaise base. Transfer mixture to a bowl.

Mix in the other ingredients one at a time, stirring well after each addition. Chill and serve.

ॐ ॐ ॐ

ALL-PURPOSE DRESSING

1 cup oil
¼ cup fresh lemon juice
1 teaspoon freshly ground pepper

¼ teaspoon dry mustard (optional)
½ teaspoon sea salt (optional)

Combine all of the ingredients in a blender and process. Or easier still, put ingredients in a jar with a tight lid and shake it well. Chill and serve.

Variation

Add one or more of these mix-ins: anchovy fillet or paste; fresh or dried parsley, dill, oregano, or basil; garlic, capers, chopped soft-boiled egg, minced onion or scallion, avocado chunks.

ॐ ॐ ॐ

Marinades

MARINADE FOR VEGETABLES

2 cups water
½ cup fresh lemon juice
3 garlic cloves, minced

1 teaspoon crushed coriander seeds
½ teaspoon freshly ground pepper

In a saucepan, bring ingredients to a boil. Add desired vegetables for your meal. Reduce heat and simmer 5 to 8 minutes or until vegetables are crisp-tender. Serve hot or cold with brown rice.

Tip

To crush small amounts of spices (like 1 teaspoon of coriander seeds), place in a plastic bag and roll over it with a rolling pin.

࿐ ࿐ ࿐

TANGY MUSTARD MARINADE

½ onion, chopped
1 cup oil
1 garlic clove, peeled and crushed
⅓ cup fresh lemon juice

1 teaspoon each of dry mustard, anise seeds,
  and dried oregano
1 teaspoon sea salt (optional)

Combine these ingredients in a blender and process until smooth.

࿐ ࿐ ࿐

SALLY'S VEGETABLE MARINADE

⅔ cup oil
½ cup fresh lemon juice
¼ cup Bragg Liquid Aminos
1 garlic clove, peeled and crushed

1 tablespoon dried parsley
¼ teaspoon each of dried oregano and basil
¼ teaspoon freshly ground pepper

In a blender, process all of the ingredients until smooth. Let stand for 1 hour while flavors blend.

Variation 1

Steam desired vegetables for 4 to 5 minutes until crisp-tender. Coat with marinade and chill them for at least 4 hours. Serve vegetables in a salad or as an appetizer.

Variation 2

Marinate kabob-style raw vegetables for at least 4 hours and alternate on skewers with chicken pieces marinated in "Marinade For Chicken and Other Poultry" (see following recipe). Barbecue kabobs.

৯ ৯ ৯

MARINADE FOR CHICKEN AND OTHER POULTRY

Mix together. Let stand 1 hour before using.

½ cup oil
¼–½ cup Bragg Liquid Aminos
1 garlic clove, minced (or

¼ teaspoon garlic powder)
1 tablespoon fresh minced onion
   (or onion flakes)

৯ ৯ ৯

Sauces

GARLIC SAUCE

2 heads of garlic, crushed and peeled
⅓ cup olive oil

⅓ cup fresh lemon juice
½ teaspoon sea salt (optional)

Process garlic in a blender for 1 minute. Add olive oil, lemon juice, and sea salt; blend until a creamy-looking sauce forms.

Chill for 1 hour before using and store in refrigerator.

              ≈ ≈ ≈

CURRY SAUCE

3 tablespoons butter or oil
½ cup diced onion
¼ cup minced garlic
⅓ cup cooked brown rice
1¼ cup water
4 whole cloves

2 teaspoons turmeric
½ teaspoon each of ground coriander and cumin
¼ teaspoon each of ground cardamom and cinnamon
¼ teaspoon cayenne (optional)

In a small pan, sauté onion and garlic in butter or oil until soft; set aside.
In a food processor or blender, purée brown rice with water and spices. Add the sautéed onion and garlic and process until smooth.

Use as a sauce, dip, or dressing for steamed or raw vegetables, chicken, seafood, meat, or salads.

              ≈ ≈ ≈

JUANA'S SALSA

TO MAKE ABOUT A GALLON

5–6 large ripe tomatoes

4–5 bell peppers (any combination of green, red, or yellow)

½ bunch celery

4 onions

1 bunch cilantro

4–5 sprigs of parsley

1 diced green or yellow ortega chili, fresh or canned

2 teaspoons dried oregano

2 teaspoons garlic powder

2 teaspoons sea salt (optional)

½ teaspoon freshly ground pepper

¼ cup oil (optional)

¾ cup fresh lemon juice (optional)

FOR A SMALLER AMOUNT

3 tomatoes

2 bell peppers

3 celery stalks

2 onions

¼ bunch cilantro

3 sprigs of parsley

½ diced green or yellow ortega chili, fresh or canned

1 teaspoon oregano

1 teaspoon garlic powder

1 teaspoon sea salt (optional)

¼ teaspoon freshly ground pepper

⅓ cup oil (optional)

⅓ cup fresh lemon juice (optional)

Using a food processor, chop the vegetables separately to the desired consistency; throw everything into a large bowl or pot as you proceed. (Process the parsley and cilantro with one of the vegetables.) Add spices, oil, and lemon juice to the mixture and combine everything well. Adjust seasoning. Store covered in the refrigerator.

Notes: While oil and lemon juice are optional, they preserve the sauce longer.

If you do not tolerate tomatoes, leave them out and use red, yellow, and/or orange bell peppers. This still makes a very tasty salsa.

Drying the salsa in a food dehydrator concentrates the great taste wonderfully.

ॐ ॐ ॐ

SALSA IN THE FAST LANE

2 cups diced tomatoes

½ cup minced onion

¼ cup minced cilantro

2–3 serrano chilies (deveined, seeds removed,
  and minced)

1 garlic clove, pressed

2 tablespoons fresh lemon juice

½ teaspoon sea salt (optional)

In a bowl, combine all of the ingredients and mix well. Serve at once.

૭ ૭ ૭

SUGAR-FREE CATSUP

1 cup sugar-free tomato sauce

½ cup sugar-free tomato paste

1½ tablespoons fresh lemon juice

⅜ teaspoon ground allspice

⅛ teaspoon garlic powder

1/16 teaspoon crushed celery seeds

¼–½ bay leaf, ground

½ teaspoon sea salt (optional)

Put everything in a blender and process until smooth. Chill for 2 hours before serving-it
tastes better! Keep refrigerated.

૭ ૭ ૭

HERB SAUCE

2 egg yolks

2 tablespoons fresh lemon juice

1 teaspoon sea salt (optional)

freshly ground pepper to taste

1 ½ cup oil

½ cup snipped fresh chives

½ cup chopped fresh parsley

1 teaspoon grated onion

In a bowl, whisk egg yolks until foamy. Add lemon juice, sea salt, and pepper; mix well.
Whisk in ½ cup of the oil a teaspoon at a time; add the remainder a tablespoon at a time.
Continue whisking until mixture is thick. Add chives, parsley, and onions. Chill.

૭ ૭ ૭

GARLICKY BARBECUE SAUCE

1 head of garlic (cloves separated, peeled, and
   crushed)
4 tablespoons oil

4 tablespoons fresh lemon juice
a pinch of sea salt (optional)
a pinch of cayenne

Combine all of the ingredients in a blender and process for 1 minute or until sauce is smooth. Keep refrigerated to use when grilling meats, poultry, seafood, and vegetables.

ॐ ॐ ॐ

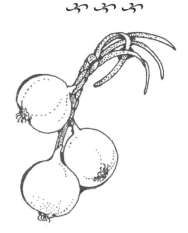

ITALIAN TOMATO SAUCE

¾ cup chopped onion
1 garlic clove, minced
1 tablespoon olive oil
4 pounds tomatoes (scalded, peeled, and
   quartered)
1 6-ounce can tomato paste (sugar-free)

½ cup water
1 dried bay leaf
1 teaspoon dried basil
½ teaspoon dried oregano
sea salt to taste (optional)

In a saucepan, sauté onion and garlic in oil until onion is soft. Add tomatoes, tomato paste, water, and bay leaf and bring to a low boil. Lower heat; stirring occasionally, simmer uncovered for 1½ hours or until sauce thickens. Add basil, oregano, and sea salt and simmer for 20 minutes more.

ॐ ॐ ॐ

Seasonings

CURRY SEASONING

2 tablespoons dried savory

1 tablespoon dry mustard

2½ teaspoons onion powder

1¾ teaspoons curry powder

1¼ teaspoons ground cumin

½ teaspoon garlic powder

In a spice grinder or with a rolling pin, pulverize the savory until it is fine enough to pass through the holes of a pepper shaker. Combine it with the other ingredients and mix well. Spoon mixture into a shaker to use on salad, raw or steamed vegetables, grains, poultry, and seafood.

ॐ ॐ ॐ

ALL-PURPOSE SPICE BLEND

5 teaspoons onion powder

2½ teaspoons each of garlic powder, paprika, and dry mustard

1¼ teaspoons white pepper

¼ teaspoon celery seed

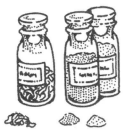

Combine the ingredients and mix well. If necessary, crush celery seeds with a rolling pin so that they can pass through the holes of a pepper shaker. Spoon into a shaker to use on salad, raw or steamed vegetables, grains, meats, poultry, and seafood.

ॐ ॐ ॐ

HERB SEASONING

2 tablespoons dried dill or basil
1 teaspoon dried oregano
¼ teaspoon dried lemon peel, grated

2 tablespoons onion powder a dash of freshly
ground pepper

In a spice grinder or with a rolling pin, pulverize basil, oregano, and lemon peel so that they are fine enough to pass through the holes of a pepper shaker. Combine well with onion powder and pepper. Spoon into a shaker to use on salads, raw or steamed vegetables, grains, meats, seafood, and poultry.

ॐ ॐ ॐ

PARSLEY RELISH

1 cup minced fresh parsley
1 tablespoon minced onion
1 large garlic clove, pressed
1 tablespoon fresh lemon juice
1 teaspoon water

¼ teaspoon dried basil
sea salt to taste (optional)
freshly ground pepper to taste
a dash cayenne

Put ingredients in a bowl and, with a wooden spoon, mix thoroughly. Before serving, chill for several hours and store in the refrigerator in a tightly covered jar.

Serve a small dollop with poultry, fish, meats, steamed vegetables, beans, or soups.

ॐ ॐ ॐ

Salads

DR. JO'S FISH SALAD

½ cup cooked fish, flaked with a fork
a dash of cayenne
1–2 teaspoons fresh lemon juice
¼ cup chopped celery
¼ cup alfalfa sprouts (or other variety
   sprouts)

1 white radish, grated
1 green onion, chopped
5–6 black olives, sliced (optional)
½ ripe avocado
sea salt to taste (optional)
freshly ground pepper

In a bowl, sprinkle the fish with cayenne and 1 teaspoon lemon juice. Add celery, alfalfa sprouts, radish, green onion, and black olives; toss. Arrange slices of avocado on a plate; sprinkle with sea salt and more lemon juice. Spoon fish salad over avocado and finish with a twist of freshly ground pepper.

ॐ ॐ ॐ

SALAD FROM THE SEA

½ pound sea scallops
2 tablespoons fresh lemon juice
¼ cup chopped sweet onion
¼ cup "Blender Mayonnaise" or "Eggless
   Mayonnaise"

2 tablespoons chopped fresh parsley
1 tablespoon minced onion
sea salt (optional)
freshly ground pepper

Wash scallops in cool water and pat dry with paper towels. In a small pan, simmer scallops in a half inch of water with 1 teaspoon lemon juice until scallops are white throughout. (Do not overcook.) Transfer scallops to a bowl and chill.

Combine mayonnaise, 1 tablespoon plus 1 teaspoon lemon juice, parsley, and onion. Season to taste with sea salt and pepper. Dress chilled scallops and serve the salad on green leaf lettuce.

Variation

Stuff ripe tomatoes with scallop salad and serve it sprinkled with paprika. Or substitute scallops for cooked fish that has been flaked with a fork.

ॐ ॐ ॐ

CHICKEN SALAD WITH BROWN RICE AND GINGER DRESSING

4 half chicken breasts, boned and skinned
¼ cup plus 2 tablespoons oil
2 tablespoons grated gingerroot (or ⅛ teaspoon ground ginger)
3 tablespoons fresh lemon juice
¾ cup chopped green onion
1 teaspoon dry mustard

½ teaspoon sea salt (optional)
¼ teaspoon freshly ground pepper
2 cups cooked brown rice (see "Grains")
½ cup chopped celery
½ cup alfalfa or mung bean sprouts
½ cup chopped red bell pepper

Slice chicken into ½-inch strips. In a heated skillet, sauté them in 2 tablespoons oil until meat is just cooked but not overcooked; set aside.

In a bowl, whisk together lemon juice, gingerroot, ¼ cup green onion, dry mustard, sea salt, and pepper. Add ¼ cup oil slowly, still whisking. Add pan drippings from the cooked chicken and whisk until mixture thickens.

In a serving bowl, combine chicken, cooked brown rice, celery, bean sprouts, red bell pepper, and remaining green onion. Toss with dressing and serve.

Variation

Use "Green Goddess Dressing" instead of the ginger dressing.

ॐ ॐ ॐ

CURRIED ARTICHOKE RICE SALAD WITH SALMON

1 artichoke
2 teaspoons butter (or oil)
1 teaspoon curry powder
¾ cup water (or "Chicken Broth")
½ cup uncooked brown rice
1 tablespoon minced onion
1 tablespoon minced celery

1 teaspoon fresh lemon juice
¼ cup "Blender Mayonnaise" or "Eggless
    Mayonnaise"
sea salt (optional)
freshly ground pepper
1 cup cooked salmon, flaked with a fork
chopped green onion to garnish

Steam-cook the artichoke for 30 to 40 minutes or until leaves pull off easily; cool. Then separate the leaves from the choke and, with a teaspoon, remove the fuzzy covering. Save the leaves for later and dice the artichoke heart; set aside.

In a pan, melt butter and stir in curry powder. Add water and rinsed brown rice; bring to a boil. Reduce heat, cover, and simmer for 30 minutes. Add onion, celery, and lemon juice; simmer for 10 to 15 more minutes or until rice is tender. Transfer it to a bowl and let it cool. Mix in artichoke heart, mayonnaise, and sea salt and pepper to taste. Arrange artichoke leaves (like flower petals) around a serving platter and spoon on curried rice. Top with salmon and sprinkle chopped green onion.

ॐ ॐ ॐ

ROOT VEGETABLE SALAD

2 cups diced potatoes
2 cups diced beets
1 cup diced carrots
¾ cup green peas
2 green onions, thinly sliced (or ¼ cup snipped
    fresh chives)

¼ cup minced fresh parsley
½ cup "Blender Mayonnaise" or "Eggless
    Mayonnaise"
2½ tablespoons fresh lemon juice
sea salt (optional)
freshly ground pepper or cayenne

Steam-cook potatoes, beets, and carrots separately; cool. Run frozen peas under warm water to thaw. Mix vegetables, green onions, and fresh parsley together in a bowl. In a smaller bowl, combine mayonnaise, lemon juice, and sea salt and pepper to taste; add to vegetables and combine. Fuller flavor is obtained from chilling the salad for a few hours.

 જી જી જી

RED LEAF SALAD

¼ cup cooked salmon, boned (optional)
red leaf lettuce
1 yellow crookneck squash, diced
½ cup cooked broccoli

1 small Jerusalem artichoke (or potato), thinly
    sliced
fresh lemon juice
sea salt (optional)
freshly ground pepper

Flake salmon with a fork and toss with the other ingredients in a salad bowl. Dress with lemon juice, sea salt, and pepper to taste.

જી જી જી

"SEVEN" SALAD

endive lettuce
grated raw sweet potato
daikon radish, sliced in thin strips
sliced celery
ripe avocado

black olives
tarragon
safflower oil
red chard to garnish

In a bowl, combine equal portions of the vegetables and olives. Mix tarragon with a little safflower oil, toss with salad, and garnish with red chard.

જી જી જી

SIMPLE SALAD

2 cups green leaf lettuce, torn in pieces
2 small Jerusalem artichokes (or potatoes),
   scrubbed and thinly sliced

½ cup mung bean sprouts (or another variety)
½ cup broccoli, cooked and cooled

Combine ingredients and toss with a favorite dressing.

৯ ৯ ৯

BROWN RICE SALAD

brown rice (see "Grains") cooked with grated
   carrot and fresh parsley
chopped purple cabbage
green peas

fresh spinach
a small green onion, thinly sliced a favorite
   dressing

In a bowl, combine equal portions of brown rice and vegetables; add green onion. Mix with your chosen dressing and serve.

৯ ৯ ৯

TWO CABBAGE SALAD

DRESSING
¼ cup fresh lemon juice
¼ cup plus
1 tablespoon olive oil (or other cold-pressed oil)
½ teaspoon thyme
½ teaspoon dry mustard
1 teaspoon sea salt (optional)
a pinch of white pepper

EQUAL PORTIONS
chopped green cabbage
chopped red cabbage
asparagus, cut in ¼-inch rounds
grated daikon radish
diced jicama
cooked tuna (optional)
cooked millet (see "Grains")

Whisk together the dressing ingredients; set aside. Prepare the vegetables and cut the tuna in chunks.

In a mixing bowl, combine equal portions of vegetables, tuna, and millet. Toss with dressing and serve.

ॐ ॐ ॐ

MILLET SALAD

2 cups cooked millet (see "Grains")
½ cup green peas
½ cup chopped celery
½ cup beet greens, washed well and finely
  chopped
½ cup grated raw yam (or sweet potato)

1 tablespoon oil
¾ teaspoon tarragon
4 teaspoons fresh lime juice
sea salt (optional)
freshly ground pepper
½ ripe avocado, diced

Mix millet, peas, celery, beet greens, and yam together in a bowl. For the dressing, whisk together oil, tarragon, and lime juice (or shake them in a tightly lidded jar). Combine salad and dressing; add sea salt and pepper to taste. Garnish with avocado and serve.

ॐ ॐ ॐ

HOT SPINACH SALAD

2 green onions, thinly sliced
1 cup chopped Swiss chard
2 cups spinach leaves, firmly packed
1–2 carrots, grated

sesame oil
sea salt (optional)
freshly ground pepper

In an oiled skillet, sauté green onions and Swiss chard over medium high heat for 2 minutes. Add spinach and carrots; sauté for 2 more minutes. If desired, serve with a drizzle of sesame oil, sea salt, and pepper.

ॐ ॐ ॐ

FISH AND AVOCADO SALAD

¼ cup cooked fish

¾ cup diced celery

¾ cup minced fresh parsley

6 tablespoons minced green onion

3–4 tablespoons "Blender Mayonnaise" or

"Eggless Mayonnaise"

½ teaspoon dried tarragon

1 ripe avocado

leaf lettuce

snipped fresh dill to garnish

Flake the cooled fish. In a bowl, mix it lightly with celery, parsley, and green onions. Stir in mayonnaise and tarragon and set aside. Slice the avocado, discard the pit, and peel each half, reserve. Arrange leaf lettuce on two salad plates and place an avocado half on each. Spoon half the fish mixture over each avocado and garnish with fresh dill.

જી જી જી

FOUR BEAN SALAD

DRESSING

¼ cup fresh lemon juice

1 teaspoon oregano

1 teaspoon dried basil (or 3 tablespoons minced fresh basil)

1 garlic clove, pressed or minced

2 tablespoons olive oil

sea salt (optional)

freshly ground pepper

2 cups cooked garbanzo beans (see "Cooking Tips" in Part 1)

2 cups cooked kidney beans

1¼ cups cooked green beans, cut in ½-inch pieces

1¼ cups cooked wax beans, cut in ½-inch pieces

1 celery stalk, diced

1 small onion, minced

Whisk the dressing ingredients together (or shake them vigorously in a tightly lidded jar). Pour them over the remaining ingredients in a large bowl and mix well. Chill for at least 1 hour before serving.

જી જી જી

EGGPLANT AND RED BELL PEPPER SALAD

4 small eggplants, about ½ pound each
3 medium red bell peppers
3 tablespoons olive oil
2 tablespoons fresh lemon juice

1 garlic clove, minced
sea salt (optional)
freshly ground pepper
2 tablespoons chopped fresh parsley

Preheat oven to 375°.

Wash and dry eggplants and red bell peppers. Place them on a broiling pan and, watching carefully, broil them for 5 to 7 minutes or until all sides are slightly charred. When cool, peel them. Cut eggplant into 1-inch cubes. Seed peppers and cut them into strips.

In a bowl, Whisk together olive oil, lemon juice, garlic, sea salt, and pepper. Add eggplant and pepper strips; mix thoroughly. Transfer to a serving platter or bowl, sprinkle with fresh parsley, and chill for at least 2 hours before serving.

Variation

Purée ingredients in a blender and use as a vegetable dip.

꒛ ꒛ ꒛

GREEN BEAN SALAD

2¼ cups green beans, cut in 2-inch pieces

2½ teaspoons fresh lemon juice

½ teaspoon minced fresh mint

2 teaspoons olive oil

½ teaspoon dried dill

1 cup celery, sliced diagonally in ¼-inch pieces

sea salt (optional)

freshly ground pepper

2 teaspoons chopped fresh parsley

1 ripe tomato, cut in wedges

Steam-cook green beans until crisp-tender. Run them under cold water to stop the cooking process; set aside. Combine lemon juice and mint; reserve. In a large skillet, heat olive oil and stir-cook dill for 20 seconds. Add green beans, celery, and salt and pepper to taste; sauté for 2 minutes. Transfer vegetables to a bowl, stir in the lemon/mint mixture and parsley; refrigerate. Before serving, garnish with tomato wedges.

ॐ ॐ ॐ

CURRIED CAULIFLOWER AND RED LENTIL SALAD

In a small pot, simmer red lentils in an inch of water for 10 to 15 minutes or until lentils are soft. Drain them well, and set them aside.

¼ cup uncooked red lentils

2 onions, diced

1 medium cauliflower, cut in florets

1 teaspoon curry powder

½ teaspoon Mexican chili powder

¼ teaspoon turmeric

1 cup water

the juice of 1 lemon

Bragg Liquid Aminos to taste

In a soup pot, heat onions with a few tablespoons of water; stirring for 4 to 5 minutes. Add cauliflower, red lentils, spices, and 1 cup water; bring to a boil. Reduce heat, cover, and simmer until cauliflower is crisp-tender. Transfer to a serving bowl and refrigerate. Before serving, stir in lemon juice and Bragg Liquid Aminos.

Variation

Serve warm with a cooked grain.

ॐ ॐ ॐ

*E*ggs provide an important source of protein in your breakfast. (See page 85)

*A*dd zucchini and tomato to your
garden vegetable soup for increased flavor.
(See page 180)

Make your salad something special; use tomato dressing for a new taste. (See page 110)

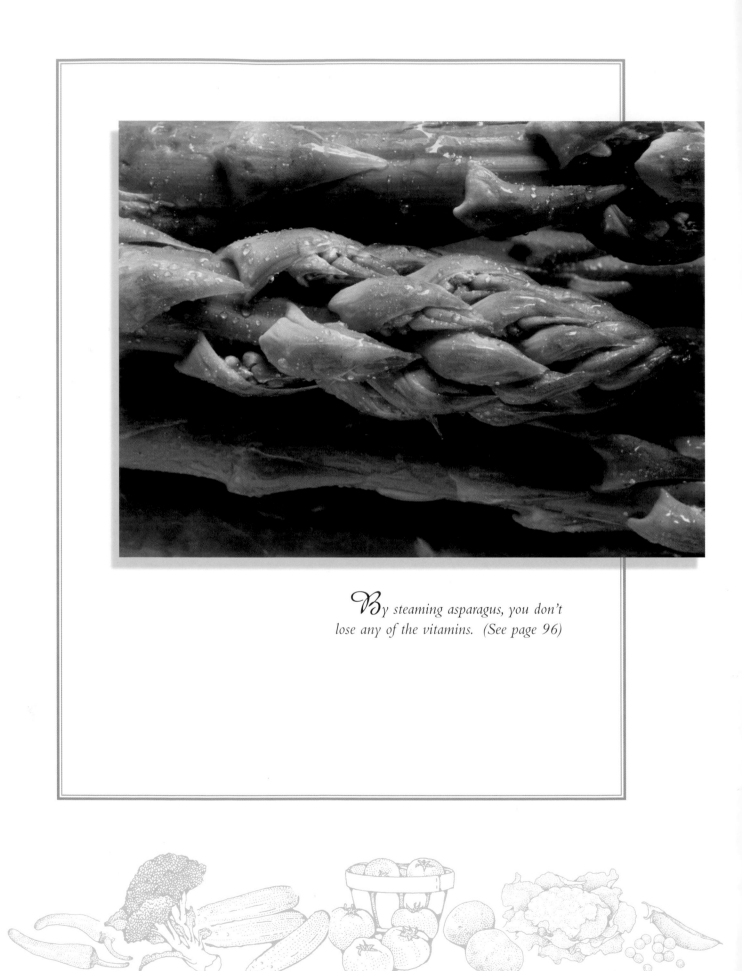

By steaming asparagus, you don't lose any of the vitamins. (See page 96)

*M*ost fish are Class A
food. They are generally
tolerated well by people who
are ill. (See page 199)

This delicious stew is a meal in itself.
(See page 230)

Try something different! Add artichokes to your pancakes for a variation on an old favorite. (See page 90)

Cornish hens contain Zinc, which helps to fight the common cold. (See page 222)

HERBED BROCCOLI SALAD

1½ pounds fresh broccoli
1 small red onion,
    thinly sliced
¼ cup oil

¼ cup fresh lemon juice
½ teaspoon dried tarragon
¼ teaspoon dry mustard
freshly ground pepper to taste

Trim rinsed broccoli into florets; cut stems into 1-inch pieces. Steam-cook broccoli until crisp-tender and immediately run it under cold water to stop the cooking process. Transfer broccoli to a bowl and add red onion. Whisk together the remaining ingredients to dress the vegetables. Cover and refrigerate for 4 to 8 hours before serving.

ॐ ॐ ॐ

KIDNEY BEAN SALAD

2½ cups cooked kidney beans (see "Cooking
    Tips" in Part 1)
1½ cups frozen or fresh cooked corn
½ cup diced green bell pepper
½ cup diced red bell pepper
½ cup sliced celery

½ cup diced onion
¼ cup oil
¼ cup fresh lemon juice
1 teaspoon mixed Italian herbs
sea salt (optional)
freshly ground pepper

Rinse and drain cooked kidney beans. Combine with the other ingredients in a large bowl; mix thoroughly. Chill before serving.

ॐ ॐ ॐ

ZUCCHINI POTATO SALAD

DRESSING
¼ cup oil
¼ cup fresh lemon juice
¼ cup "Vegetable Stock" (or water)
2 tablespoons snipped fresh chives or dill
½ tablespoon minced fresh tarragon
   (or ½ teaspoon dried tarragon)

teaspoon sea salt (optional)
½ teaspoon freshly ground pepper

5 cups new red potatoes, cut in cubes
3 cups (or 3 medium) zucchini, cut in ½-inch
   slices
2 tablespoons oil

For dressing: Combine oil, lemon juice, vegetable stock, herbs, and spices in a jar with a tight lid. Shake it well and refrigerate it for at least 2 hours to blend the flavors.

   Meanwhile, steam-cook potatoes until they are done but still retain their shape. Plunge them in cold water to stop the cooking process, drain them well, and transfer them to a bowl. Shake the dressing jar, pour contents over potatoes, and mix well.

   Stir-cook zucchini in oil over medium heat for 3 minutes or until crisp-tender. Remove from heat and cool slightly. Add to potatoes mixture, toss, and serve.

ᔓ ᔓ ᔓ

LEMON RICE SALAD WITH LAMB

4 shoulder lamb chops
½ cup plus 1 tablespoon oil
½ cup "Chicken Broth"
¼ cup plus 1 tablespoon fresh lemon juice
1½ cups water
1 cup uncooked brown rice
1 tablespoon butter
1½ teaspoons sea salt (optional)

1 cup fresh spinach, torn in bite-size pieces
   and firmly packed
1 small red bell pepper, cut into ¼-inch strips
¼ cup diced onion
1½ teaspoons minced fresh dill
   (or ¼ teaspoon dried dill)
1 garlic clove, minced
freshly ground pepper

In a skillet over medium-low heat, brown lamb chops in 1 tablespoon oil for 5 minutes on each side; drain off excess oil. Add chicken broth and 1 tablespoon lemon juice, cover, and simmer for 20 to 25 minutes or until chops are tender. Transfer chops to a plate to cool.

Meanwhile, bring water to a boil in a medium saucepan. Stir in brown rice, butter, and 1 teaspoon sea salt. Reduce heat, cover, and simmer for 40 minutes. Remove from heat and let stand until water is absorbed (about 5 minutes). Put rice in a bowl; cool to room temperature.

Removing fat and bone, slice meat into ¼-inch strips. Add to the brown rice along with spinach and red bell pepper. Separately, whisk together the remaining ½ cup oil, onion, ¼ cup lemon juice, dill, garlic, sea salt, and pepper. Combine dressing with the salad and chill it before serving.

Note: This salad is also wonderful without lamb.

ॐ ॐ ॐ

PARSLEY POTATO SALAD

5 pounds new potatoes
2 garlic cloves, minced
3 tablespoons chopped fresh parsley

3 tablespoons olive oil
2 tablespoons fresh lemon juice
freshly ground pepper to taste

Wash potatoes and cut them in cubes (or, depending on their size, slice or quarter them). Steam-cook them until tender when pierced with a fork. Run them under cool water to stop the cooking process; set aside. In a small bowl, whisk together garlic, fresh parsley, olive oil, lemon juice, and pepper. Pour over potatoes and mix well. Refrigerate for 2 hours, stirring occasionally, before serving.

ॐ ॐ ॐ

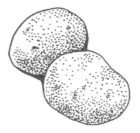

QUINOA SALAD

DRESSING
1 garlic clove, pressed
¼ cup fresh lemon juice
¼ cup olive oil
½ teaspoon sea salt (optional)
¼ teaspoon freshly ground pepper
1 cup chopped fresh parsley (or 1 tablespoon
   snipped fresh chives)

2 tablespoons chopped fresh mint
   (or 1 teaspoon dried mint)
½ teaspoon basil

2 cups cooked quinoa (see "Grains")
½ cup chopped green onions
leaf lettuce
sliced black olives to garnish

Whisk the dressing ingredients together in a bowl. Add the quinoa and green onions and mix thoroughly; chill for 1 hour. Line a salad bowl with leaf lettuce, spoon in the quinoa salad, and garnish with black olives.

Variations

Add chopped tomatoes and/or cucumber to the salad. Or serve it on cucumber rounds as an appetizer. Or prepare a quinoa spread by blending the mixture in a food processor.

৯ ৯ ৯

CHILLED SPAGHETTI SQUASH AND GARBANZO SALAD

3 cups cooked spaghetti squash
1 cup cooked garbanzo beans (see "Cooking
   Tips" in Part 1)
¼ cup carrot, finely diced
4 teaspoons fresh lemon juice

2 teaspoons olive oil
1 teaspoon chopped fresh parsley
½ teaspoon sea salt (optional)
freshly ground pepper to taste

Spaghetti squash is also known as cucuzzi, calabash, and sussa melon. It is not a true squash but an edible gourd. After cooking (see "Cooking Tips" in Part 1), the pulp assumes the appearance of spaghetti and is delicious dressed with various sauces.

Prepare the cooked spaghetti squash by shredding it with a fork so that it resembles its pasta namesake. Combine it with drained garbanzo beans and carrot. Whisk the remaining ingredients together in small bowl and pour them over the squash mixture. Cover bowl and refrigerate for at least 1 hour. Toss before serving.

ᔧ ᔧ ᔧ

HEAD OF CAULIFLOWER SALAD

1 medium cauliflower
¼ cup fresh lemon juice
¼ cup olive oil (or other cold-pressed oil)
½ teaspoon dried thyme

½ teaspoon dry mustard
1 teaspoon sea salt (optional)
a pinch of white pepper
radishes and fresh parsley sprigs to garnish

Remove leaves and rinse cauliflower well in cool water. With a paring knife, cut out the core. Place the head of cauliflower in a steamer basket, cover, and steam-cook until crisp-tender (about 10 minutes). Run under cold running water to stop the cooking process, drain, and set aside to cool.

In a deep bowl, whisk together lemon juice, olive oil, and seasonings. Place cooled cauliflower in the bowl with the dressing and turn it several times until it is well saturated with the mixture. Cover the bowl and let it sit for several hours at room temperature (or overnight in the refrigerator). Turn several times. Serve the head of cauliflower at room temperature drizzled with the remaining dressing and garnished with radishes and sprigs of parsley.

ᔧ ᔧ ᔧ

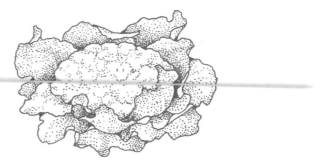

RICE AVOCADO SALAD

2 cups cooked brown rice (see "Grains")
1 ripe avocado, peeled and diced
½ cup diced onion
½ cup grated carrots or red bell pepper strips

1–2 tablespoons oil
1 teaspoon fresh lemon juice
sea salt to taste (optional)

Mix ingredients together and continue stirring until avocado begins to coat the mixture like a dressing.

Variations

Use other vegetables (for instance, spinach or green peas) or add cooked chicken or shrimp. Vary the herbs and spices (perhaps curry, dill, tarragon, or thyme). You can even use the salad to stuff ripe tomatoes.

꒜ ꒜ ꒜

SHRIMP SALAD FOR A CROWD

6 cups cooked brown rice (see "Grains")
2–4 cups cooked shrimp
1¼ cups grated carrot
2 ripe avocados, peeled and diced
1¼ cups chopped green onion

2–4 tablespoons oil
1–2 tablespoons fresh lemon juice
sea salt (optional)
freshly ground pepper
fresh spinach or bean sprouts to garnish

In a large bowl, combine the ingredients and mix until avocado begins to coat the mixture like a dressing. Season to taste and serve on a bed of fresh spinach or bean sprouts.

Variations

Try adding different herbs and spices. Or use green peas instead of shrimp.

ॐ ॐ ॐ

SPINACH SALAD WITH BLACK-EYED PEAS

2 cups cooked black-eyed peas (see "Cooking
   Tips" in Part 1) or 2 cups black-eyed peas
   sprouted for 3 days
1 cup fresh spinach, finely shredded and firmly
   packed
1 carrot, coarsely grated
¼ cup minced green onion (white part only)

juice and chopped pulp of ½ lemon
2 teaspoons oil
½ teaspoon dried tarragon
¼ teaspoon dried oregano
a pinch of dry mustard
freshly ground pepper to garnish

Rinse and drain black-eyed peas; add them to spinach, carrot, and onion in a large bowl.
Separately, whisk together lemon juice and pulp, oil, and seasonings. Pour dressing over the
beans and vegetables, transfer to a serving bowl, and sprinkle with freshly ground pepper.

ॐ ॐ ॐ

MOLDED JICAMA SALAD

3 cups cooked brown rice (see "Grains")

1½ cups cubed jicama

1½ cups green peas

1 cup diced celery

½ cup diced green onion

¼–½ cup diced red bell pepper

2 envelopes unflavored gelatin (or agar-agar)

½ cup "Vegetable Stock"

½ cup "Blender Mayonnaise" or "Eggless Mayonnaise"

1 tablespoon fresh lemon juice

2 teaspoons sea salt (optional)

1 teaspoon seasoned pepper

a bed of salad greens

In a large mixing bowl, combine cooked brown rice, jicama, peas, celery, onions, and red bell pepper; set aside. Stir gelatin into vegetable stock to soften; heat it to dissolve. In a small bowl, stir stock into mayonnaise, lemon juice, sea salt, and seasoned pepper. Add to the rice salad, mixing well. Spoon mixture into a 6-cup mold or individual molds. Chill until set. Unmold onto a platter with a bed of salad greens.

Variation

Instead of jicama and vegetable stock, use diced chicken and chicken broth. Or substitute pimento for red bell pepper.

ॐ ॐ ॐ

MOLDED SPRING SALAD

3 cups water

½ cup green beans, cut in ½-inch pieces

½ cup broccoli florets

½ cup carrots, cut in 3-inch matchsticks

½ cup sliced zucchini

½ cup cauliflower florets

¾ cup shredded savoy cabbage

½ cup corn (fresh or frozen)

1 small red chili pepper

1 teaspoon fresh lemon juice

2 tablespoons chopped fresh parsley

2 cups "Chicken Broth"

4 envelopes unflavored gelatin (or agar-agar)

sea salt to taste (optional)

Prepare this salad a day ahead.

Chill a 6-cup mold in the refrigerator. In a large stockpot, bring water to a boil, and drop in green beans. Remove them with a slotted spoon once their color changes and plunge them into a bowl of ice water. Use the same procedure for broccoli, carrots, zucchini, cauliflower, and savoy cabbage. Set vegetables aside.

Add chili pepper, lemon juice, and parsley to the stockpot. Boil cooking liquid until it is reduced to 1 cup; pour it through a strainer into a bowl with the chicken broth. Add gelatin and let stand for 5 minutes to soften. Heat mixture in a clean pan until the gelatin dissolves completely, adding sea salt if desired.

Place the chilled mold in ice water. Spoon in a few tablespoons of gelatin mixture and swirl the mold to coat the inside. (It sets quickly.) When the mold is coated, arrange a layer of vegetables (except savoy cabbage) in an attractive pattern. Layer the mold with the remaining vegetables with savoy cabbage last. Pour in the gelatin mixture, cover mold with plastic wrap, and refrigerate overnight.

Use a sharp knife to trim any errant vegetables that poke out from the bottom of the gelatin. Dip the mold in hot water for a few seconds (being careful not to wet the gelatin). Unmold the salad onto a serving dish. Voila!

ॐ ॐ ॐ

WATERCRESS AND EGG SALAD

2 bunches deep green watercress
1 teaspoon dry mustard
2 tablespoons fresh lemon juice
⅛ teaspoon sea salt (optional)
a dash of freshly ground pepper

6 tablespoons oil
2 soft-cooked eggs, peeled and sliced
2 tablespoons chopped red onion
1 tablespoon minced fresh parsley

Trim off the tough ends of the watercress and discard them. Rinse the leaves and tender stems in cool water, drain, and pat dry between paper towels. Combine dry mustard, lemon juice, sea salt, and pepper in a salad bowl; whisk. Slowly add oil, still whisking. Add watercress, sliced egg, red onion, and parsley. Toss gently and serve.

ॐ ॐ ॐ

PARSLEY SHRIMP SALAD WITH DAIKON

2 cups cooked tiny shrimp

2 cups chopped fresh parsley

1 cup shredded daikon radish

3 tablespoons olive oil

3 tablespoons fresh lime juice

1 tablespoon chopped fresh mint

2 teaspoons Bragg Liquid Aminos (optional)

Bibb lettuce leaves, washed and dried

¼ cup black olives, pitted and halved

4 day lily blossoms or other edible flowers, torn into pieces (optional)

Combine shrimp, parsley, and daikon radish in a large bowl. In a separate bowl, whisk together olive oil, lime juice, mint, and Bragg Liquid Aminos. Toss the dressing with the salad and arrange on a bed of Bibb lettuce. Garnish with black olives and flowers.

ॐ ॐ ॐ

MIXED SEAFOOD SALAD

1 cup cooked shrimp

1 cup flaked cooked tuna

3 cups brown rice, cooked and cooled see "Grains")

3 soft-cooked eggs, chopped

½ cup diced onion

1½ cups celery, thinly sliced

¼ cup pimentos, drained and diced

cup "Blender Mayonnaise" or "Eggless Mayonnaise"

tablespoon fresh lemon juice

sea salt (optional)

freshly ground pepper

salad greens and tomato wedges to garnish

Combine shrimp, tuna, brown rice, eggs, onion, celery, and pimentos in a bowl; toss gently. Whisk together mayonnaise and lemon juice and stir into the salad mixture. Season to taste with sea salt and pepper; chill. Serve on salad greens and garnish with tomato wedges.

ॐ ॐ ॐ

SPICY ORIENTAL RICE SALAD

2 cups cooked brown rice (see "Grains")
1 cup fresh snow peas, cut diagonally into
    1-inch pieces
2 cups cooked chicken or turkey (optional)
1 carrot, cut in matchsticks
2 green onions with tops, sliced

¼ cup oil
¼ cup fresh lemon juice
1 garlic clove, minced
2 tablespoons Bragg Liquid Aminos
2 teaspoons grated gingerroot
½ teaspoon crushed red pepper flakes

Put brown rice in a large bowl to cool. Steam-cook snow peas for 2 minutes; run them under cold water to stop the cooking process; set aside. Cut chicken into cubes and mix with the rice; add carrots, green onions, and snow peas. Separately, whisk together oil, lemon juice, garlic, Bragg Liquid Aminos, gingerroot, and red pepper flakes. Pour dressing over rice mixture and mix well. Cover and chill salad for 3 hours before serving.

ॐ ॐ ॐ

A SPRING BOUQUET SALAD

1 cup each of tender young things: purple-
    tinged kale, romaine lettuce, beet greens, and
    red and green leaf lettuces
½ cup peppery arugula and its flowers
½ cup alfalfa sprouts
¼ cup ruby red beet stems, cut in matchsticks
    and steamed

oil and lemon juice to taste
assorted edible flowers not sprayed with
    pesticides: Johnny-jump-ups, blue-star borage
    (cucumber flavor), nasturtiums, and early-
    blooming day lilies

Rinse the tender young things and arugula in cool water and pat them dry between paper towels. Transfer them to a lovely pottery or wooden salad bowl; gently mix in alfalfa sprouts and beet stems. Drizzle lightly with oil and fresh lemon juice, and again gently toss. Sprinkle salad with the edible flowers and serve.

ॐ ॐ ॐ

SALADE NIÇOISE

1 cup cooked millet, rice, or quinoa
  (see "Grains")

1 cup cooked garbanzo beans (see "Cooking
  Tips" in Part 1)

1 head of romaine lettuce, torn in small pieces

1 cup cooked potatoes, cut in cubes

1 cup celery, thinly sliced

1 cup red bell pepper, thinly sliced

1 cup cooked tuna, cut in chunks or flaked with
  a fork

½ pound tomatoes, quartered and seeded

6 radishes, thinly sliced

DRESSING

3 tablespoons fresh lemon juice

½ cup olive oil

1 garlic clove, pressed

⅛ teaspoon sea salt (optional)

a dash of freshly ground pepper

2–4 hard-cooked eggs

black olives to garnish

Cool the cooked grain, rinse and drain the garbanzo beans; reserve. Prepare the vegetables
and tuna, placing them together in a large bowl as you proceed. Put dressing ingredients
in a jar with a tight lid, shake them vigorously, and pour over the salad; mix gently. Add
grain and tuna. Transfer salad to a large platter and garnish with wedges of hard-cooked
egg and black olives.

ॐ ॐ ॐ

DUNGENESS CRAB SALAD

¼ pound cooked Dungeness crabmeat

"Green Goddess Dressing"

6 cups mixed salad greens (romaine lettuce,
  spinach, watercress, endive, and arugula)

freshly ground pepper cherry tomatoes to
  garnish

Moisten crabmeat with a little dressing; set aside. In a separate bowl, toss the mixed salad
greens with dressing to taste and divide onto four chilled plates. Top each plate with a quarter of the crabmeat and a generous sprinkling of pepper. Garnish plates with cherry tomato halves.

ॐ ॐ ॐ

MARINATED GARDEN VEGETABLE SALAD

DRESSING

6 tablespoons fresh lemon juice

1 tablespoon oil

1 small garlic clove, pressed

⅛ teaspoon sea salt (optional)

freshly ground pepper to taste

a pinch of dry mustard

2 cups shredded green cabbage

1 cup cucumbers, seeded and diced

1 cup diced tomatoes

1 cup sliced carrots

½ cup diced green or red bell pepper

½ cup sliced radishes

¼ cup chopped onion

In a large bowl, whisk the dressing ingredients until smooth. Add the vegetables and mix thoroughly. Cover and refrigerate for a few hours or overnight. Toss and serve.

Variation

Add to or replace the above vegetables with chopped raw broccoli or cauliflower, diced celery, zucchini slices, or cooked or sprouted garbanzo beans.

ॐ ॐ ॐ

Soups, Stews, and Stocks

BEEF OR TURKEY STOCK

4 pounds cracked beef marrow bones
   (or bones from a roasted turkey)
3 pounds beef chuck (or turkey meat)
1 large onion, quartered
1 cup chopped celery
6 quarts water

1 bay leaf
½ cup chopped fresh parsley
½ cup grated carrots
12 cracked peppercorns
1 tablespoon sea salt (optional)

Preheat oven to 450°.

To heighten the stock's flavor, first brown bones, meat, onion, and celery in a roast pan for 45 minutes. Transfer to a stockpot and add the other ingredients. Bring to a boil, skimming off foam as it rises. Reduce heat, cover, and simmer for 2½ hours. Remove from heat and allow to cool to room temperature. Strain stock through cheesecloth or a fine sieve and discard the now overcooked vegetables and meat. Chill stock and skim off the fat. Keep it in the refrigerator or freeze it in small containers to use as needed.

ꕔ ꕔ ꕔ

VEGETABLE BROTH

1 quart water
2 medium onions, peeled and quartered
1 small carrot
leafy tops from 2 celery stalks

a pinch each of rosemary, marjoram,
   tarragon, and basil
1 bay leaf
½ teaspoon freshly ground pepper
½ teaspoon sea salt (optional)

In a soup pot, bring the ingredients to a boil; reduce heat, cover, and simmer for 20 minutes. Pour broth though a strainer (or cheesecloth) and discard the now overcooked vegetables. Use at once or cool and refrigerate. (You may also freeze the stock in individual portions.)

POULTRY STOCK

poultry neck, wing tips, backs, giblets, bones　　*½ large onion (peel left on to color stock)*
water to cover　　*1 bay leaf*
1 carrot　　*several sprigs of parsley*
1 leafy celery stalk　　*sea salt (optional)*

Place all ingredients in a stockpot and cover with water; bring to a boil. Reduce heat, cover, and simmer for 1 hour, skimming off the foam as it rises. Remove from heat and allow to cool slightly. Strain the stock through cheesecloth; discard the bones and overcooked vegetables. Chop the meat and giblets and return them to the stock. Keep refrigerated or frozen in ready-to-use portions.

To make a soup:

Add freshly chopped onion and carrots and a handful of brown rice. Bring soup to a boil, reduce heat, cover, and simmer for 20 minutes. Add additional poultry meat, green peas, and some chopped fresh parsley. Cook for 10 more minutes or until rice is done. Adjust seasoning and serve with freshly ground pepper.

CHICKEN BROTH

1 chicken, cut up and skinned
6 quarts water
1 white onion, peeled and chopped
2 cups chopped celery

2 cups diced carrots
½ cup chopped fresh parsley
6 whole peppercorns
sea salt to taste (optional)

Wash chicken pieces in warm water; after removing the skin, place them in a stockpot. Add water, vegetables, and peppercorns; bring to a boil. Reduce heat, cover, and simmer for 1 hour. (After 45 minutes, add sea salt.) Remove from heat. Retrieve the chicken pieces from the pot, discard the bones, and reserve the meat for soup. Discard the overcooked vegetables. Strain the broth through cheesecloth, adjust seasoning, and serve (or cool, refrigerate, and freeze in small portions).

ও ও ও

GOOD OLD CHICKEN SOUP

4 cups "Chicken Broth"
2 cups cooked chicken, cubed (from the broth)
2 cups cooked brown rice (see "Grains")
1 cup sliced carrots
1 cup cubed potato

1 cup broccoli florets
1 cup shredded cabbage
1 cup cauliflower florets
1 tablespoon arrowroot flour (optional)
minced fresh parsley to garnish

Prepare the chicken broth, chicken meat, and brown rice; set aside.

In a steamer basket over boiling water, steam-cook the vegetables until they are crisp-tender. Begin with those that take the longest cooking time and add the others at the appropriate time. Try not to steam them longer than necessary because their nutrients will be lost.

If you prefer a thicker broth, mix arrowroot flour into ¼ cup cold water. Blend well and slowly add to the hot broth, stirring until the broth thickens and turns transparent.

To serve, spoon brown rice into each soup bowl and top with chicken and steamed vegetables. Ladle in the heated broth and garnish with parsley.

ও ও ও

COCKALEEKIE SOUP

1 fowl (about 6 pounds)
3 pounds leeks, washed and trimmed
6 fresh parsley sprigs
½ teaspoon thyme
1 bay leaf

6 peppercorns
1 quart "Poultry Stock," "Beef Stock," or water
sea salt (optional)
fresh chives to garnish

Rinse fowl thoroughly in cool water; place in a large stockpot and surround with half of the leeks. Tie parsley, thyme, bay leaf, and peppercorns in a piece of cheesecloth and put it in the pot. Add stock or water to cover and bring to a boil. Skim off foam, reduce heat, and simmer partially covered for 1 hour or until the meat is tender. Remove herb bundle and discard. Remove leeks and purée in a food processor or blender; reserve. Remove fowl, cool it, and take the meat from the bones leaving it in large chunks. Degrease the broth. Stir leek purée into the broth to simmer, reduce, and thicken. Chop remaining leeks into ½-inch rounds, add them to the broth, and cook for 10 minutes. Add chicken meat to broth and cook for 15 minutes more. Add more sea salt if needed and serve garnished with snipped fresh chives.

る る る

GARBANZO BEAN AND POTATO SOUP

2 tablespoons canola oil
2 medium onions, chopped
2 garlic cloves, grated or minced
¼ cup minced fresh chives
a 16-ounce can of stewed tomatoes (sugar-free)
2 medium potatoes, peeled and diced

½ teaspoon sea salt (optional)
¼ teaspoon freshly ground pepper
a pinch of cayenne
2 cups cooked garbanzo beans (see "Cooking Tips" in Part 1)
reserved cooking liquid from beans

In a stockpot, heat oil and sauté onions and garlic until softened. Add chives and sauté for 2 minutes. Add vegetables, spices, garbanzo beans, and cooking liquid. Add additional water to come to 1 inch above the ingredients; bring to a boil. Cook over medium heat for 20 minutes or until potatoes are crisp-tender. Thin soup with more water if desired.

る る る

VEGETABLE SOUP WITH SPLIT PEAS

2 quarts water
1 cup cooked split peas (or green lentils)
2 medium onions, chopped
1 cup sliced carrots
1 cup sliced celery
1 cup diced potatoes
1 cup chopped fresh parsley

1 garlic clove, minced
2 tablespoons oil
2 bay leaves
1 teaspoon Italian seasoning
½ teaspoon thyme
½ teaspoon sea salt (optional)
freshly ground pepper to taste

Combine all of the ingredients in a large stockpot, bring to a boil, and cook over low heat until the vegetables are crisp-tender.

Variation

Prepare the soup in a Crock-Pot.

ॐ ॐ ॐ

A LOT OF ITALIAN VEGETABLE SOUP

6 quarts "Beef Stock"
2 cups beef, cut in cubes
1 cup uncooked brown rice
3 medium onions, chopped
1 teaspoon sea salt (optional)
7 carrots, chopped
1 cup chopped celery
1 cup trimmed green beans
2 garlic cloves, chopped

½ cup chopped fresh parsley
2 teaspoons Italian seasoning
¼ teaspoon cayenne (optional)
1 cup chopped green bell pepper
1 cup cooked lima beans (or green lentils)
1 cup green peas
1 cup diced yellow banana squash
1 cup diced jicama
6 large tomatoes, quartered

In a stockpot, combine beef stock, meat, rinsed brown rice, onion, and sea salt. Bring to a boil, reduce heat, and simmer for 30 minutes. Add carrots, celery, green beans, garlic, parsley, Italian seasoning, and cayenne; cook for 10 minutes. Add remaining ingredients and continue cooking for 10 minutes or until the vegetables are crisp tender.

Variation

Steam vegetables separately and add them to the soup before serving. See "Good Old Chicken Soup" for directions.

ॐ ॐ ॐ

NORWEGIAN SWISS CHARD SOUP

1 cup cooked brown rice (see "Grains")
2 quarts "Poultry Stock" or "Vegetable Broth"
2 tablespoons melted butter
1 carrot, sliced
½ teaspoon sea salt (optional)
a pinch of ground mace

¼ teaspoon freshly ground pepper
2 pounds Swiss Chard, sliced
1 red bell pepper, chopped
1 zucchini, sliced
½ pound snow peas

Place brown rice, 2 cups of the chicken stock, and butter in a blender and pureé, adding more stock if necessary; set aside. In a large pot, combine the remaining stock, carrot, sea salt, mace, and pepper. Bring to a boil, reduce heat, and simmer until carrots begin to soften. Add Swiss chard, red bell pepper, zucchini, snow peas, and puréed mixture. Simmer until the vegetables are crisp-tender.

ॐ ॐ ॐ

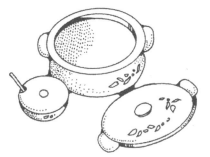

HEARTY VEGETABLE SOUP

½ cup cooked brown rice (or millet)

1 quart soup stock of choice

2 tablespoons butter

4 carrots, thinly sliced

3 new red potatoes, diced

2 cups cauliflower florets

2 cups broccoli florets

¼ cup daikon radish, thickly sliced

1 cup green peas

¼ pound spinach, chopped

1 teaspoon sea salt (optional)

2 tablespoons minced fresh dill (or ½ teaspoon dried dill)

freshly ground pepper

Purée brown rice with ¼ cup of stock; reserve.

In a pot, melt butter and stir-cook the vegetables until crisp-tender, adding green peas and spinach last. Add the remaining stock and sea salt; bring to a boil. Reduce heat, add brown rice purée, and simmer until soup thickens. Serve garnished with dill and freshly ground pepper.

ॐ ॐ ॐ

JULIE'S VEGETABLE SOUP

3 cups water

½ cup cooked lima beans (see "Cooking Tips" in Part 1)

½ cup sliced carrots

½ cup sliced zucchini

¼ cup chopped broccoli (or cabbage)

1 cup fresh or frozen corn

1 tablespoon minced fresh parsley (or 1 teaspoon dried parsley)

1 teaspoon Bragg Liquid Aminos (optional)

¼ teaspoon sea salt (optional)

Combine water, lima beans, and carrots in a soup pot. Bring mixture to a boil, reduce heat, and simmer for 10 minutes. Add zucchini and broccoli; simmer 5 minutes. Add corn, parsley, and seasonings. Heat thoroughly and serve.

ॐ ॐ ॐ

SPLIT PEA SOUP

2 cups uncooked split peas
6 cups water
1 teaspoon baking soda
4 cups water
½ cup chopped celery leaves
1 onion, chopped

1 strip dried kombu seaweed
1 bay leaf
5 peppercorns (or
½ teaspoon freshly ground pepper)
½ teaspoon sea salt (optional)

Soak rinsed split peas overnight in 6 cups water with baking soda. In the morning, rinse split peas three times in fresh water to decrease gas formation.

Place in a Crock-Pot with 4 cups water, celery leaves, onion, kombu, bay leaf, peppercorns, and sea salt. Cook on the "low" setting for 10 to 12 hours or on the "high" setting for 5 to 6 hours.

ॐ ॐ ॐ

BUTTERNUT SQUASH SOUP

1 butternut squash
1 cup broccoli florets
1 cup cooked chicken, cut in cubes

sea salt (optional)
freshly ground pepper
minced fresh parsley to garnish

Peel squash with a potato peeler and carefully, because it will be slippery, cut it into cubes. In a soup pot with water to cover, simmer squash until soft. Purée it with its cooking liquid in a blender or food processor. Return mixture to the pot, stir in broccoli and chicken, and season to taste with sea salt and pepper. Warm soup and serve garnished with parsley.

ॐ ॐ ॐ

CLAM CHOWDER FOR A CROWD

4 medium onions, peeled and chopped

1 small garlic clove, minced

4 tablespoons butter

5 large potatoes, diced

4 large carrots, diced

2 tablespoons diced green bell pepper

2–3 bottles clam juice

a 28-ounce can of stewed tomatoes (sugar-free)

1 teaspoon dried thyme

freshly ground pepper

a pinch of cayenne

24 clams and juice

1 cup corn

In a stockpot, sauté onions and garlic in butter until softened. Add potatoes, carrots, and green bell pepper; stir-cook for 2 minutes. Stir in clam juice, roughly chopped tomatoes, and seasoning; simmer for 20 minutes. Chop clams coarsely and add to the chowder for the last 15 minutes; add corn last.

Note: If the chowder is too thick, thin it with a little boiling water. If too thin, stir in 1–2 tablespoons arrowroot flour mixed with cold water to form a smooth paste.

ॐ ॐ ॐ

ZINGY CHICKEN SOUP

¼ cup oil

1 ½ pound chicken, boned and cut in cubes

1 medium onion, chopped

2 garlic cloves, chopped

1 hot pepper, minced

6 cups water

6 fresh tomatoes, chopped

½ teaspoon sea salt (optional)

½ teaspoon freshly ground pepper

½ teaspoon ground cumin

1 large zucchini, cubed

¼ cup fresh basil, finely chopped

In a large pot, heat oil and sauté chicken over medium heat until lightly browned. Add onion, garlic, and hot pepper; stir-cook for 10 minutes. Add water, tomatoes, and seasoning; bring mixture to a boil. Reduce heat, cover, and simmer for 10 minutes. Add zucchini and cook for 10 minutes more. Remove from heat, stir in basil, and serve.

ॐ ॐ ॐ

ELEGANT BLACK BEAN SOUP

*3 cups cooked black beans (see "Cooking Tips"
   in Part 1)*
½ cup diced celery
½ cup diced onion
½ cup grated carrot
1 teaspoon minced garlic
2 bay leaves

2 cups soup stock or water
2 tablespoons fresh lemon juice
2 tablespoons snipped fresh parsley
a pinch of marjoram or thyme
a dash of cayenne
sea salt to taste (optional)
thin lemon slices to garnish

In a stockpot, combine black beans, celery, onion, carrot, garlic, bay leaves, and stock; bring to a boil. Reduce heat, cover, and simmer for 20 minutes. Remove bay leaves. Purée mixture in a food processor or blender; return it to the stockpot. Stir in fresh lemon juice, parsley, and seasoning. Serve soup hot or chilled, garnished with lemon slices.

かかか

GRANNY'S VEGETABLE SOUP

2 medium potatoes, diced
2 celery stalks with leaves, chopped
1 small zucchini, cut in cubes
½ large onion, chopped
½ green bell pepper, diced
a small wedge of cabbage, shredded
4 cups chopped tomatoes
2 cups mixed vegetables (fresh or frozen)

¾ cup cut green beans (fresh or frozen)
½ cup corn (fresh or frozen)
4 cups soup stock or water
1 teaspoon sea salt (optional)
2 tablespoons uncooked millet
minced fresh parsley
freshly ground pepper

Prepare the vegetables and set them aside.

   In a large stockpot, bring water and sea salt to a boil; add millet. Add the prepared vegetables. Reduce heat, cover, and simmer until the vegetables are crisp-tender and still retain their bright colors. Stir in parsley and pepper to taste.

かかか

DR. JO'S VERSION OF GRANNY'S VEGETABLE SOUP

4 cups water

1 teaspoon sea salt (optional)

2 tablespoons uncooked millet

1¼ cups frozen lima beans

2 medium potatoes, chopped

½ large onion, chopped

2 celery stalks, chopped

¼ medium green bell pepper, chopped

1¼ cups frozen green beans

¼ cup fresh parsley

leafy celery tops

a small wedge of cabbage

a 16-ounce can of tomatoes

1 small zucchini, diced

1¼ cups frozen corn

1¼ cups frozen green peas

¼ teaspoon freshly ground pepper

In a soup pot, bring water to a boil with sea salt and millet. Add lima beans, potatoes, onion, celery, green bell pepper, and green beans in sequence. Reduce heat, cover, and simmer until vegetables are crisp-tender; set aside.

In a food processor, chop parsley, celery tops, and cabbage into fine particles; add tomatoes and chop coarsely. Stir this mixture into the soup. Add zucchini, corn, peas, and pepper. Heat and serve.

ॐ ॐ ॐ

BLACK-EYED PEA SOUP

1½ cups uncooked black-eyed peas

6 cups water

3 tablespoons Bragg Liquid Aminos

1 teaspoon basil

1 teaspoon dried dill

2 garlic cloves, minced

1½ cups Jerusalem artichokes or potatoes, peeled
    and diced

3 celery stalks, sliced

2 carrots, sliced

1 medium onion, chopped

1 cup cooked brown rice

¼ teaspoon freshly ground pepper

Rinse black-eyed peas thoroughly and put them in a large pot with plenty of water to soak overnight.

The next day, drain the beans and add 6 cups fresh water, Bragg Liquid Aminos, basil, and dill. Bring to a boil; reduce heat, cover, and simmer for 45 minutes. Stir occasionally, mashing beans against the sides of the pot to thicken the mixture. Add garlic, vegetables, and cooked rice; simmer for 10 to 15 minutes or until vegetables are crisp-tender. Add pepper and serve.

Note: Bean soups tend to burn easily, so be diligent about stirring occasionally from the bottom of the pot.

ళు ళు ళు

CHILLED GREEK LEMON SOUP

HERBS
1 bay leaf
½ teaspoon each of thyme, rosemary, and basil
4 sprigs of parsley
4 peppercorns

8 cups "Chicken Broth"
3 cups chopped celery with leaves

1 onion, chopped
½ cup uncooked brown rice
4 eggs
6 tablespoons fresh lemon juice
1 teaspoon sea salt (optional) chopped celery
*   leaves to garnish*
paper-thin lemon slices

Wrap herbs in a square of cheesecloth to make a bag; tie securely.

In a stockpot, bring chicken broth to a boil; add celery, onion, and brown rice. Toss in the bag of herbs. Reduce heat, cover, and simmer for 40 minutes. Remove from heat, discard the herb bag, and purée the broth in a blender a little at a time. (Be careful not to overfill the blender and scald yourself!) Return the broth to the pot.

In a bowl, whisk eggs thoroughly, add lemon juice and (gradually) 2 cups of hot broth. Add this mixture to the pot and heat slowly, stirring until the mixture thickens. (Caution: Do not let it boil.) First cool and then refrigerate the soup for 6 hours. Season to taste and serve garnished with chopped celery leaves and lemon slices.

Variation

This Greek-style lemon soup is also good warm.

ళు ళు ళు

LENTIL AND SWISS CHARD SOUP

2 cups green lentils

4 cups "Beef Stock" or "Vegetable Broth"

4 cups water

1 tablespoon oil

1 teaspoon minced garlic

1 cup chopped leeks

½ cup chopped carrots

½ cup chopped onions

½ cup diced celery

7 cups Swiss chard, cut in ½-inch strips

1 teaspoon fresh lemon juice

Wash lentils and remove any bad ones. In a large pot, bring broth and water to a boil; add lentils. Reduce heat and simmer, partially covered, for 30 minutes.

Meanwhile, heat a skillet, add oil, and stir-cook garlic, leeks, carrots, onion, and celery for 1 minute; reserve. When lentils have cooked for 30 minutes, add the sautéed vegetables and simmer for 10 minutes or until lentils are soft. Add Swiss chard and simmer for 5 minutes. Stir in lemon juice and season with sea salt and pepper to taste. Delicious!

ॐ ॐ ॐ

SEVENTEEN (THAT'S RIGHT!) BEAN SOUP

1 CUP EACH

brown beans

large lima beans

small lima beans

navy beans

split lentils

green split peas

black-eyed peas

pinto beans

great northern beans

kidney beans

yellow split peas

½ CUP EACH

black beans

garbanzo beans

red beans

field beans

yellow-eyed beans

cranberry beans

1 large onion, chopped

1 ½ tablespoons fresh lemon juice

½ teaspoon sea salt (optional)

¼ teaspoon freshly ground pepper

This is a great way to become familiar with the variety of dried beans available. (Of course, you can buy a prepackaged bean mix instead.) After making this recipe, you will have 12 cups of beautiful mixed dried beans on hand. Display them in a glass canister or distribute them in small bags to friends.

Prepare a "Seventeen Bean" mix by putting all of the beans (in their assigned proportions) in a bowl. Using your hands, mix them well.

Take out 2 cups of mixed beans. Pick over them and remove any debris or broken beans, rinse them thoroughly in cool water, drain, and place them in a pan. Cover them with plenty of water and let them soak overnight. The next day, drain beans and rinse them well. In a stockpot, combine beans with 8 cups of water (or to cover); bring to a boil, reduce heat, cover, and simmer for 3 hours. Add onion, lemon juice, sea salt, pepper, and additional water to thin the soup. Simmer for 30 minutes more.

Variations

Simmer a leftover turkey carcass with the beans, removing the bones before adding the final ingredients. Or instead of thinning with water at the end, add a 16-ounce can of tomatoes, coarsely chopped, and a red chili pepper or 1 teaspoon chili powder.

ॐ ॐ ॐ

BROCCOLI POTATO SOUP

5 tablespoons oil

2 onions, chopped

1 garlic clove, minced

6 potatoes, diced

2 large broccoli stalks, cut into florets and
stems sliced

5 cups water or "Vegetable Broth"

2½ tablespoons fresh lemon juice

½ teaspoon curry powder

¼ teaspoon powdered basil

½ teaspoon sea salt (optional)

freshly ground pepper to taste

Heat oil in a pot and sauté onions until transparent. Add garlic and potatoes; stir-cook for 5 minutes. Add broccoli and water; bring to a boil, reduce heat, and simmer until potatoes are tender. Purée mixture in a blender or food processor and return it to the pot. Stir in lemon juice, curry powder, basil, sea salt, and pepper. Serve hot or chilled.

ॐ ॐ ॐ

POTATO CHIVE SOUP

4 white potatoes, cubed

2 carrots, coarsely grated

1 onion, chopped

1 celery stalk, chopped

2 tablespoons butter

1 teaspoon arrowroot flour

½ small garlic clove, minced

½ teaspoon minced fresh dill

sea salt (optional)

freshly ground pepper to taste

3 tablespoons snipped chives

Put potatoes, carrots, onion, and celery in a stockpot with water to cover; bring to a boil. Reduce heat, cover, and simmer until vegetables are crisp-tender; set aside. Heat a skillet and melt butter; add arrowroot flour and stir constantly for 1 minute. Slowly whisk in a cup of cooking liquid from the pot, ¼ cup at a time; continue whisking to make a smooth paste. Then whisk the arrowroot mixture into the soup. Season with garlic, dill, sea salt, and pepper; simmer for 5 minutes. Serve the soup garnished with chives.

ॐ ॐ ॐ

ZESTY RED BELL PEPPER SOUP

8 red bell peppers

3 carrots, sliced

½ cup chopped onion

2 tablespoons minced garlic

1 tablespoon oil

4 tablespoons butter

4 cups "Poultry Stock"

1 teaspoon crushed red pepper flakes

a dash of cayenne

sea salt (optional)

freshly ground pepper to taste

fresh tarragon to garnish

Preheat oven to 375°.

Thinly slice 6 of the 8 red bell peppers. In a stockpot, stir-cook the red pepper strips with carrots, onion, and garlic for 10 minutes over medium-low heat. Add stock, red pepper flakes, and cayenne. Bring the mixture to a boil, reduce heat, and simmer for 10 minutes.

Watching carefully, roast the remaining 2 red bell peppers under the broiler until they are completely charred on all sides. Remove and place them in a brown paper bag to sweat for 5 minutes. Under cold running water, use your hands to rub off the blackened pepper skin. Cut peppers in half, remove and discard the seeds, and drain peppers well.

In a blender or food processor, purée the soup mixture with one of the roasted red bell peppers. Return soup to the pot and reheat over low heat, seasoning to taste with sea salt and pepper. Stir in the last red bell pepper cut in julienne strips. Garnish with tarragon and serve.

ॐ ॐ ॐ

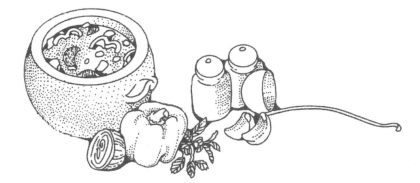

GRANDMOTHER'S CHICKEN SOUP

BROTH FIXINGS

1 whole chicken, skinned

1 garlic clove, pressed

1¼ cups "Chicken Broth" or water

1 onion, unpeeled and stuck with

2 whole cloves

1 medium parsnip, diced

1 large white turnip, diced

1 celery stalk with leaves, cut in 3-inch pieces

3 sprigs of parsley

10 peppercorns

1 bay leaf

1 teaspoon sea salt (optional)

SOUP VEGETABLES

1 small onion, diced

2 small potatoes or Jerusalem artichokes, cubed

1 large carrot, diced

dill to garnish

Rinse and dry the chicken. Rub it with garlic, place it in a large stockpot, and add chicken broth or water to cover; bring to a boil. Add the remaining broth fixings, reduce heat, cover, and cook for 50 minutes or until chicken is tender. Skim off fat during this cooking time.

Remove the chicken; cool it slightly and remove the bones. Cut meat into bite-sized pieces; reserve. Return bones to the pot, bring broth to a rolling boil, and cook uncovered until volume reduces by one-fourth. Strain the mixture, discarding the bones and now overcooked vegetables.

Return broth to the pot and add the fresh soup vegetables. Cook over medium heat for 15 minutes or until vegetables are crisp-tender. Sprinkle with dill and serve.

ဆ ဆ ဆ

JULIE'S QUICK AND EASY CHILI

4 cups cooked beans of choice

water, cooking liquid from the beans, or

  tomato juice

1 tablespoon prepared chili powder

¼ teaspoon garlic powder

sea salt to taste (optional)

Combine all of the ingredients in a pot. Add water, reserved cooking liquid from the beans, or tomato juice to cover. Bring mixture to a boil, reduce heat, and simmer for 5 to 10 minutes.

ဆ ဆ ဆ

KIDNEY BEAN STEW

2 cups cooked kidney beans (see "Cooking
   Tips" in Part 1)
1 garlic clove, peeled
½ large onion, wedged
½ teaspoon sea salt (optional)
1 potato, cut in cubes

1–2 carrots, sliced or grated
1 cup cut green beans
¼ teaspoon freshly ground pepper
½ cup shredded cabbage
½ cup corn

Combine kidney beans, garlic, onion, and sea salt in a large soup pot. Cover with water and bring to a boil; reduce heat, cover, and simmer for 40 minutes. Add potato, carrots, green beans, and pepper; simmer for 10 minutes. Stir in cabbage; simmer for 5 minutes. Finally, add corn and serve when warmed.

శ్రీ శ్రీ శ్రీ

ARMENIAN LAMB STEW

1½ pounds boned lean lamb, cut in 1-inch cubes
1 tablespoon vegetable oil
½ cup diced onion
1 garlic clove, minced
2 cups tomatoes, peeled and chopped
1 cup carrots, cut in ¼-inch slices
1 medium red bell pepper, cut in 1-inch pieces

5 cups eggplant, cut into 1-inch cubes
2 medium zucchini, cut in half lengthwise and
   then in ¼-inch slices
½ teaspoon paprika
½ teaspoon ground cumin
¼ teaspoon sea salt (optional)
freshly ground pepper

Preheat oven to 375°.

Place lamb on the rack of a broiling pan; broil for 10 minutes Turn meat over and broil for 5 minutes more; set aside.

Heat oil in a large saucepan; sauté onion and garlic until softened. Add lamb, tomatoes, carrots, and red bell pepper. Cook for 5 minutes, stirring occasionally. Add eggplant, zucchini, paprika, cumin, sea salt, and pepper to taste and mix well. Cover stew and simmer for 5 minutes or until eggplant and zucchini are cooked.

శ్రీ శ్రీ శ్రీ

FIVE-HOUR BEEF STEW

2 pounds beef stew meat, cubed
1 medium onion, diced
3–4 carrots, sliced
2–3 potatoes, thickly sliced
½–¼ cup water

¼ teaspoon garlic powder
2–3 tablespoons arrowroot flour
½ cup green peas
½ cup corn

Preheat oven to 250°.

In large casserole dish, arrange layers of beef, onion, carrots, and potatoes in that order. Whisk together the water, garlic powder, and arrowroot flour and pour the mixture over the beef and vegetables. Cover and bake for 5 hours. Remove lid, spread green peas and corn over the stew, and return to the oven uncovered until these last vegetables are warmed.

ঌ ঌ ঌ

LENTIL AND BROWN RICE STEW

1 cup uncooked brown rice
¾ cup uncooked green lentils
3¾ cups "Chicken Broth" or water
a 16-ounce can of whole tomatoes, chopped
1 garlic clove, minced
1 ½ teaspoon Italian seasoning

1 bay leaf
¾ cup chopped onions
¾ cup diced celery
¾ cup sliced carrots
½ cup chopped fresh parsley

Rinse and drain brown rice and lentils. In a stockpot, combine them with chicken broth, tomatoes with their juice, garlic, Italian seasoning, and bay leaf. Bring the mixture to a boil. Reduce heat, cover, and simmer for 30 to 35 minutes, stirring occasionally. Add onions, celery, carrots, and parsley and simmer for 8 minutes or until vegetables are crisp-tender.

ঌ ঌ ঌ

CAJUN SEAFOOD STEW

2 tablespoons olive oil

1 medium yellow onion, diced

½ small green bell pepper, diced

1 cup diced celery

a 16-ounce can of stewed tomatoes (sugar-free)

2 8-ounce cans of tomato sauce (sugar-free)

1 cup water

6 parsley sprigs, minced

2 garlic cloves, pressed

½ teaspoon ground cumin

½ teaspoon cayenne

½ teaspoon sea salt (optional)

¼ teaspoon oregano

2 cups potatoes, cubed

a 6-ounce can of whole clams

1 ½ pounds uncooked red snapper, boned
    and cubed

½ pound small cooked shrimp

freshly ground pepper to garnish

In a stockpot, heat olive oil and stir-cook onion, green bell pepper, and celery over low heat until lightly browned. Add chopped stewed tomatoes, tomato sauce, water, parsley, garlic, and seasonings; bring mixture to a boil. Reduce heat, cover, and simmer for 5 minutes. Add potatoes and clams with juice; simmer for 15 minutes. Add red snapper and simmer until the fish is just cooked. Stir in shrimp and garnish with pepper. Serve at once.

Caution: Do not overcook seafood or it will be tough.

ॐ ॐ ॐ

Grains

SOME GENERAL INFORMATION

The variety of whole grains available may surprise you. Most of us, of course, have been raised on wheat, oats, and white rice—none of which are on the "Get Healthy Eating Plan." However, our "alternative" grains are wonderfully nourishing and delicious.

Before presenting the recipes, I would like to introduce some general information about these grains. While brown rice is commonly used in *The New Natural Healing Cookbook* recipes, you will find that you can easily substitute amaranth, millet, quinoa, teff, and wild rice. Lastly, remember that beans and grains together make a complete protein.

Amaranth

Amaranth, a broad-leaved annual, is part of the Carophyllales family that includes beets, chard, spinach, sweet William, pinks, and baby's breath. It produces thousands of tiny seeds that are harvested, dried, and ground into flour or used whole like a grain. It is high in protein, fiber, and vitamin C and has notable levels of calcium and iron.

The Aztecs grew amaranth for food and religious ceremonies. After Cortez conquered Montezuma and his people in 1519, he banned the growth of amaranth. Today amaranth is regaining popularity and is available in natural food stores across the country.

◆ *To make flour:* Mix 3 cups amaranth with 1 cup arrowroot flour or tapioca starch. Process in a flour or spice grinder.

◆ *Cooking method 1:* Combine ¾ cup amaranth seeds, 3½ cups cool water, and ¼ teaspoon sea salt (optional). Cook overnight in a Crock-Pot on the "low" setting. Before serving, beat cereal for uniform creaminess.

◆ *Cooking method 2:* Combine 1 cup amaranth and 3 cups water, bring to boil, and simmer for 25 minutes stirring occasionally.

◆ One cup uncooked amaranth yields 3 cups cooked.

Millet

Millet is related to sorghum, a grain that produces a molasses-like syrup. It is one of the oldest foods known to humankind. Although many people think of it as birdseed, it is delicious cooked like rice and used with vegetables and beans. Millet is available in natural food stores.

Ground millet can be substituted for flour in most recipes—unless the recipe requires rising. Because millet lacks gluten, when making pancakes or biscuits, you can combine millet flour with another starch to hold the dough together. (Note: Cooked millet does not freeze well.)

◆ *To cook:* Wash 1 cup millet until the water runs clear. Combine in a saucepan with 2 cups water and a pinch of sea salt (optional). Bring to a boil, cover, reduce heat, and simmer for 30 to 45 minutes.

◆ One cup uncooked millet yields 4 cups cooked.

Quinoa

Quinoa (pronounced "keen-wah") is an annual herb in the Chenopodium family and produces thousands of small seeds. It is higher in protein than any other grain and also supplies good amounts of calcium, phosphorus, iron, vitamin E, and some of the B vitamins.

It was sacred to the Incas who cultivated it as early as 3000 B.C. Like millet, quinoa contains no gluten. However, it can be used as a substitute flour in almost any recipe if you combine it with another grain or starch.

◆ Before *cooking:* Wash quinoa in cool water until it no longer foams. Quinoa has a natural bitter coating called saponin that is usually washed off during processing. However, you should wash it again to ensure that all bitterness is removed.

◆ *To cook:* Place 1 cup washed quinoa in a saucepan with 2 cups water and a pinch of sea salt (optional). Bring to a boil, reduce heat, cover, and simmer for 15 to 20 minutes or until all water is absorbed.

◆ One cup uncooked quinoa yields 3½ cups cooked.

Brown Rice

Rice has been cultivated for over 5,000 years and remains one of the world's most important staples. In fact, over half of the earth's human population consumes rice regularly.

Brown rice is the most nutritious form of rice because only the hull has been removed. It is high in fiber, vitamins, and minerals and comes in interesting varieties. Short-grain rice's starchy, round form cooks up stickier than the medium- or long-grain varieties. Long-grain rice cooks up as fluffier, more separated grains. Basmati brown rice is a long-grain variety with a fragrant aroma and taste, particularly coveted in Indian and Thai cuisine.

Brown rice can also be ground into flour for use in recipes that do not require gluten.

◆ *To cook:* Place washed brown rice in a pot and add water in the proportions that follow. Bring to a boil, cover, reduce heat, and simmer for 35 to 45 minutes. (Note: Do not stir rice while cooking or it will become gummy.)

> 1 cup short-grain brown rice + 2½ cups water
> 1 cup medium-grain brown rice + 2 cups water
> 1 cup long-grain brown rice + 1½ cups water
> 1 cup basmati brown rice + 2 cups water

◆ Alternate method: Place 1 cup washed brown rice in a pot and cover with 1 inch of water. Add ¼ teaspoon sea salt (optional). Bring to a boil, cover, reduce heat, and simmer for 35 to 45 minutes. Do not stir while cooking.

◆ One cup uncooked brown rice yields 2½ cups cooked.

Teff

Teff is an Ethiopian staple and the world's smallest grain. It is high in protein, iron, and minerals with seventeen times the calcium content of wheat or barley!

Brown in color, teff is used in seed form or ground into flour. Teff flour must be combined with another non-grain—like arrowroot flour or tapioca starch—to provide the necessary starch to hold the mixture together.

To cook: Place ½ cup teff, 2 cups water, and a pinch of sea salt (optional) in a pot. Bring to a boil, lower heat, cover, and simmer for 15 to 20 minutes. Stir occasionally.

Wild Rice

Wild rice is the only grain native to North America—and it is not a type of rice. It is the seed of an aquatic grass, *Zizania aquatica.* While you can still find wild rice harvested by traditional Native American methods, most crops today are cultivated on modern farms that produce a reliably clean and uniform wild rice harvest. This grain is high in protein, rich in B-complex vitamins, low in fat, and a good source of bran fiber.

It is easy to prepare wild rice. You can also cook it for varied lengths of time to vary its texture. Cook it in broth or stock or add sliced vegetables to enhance the flavor. Combine it with brown rice to make a tasty and economical pilaf.

Stored in an airtight container, uncooked wild rice will keep for an indefinite period of time. It is available in natural food stores and many groceries.

◆ *To cook:* Pour 3½ cups boiling water over 1 cup washed wild rice in a pot. Bring to a boil, reduce heat, cover, and simmer for 40 to 45 minutes or until kernels puff open.

◆ One cup uncooked wild rice makes approximately 4 cups cooked.

AMARANTH TORTILLAS

1 cup amaranth flour   *¼–½ cup water*
¼ cup oil

In a small bowl, use a fork to mix together amaranth flour and oil. Add water a tablespoon at a time until you can pat the dough into a tortilla shape between your palms. Cook quickly on both sides over medium-high heat in a nonstick skillet.

ॐ ॐ ॐ

CARAWAY AND MILLET MASHED POTATOES

4 potatoes, peeled and cut in cubes   *½ teaspoon sea salt (optional)*
1 cup uncooked millet   *3 cups water*
2 teaspoons caraway seeds   *chopped fresh parsley for garnish*
1 tablespoon butter or oil (optional)

Place potatoes in a pot with millet that has been washed until the water runs clear. Add caraway seeds, butter or oil, sea salt, and water. Bring to a boil, lower heat, cover, and simmer for 20 to 30 minutes or until the water is absorbed. If millet is still chewy, add ½ cup water and simmer for 5 more minutes. Mash the mixture by hand or in a food processor. Serve garnished with chopped fresh parsley.

Variations

Use cauliflower instead of potatoes or a favorite herb instead of caraway seeds.

ॐ ॐ ॐ

PETITE QUINOA AND POTATO CROQUETTES

2 cups warm mashed potatoes

2 cups cooked quinoa

2 beaten eggs

½ cup chopped onion

¼ cup chopped fresh parsley

½ teaspoon sea salt (optional)

½ teaspoon ground cumin

½ teaspoon dried oregano

freshly ground pepper to taste

Preheat oven to 375°.

Combine all of the ingredients in a bowl and mix thoroughly. Form into 1-inch balls or cones between your palms. Place croquettes on a nonstick baking pan and spray them lightly with oil. Broil in the oven for a few minutes or until they turn brown. Watch carefully to prevent them from burning.

ॐ ॐ ॐ

TEFF BURGERS

1 cup uncooked teff

3 cups water

1 teaspoon thyme

2 garlic cloves, minced

¼ teaspoon sea salt (optional)

½ cup chopped green onions, white part only

freshly ground pepper to taste

large lettuce leaves, tomato and onion slices, etc.

Combine teff, water, and seasonings in a pot. Bring to a boil, reduce heat, cover, and simmer for 15 minutes. Stir the mixture and spread it out on a shallow pan to cool.

Then, adding green onions and pepper, form into patties. Sauté in a heated oiled skillet until nicely browned on each side.

To serve, wrap burgers in large lettuce leaves accompanied with assorted garnishes such as sliced tomatoes and onions and "Sugar-Free Catsup" (see recipe).

ॐ ॐ ॐ

BROWN RICE WITH ADZUKI BEANS

¾ cup adzuki beans
1 cup uncooked brown rice

1¼ cups water
a pinch of sea salt (optional)

Rinse adzuki beans and brown rice thoroughly and place them in a saucepan with salted water. Bring to a boil, reduce heat, cover, and simmer for 35 to 40 minutes without stirring.

Note: These small red beans originated in China and Japan and are available from natural food stores or oriental markets.

ॐ ॐ ॐ

CRUNCHY RICE AND SPINACH PILAF

2 tablespoons olive oil
3 tablespoons uncooked wild rice
1 cup uncooked long-grain brown rice
1 garlic clove, peeled and crushed
1 ¾ cups water
1 teaspoon sea salt (optional)

1 teaspoon dried oregano
¼ teaspoon thyme
2 cups chopped fresh spinach
2 tablespoons minced fresh parsley (or
½ tablespoon dried parsley)
    freshly ground pepper

Heat olive oil in a saucepan or deep skillet. Stir-cook thoroughly rinsed, well-drained wild rice and brown rice with garlic until rice turns translucent. Reduce heat; add water, salt, oregano, and thyme. Cover and simmer for 45 minutes without stirring. Remove from heat and mix in spinach and parsley so that they barely wilt. Serve at once garnished with freshly ground pepper.

ॐ ॐ ॐ

CURRIED BEANS AND RICE

1 tablespoon oil
1 small white onion, chopped
1 garlic clove, minced
1 teaspoon curry powder
½ teaspoon sea salt (optional)

a dash of cayenne
1 cup cooked kidney beans
1 cup cooked white beans
¼ cup cooking liquid from beans (or water)
2 cups cooked brown rice

Heat oil in a skillet and sauté onion and garlic until softened. Stir in spices and add cooked beans and cooking liquid to moisten. Heat the mixture over low heat for 5 to 10 minutes, stirring occasionally. Serve over warm brown rice.

෴ ෴ ෴

LENTILS AND BROWN RICE

1 tablespoon oil
2 tablespoons chopped green onion, white
   part only

½ cup uncooked brown rice
2 cups water
¼ cup uncooked green lentils

In a skillet, heat oil and sauté onions. Add washed brown rice and stir-cook for 2 to 3 minutes. Slowly add water and stir in rinsed lentils. Bring mixture to a boil, reduce heat, cover, and simmer for 20 to 25 minutes or until all liquid is absorbed.

෴ ෴ ෴

LEMON RICE STUFFING

1½ cups uncooked brown rice

2½ cups water

¼ cup fresh lemon juice

2 teaspoons grated lemon peel

¼ teaspoon thyme

3 tablespoons butter

1 small onion, chopped

1 cup sliced celery

½ teaspoon sea salt (optional)

freshly ground pepper

Combine washed brown rice, water, lemon juice, lemon peel, and thyme in a pot. Bring to a boil, reduce heat, cover, and simmer for 40 minutes or until rice is cooked.

Meanwhile, melt butter in a small pan and sauté onion and celery until softened.

Remove from heat and reserve. When rice is done, remove the lid and allow the steam to dissipate for a few minutes. Mix in the onions and celery with sea salt and pepper to taste.

Use to stuff poultry, fish, zucchini, bell peppers, and so forth—or as a sidedish.

క్రు క్రు క్రు

BROWN RICE BURGERS

2 cups cooked brown rice

2 beaten eggs

½ cup brown rice flour

1 garlic clove, minced (or

¼ teaspoon garlic powder)

1 cup grated carrots

½ cup diced onion

¼ cup chopped fresh parsley

½ teaspoon sea salt (optional)

¼ teaspoon freshly ground pepper

After preparing the ingredients, combine everything together in a bowl. Use your hands first to mix and then to form 12 firm patties. In a heated and heavily oiled skillet, cook on both sides over medium heat until browned.

Variation

Instead of cooking in oil, bake patties on a nonstick baking sheet in a preheated 350° oven until browned.

క్రు క్రు క్రు

HERB RICE

1 cup uncooked brown rice (or ¾ cup brown
    rice and ¼ cup wild rice)
2 tablespoons oil
1 garlic clove, minced
1½ cups boiling water
½ teaspoon sea salt (optional)

1 tablespoon minced fresh parsley (or teaspoon
    dried parsley)
½ teaspoon dried sweet basil
½ teaspoon tarragon
freshly ground pepper to taste

Rinse brown rice and drain well. Heat oil in a pot (or electric skillet) and stir-cook brown rice and garlic over medium-high heat until rice looks transparent. Carefully stir in boiling water and seasonings. Lower heat, cover, and simmer for 40 minutes. Remove the lid to allow the steam to escape. After a few minutes, stir lightly with a fork to separate the grains.

ॐ ॐ ॐ

HERB RICE WITH CHICKEN

1 chicken

"Herb Rice" (previous recipe)

Prepare a chicken by cutting it in pieces, washing it, and removing the skin; set it aside.

    Please refer to the previous recipe for "Herb Rice." After stir-cooking the brown rice, arrange the chicken pieces over it and sprinkle with seasonings. Pour in the boiling water, cover, and simmer for 40 minutes or until chicken is cooked through but still tender.

ॐ ॐ ॐ

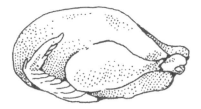

WILD RICE AND BROCCOLI

2 tablespoons butter
2 cups broccoli florets
¼ cup chopped red bell pepper

2½ cups cooked wild rice
sea salt (optional)
freshly ground black pepper

Melt butter in a deep skillet over medium heat and stir-cook broccoli for 3 to 5 minutes or until crisp-tender. Add red bell pepper and cook for another minute. Add cooked wild rice and stir gently until rice is heated. Season to taste with sea salt and pepper.

ﾞ ﾞ ﾞ

CHICKEN FRIED RICE

3 cups cooked brown rice
1 cup cooked chicken meat, diced
1 garlic clove, minced
1½ cups celery, thinly sliced
½ cup diced green onion
2 eggs, beaten separately

¼ cup "Chicken Broth"
¼ cup oil
¼ cup Bragg Liquid Aminos
¼ teaspoon ground ginger
1 cup fresh bean sprouts (mung or alfalfa)

For this recipe, you can use leftover brown rice. However, if rice is freshly prepared, spread it on a baking sheet and refrigerate it uncovered for 2 hours.

Prepare chicken, garlic, celery, and green onion; set aside. Whisk 1 egg lightly into chicken broth; set aside.

In a wok or skillet, heat 2 tablespoons of oil over medium heat. Add the remaining beaten egg and, without stirring, allow it to spread out and cook like a thin omelette. Turn it once. Remove the egg, roll it up in jelly-roll fashion, and cut it into ⅓-inch strips; reserve.

Heat the remaining 2 tablespoons of oil. Sauté garlic, green onion, and celery until crisp-tender. Add brown rice and stir-cook until it is coated with oil. Add diced chicken, broth mixture, and seasonings; cook until thoroughly heated. Transfer to a bowl or platter, toss with egg strips and bean sprouts, and serve.

Vegetarian Alternative

Substitute chicken broth, diced chicken, and eggs with "Quick Vegetable Broth" and frozen peas, diced red bell pepper, or other chosen vegetables.

৵ ৵ ৵

ASPARAGUS RISOTTO

1 pound fresh asparagus
reserved cooking liquid from asparagus
1 tablespoon oil
1 cup diced onions
1 garlic clove, minced

1 cup uncooked brown rice (short grain
   preferred)
½ teaspoon sea salt (optional)
¼ cup chopped fresh parsley
freshly ground black pepper

Wash asparagus, trim stems, and remove tough part of stalks with a potato peeler. Steam-cook for 12 minutes. Reserve cooking liquid. Cut off asparagus tips; set aside.

Heat oil in a deep skillet; sauté onions and garlic over medium-high heat until softened. Add brown rice and stir-cook for 2 to 3 minutes. Add 1 cup reserved asparagus liquid and salt. Cook, uncovered, stirring frequently, until liquid is absorbed. One cup at a time, add remaining asparagus liquid and water to make up to 5 cups. Allow each addition to be absorbed before adding more liquid. Rice should be tender and mixture should have a creamy consistency. Stir in asparagus tips and parsley, garnish with pepper, and serve.

৵ ৵ ৵

Vegetables

BAKED EGGPLANT SLICES

8 eggplant slices, ½-inch thick
sea salt (optional)
2 small garlic cloves

½ teaspoon oregano
a pinch of freshly ground pepper

Preheat oven to 350°.

Sprinkle eggplant with salt; place slices in a colander, weigh them down with a heavy plate, and let them drain for ½ hour. Pat slices dry with paper towels. In small bowl (or with a mortar and pestle), mash garlic with ¼ teaspoon salt to form a paste; add oregano and pepper. Arrange eggplant slices on a nonstick baking sheet and, using half of the garlic mixture, season each slice equally. Bake for 5 minutes. Turn slices and season with remaining garlic mixture; bake for 5 to 10 minutes or until eggplant is soft.

৵ ৵ ৵

BAKED SQUASH

1 butternut or acorn squash
2 tablespoons almond oil

¼ teaspoon ground ginger (optional)

Preheat oven to 350°.

Cut squash in half and scrape out the seeds. Combine almond oil and ground ginger; brush on squash. Place squash, flesh side up, on a nonstick baking sheet; bake for 20 minutes or until it is tender.

Variations

Stick a whole clove in the flesh of each squash half before baking. Or serve with finely chopped chestnuts.

వు వు వు

BAKED VEGETABLE STUFFING WITH LENTILS AND HERBS

2 cups chopped onion
2 cups diced celery
2 cups diced red bell pepper
2 cups chopped yellow squash
2 cups mixed fresh herbs (minced parsley,
  marjoram, thyme, sage)

¼ cup butter
¼ fresh lemon
2 eggs, beaten
2 cups cooked green lentils
sea salt (optional)
freshly ground pepper

In a large pot, sauté the combined vegetables and herbs in butter until vegetables are crisp-tender; add a squeeze of lemon. Mix in eggs, well-drained lentils, and sea salt and pepper to taste. Use the stuffing for vegetables (like green peppers) or a fowl of choice. Or place stuffing in a nonstick loaf pan and bake in a preheated 350° oven for 35 to 45 minutes.

Simple sauce for stuffed vegetables

Sauté 1 cup chopped onion and 1 minced garlic clove in 1 tablespoon oil. Purée mixture with ¾ cup cooked brown rice or millet, adding a little stock or water to thin. Season with sea salt.

వు వు వు

BEAN SPROUTS AND BROCCOLI

1 bunch broccoli, cut in florets and stems sliced

1 teaspoon grated gingerroot

1 large garlic clove, minced

2 tablespoons oil

12 ounces fresh bean sprouts

2 tablespoons Bragg Liquid Aminos

1 teaspoon sesame oil

In a wok or large skillet, stir-cook broccoli, gingerroot, and garlic in heated oil for 2 minutes. Stir vigorously over high heat for 2 minutes more. Add bean sprouts and Bragg Liquid Aminos; stir-cook until bean sprouts wilt. Remove from heat and sprinkle with sesame oil. Toss and serve.

✂ ✂ ✂

BEAUTIFUL STEAMED VEGETABLES

1 pound small carrots, peeled

5 medium-sized new potatoes, quartered

1 large stalk of broccoli, cut in florets

1 tablespoon melted butter

1 tablespoon fresh lemon juice

½ teaspoon sea salt (optional)

a pinch of freshly ground pepper

2 large tomatoes, cut in wedges

4 sprigs of fresh parsley

Place carrots and potatoes in a steamer basket over 2 inches of boiling water, cover, and steam-cook for 6 minutes. Add broccoli and steam-cook for 5 more minutes or until vegetables are crisp-tender. Transfer vegetables to a serving platter.

Combine melted butter, lemon juice, sea salt, and pepper; pour over steamed vegetables. Garnish the platter with tomato wedges and sprigs of parsley.

✂ ✂ ✂

BRAISED LEEKS

6 tablespoons butter or oil
4 cups chopped leeks
3 celery stalks, chopped

sea salt (optional)
freshly ground pepper

Heat butter or oil in a saucepan. Sauté leeks and celery over low heat for 6 minutes, stirring frequently to avoid burning the vegetables. Season to taste with sea salt and pepper.

Note: To reduce the amount of butter or oil, use half the amount called for and instead add "Chicken Broth" or water during the last half of cooking.

જ જ જ

BROASTED POTATOES

potatoes of choice

Steam potatoes first and quarter them lengthwise (or slice them like French fries). Arrange them, skin side down, on a baking sheet; lightly brush with melted butter or spray with oil. Place under a preheated broiler until browned. If desired, sprinkle with an herb or spice (tarragon, curry, paprika, chili powder, etc.).

જ જ જ

BROCCOLI PROVENÇAL

1 teaspoon olive oil
½ cup diced onion
1 garlic clove, minced
3 cups broccoli florets
2 medium tomatoes, cut in thick slices

½ cup water
½ teaspoon oregano
¼ teaspoon sea salt (optional)
freshly ground pepper to taste

Heat olive oil in a skillet and sauté onion and garlic for 2 minutes. Add broccoli and stir-cook for 2 minutes. Add tomato slices, water, and seasonings; bring to a boil. Cover, reduce heat, and simmer for 5 minutes or until broccoli is crisp-tender.

જ જ જ

BUTTERNUT SQUASH AND PUMPKIN PURÉE

butternut squash　　　　　　　　　*ground cloves*
pumpkin　　　　　　　　　　　　　*ground ginger*

Peel butternut squash and pumpkin with a sturdy potato peeler; cut flesh into 1-inch chunks. First steam-cook and then purée equal amounts of the two vegetables together, adding ground cloves and ginger to taste.

　　Note: Be sure to purchase only edible, unsprayed pumpkin—not the ornamental variety. If uncertain, ask your grocer.

ॐ ॐ ॐ

BUTTERED POTATO BALLS

4 large potatoes　　　　　　　　　*freshly ground pepper*
2–4 tablespoons butter　　　　　　*minced fresh parsley to garnish*
sea salt (optional)

With a medium melon ball cutter, make as many potato balls as you can. Place them in a bowl of cold water as you proceed to prevent them from discoloring. (This also removes excess starch and makes them crisper.) When you are ready to cook them, pat the potato balls dry with paper towels and melt butter in a skillet. Stir-cook over medium-high heat until golden brown. Season to taste with sea salt and pepper. Serve garnished with parsley.

ॐ ॐ ॐ

CARAWAY CABBAGE

4 cups shredded cabbage　　　　　*freshly ground pepper to taste*
½ cup "Chicken Broth"　　　　　　*½ teaspoon caraway seed*
½ cup carrots, coarsely grated

Combine cabbage, chicken broth, carrots, and pepper in a skillet over medium heat. Cook for 8 minutes. Add caraway seeds and continue cooking for 2 minutes or until cabbage is tender but not limp.

᧞ ᧞ ᧞

CARROTS AND ZUCCHINI SAUTÉ

1 tablespoon oil
1 small garlic clove, pressed
2 cups carrots, thinly sliced

2 cups zucchini, thinly sliced
2 tablespoons minced fresh parsley

Slowly heat oil in a wok or skillet; sauté garlic taking care not to burn it. Add the carrots and stir-cook over medium heat for 2 minutes. Add zucchini and 1 tablespoon parsley; cook for 3 minutes. Transfer vegetables to a serving bowl and sprinkle with the remaining parsley.

᧞ ᧞ ᧞

CRUNCHY GREEN BEANS

½ cup water
½ teaspoon sea salt (optional)
½ pound trimmed green beans
½ cup sliced water chestnuts, drained
2 tablespoons snipped fresh chives

2 tablespoons diced pimento
1 tablespoon fresh lemon juice
1 teaspoon minced fresh dill
freshly ground pepper

Combine water, salt, and green beans in a saucepan. Cover and steam-cook until green beans are crisp-tender. Add the remaining ingredients, stir lightly to heat, and serve.

᧞ ᧞ ᧞

DUKE & DUCHESS POTATOES

2 large potatoes
2 egg yolks

sea salt (optional)
melted butter

Preheat oven to 425°.

Wash, peel, and cut potatoes in pieces; boil them in lightly salted water until tender. Mash them with egg yolks, beating until smooth. Place mixture in a pastry bag with a star-shaped tip. Pipe potatoes onto a nonstick baking sheet and brush them lightly with melted butter. Bake for 20 minutes or until potatoes turn golden brown.

ॐ ॐ ॐ

GARDEN VEGETABLE STEW

3 tablespoons oil
½ cup chopped onion
1 small garlic clove, minced
3 cups zucchini, cut in 1-inch cubes
2 cups yellow squash, cut in 1-inch cubes
2 cups chopped tomatoes
sea salt (optional) to taste

freshly ground pepper to taste
3 tablespoons minced celery leaves
½ teaspoon minced fresh thyme (or ¼ teaspoon dry thyme)
¼ teaspoon marjoram
¼ teaspoon oregano

Heat oil in a large saucepan and sauté onion and garlic until softened. Add zucchini, yellow squash, and tomatoes and season to taste with sea salt and pepper. Stir-cook for 4 minutes. Sprinkle herbs over the mixture, cover, and simmer for 5 minutes more.

ॐ ॐ ॐ

GARLIC SCALLOPED POTATOES

1 large garlic clove, peeled
4 large potatoes
sea salt (optional)

freshly ground pepper
"Beef Stock" or "Chicken Broth"
butter

Preheat oven to 375°.

Rub garlic on the inside of a shallow baking dish. Wash, peel, and cut potatoes in thin slices; layer them in the baking dish to a depth of 1½ inches. Sprinkle with sea salt, pepper, and any remaining garlic. Carefully pour in enough broth to reach the top of the potatoes; dot with butter. Bake until the top layer is browned and crisp.

ॐ ॐ ॐ

GREEN BEAN, SQUASH, AND TOMATO COMBO

2 cups sliced fresh green beans
1 medium onion, cut in wedges
2 cups sliced zucchini

2 cups sliced summer squash
2 large tomatoes, cut in wedges
Italian seasoning (basil, oregano, marjoram, etc.)

In a covered saucepan, cook green beans and onions in a little water for 8 minutes. Add zucchini and summer squash and cook for 5 more minutes. Add tomatoes and heat through. Sprinkle with Italian seasoning and serve.

ॐ ॐ ॐ

HURRY-UP BEETS

4 medium beets, peeled and grated
1 small garlic clove, pressed
1 tablespoon oil
1 tablespoon fresh lemon juice

sea salt (optional)
freshly ground pepper
water as needed
butter

Combine beets, garlic, oil, and lemon juice in a saucepan. Stir-cook over medium heat for 10 minutes or until tender. If mixture seems dry, add a little water. Transfer beets to a serving bowl, season with sea salt and pepper, and add a smidgen of butter.

ॐ ॐ ॐ

JICAMA AND FRESH BROCCOLI

1 bunch of broccoli

2 tablespoons oil

1 teaspoon minced gingerroot

½ teaspoon sea salt (optional)

1 cup "Chicken Broth"

2 tablespoons butter

2 tablespoons fresh lemon juice

2 cups jicama, cut in small cubes

Rinse broccoli, trim into florets, and peel and cut stalks in 1-inch pieces. In a wok or skillet, heat oil and stir-cook gingerroot for about 10 seconds. Add broccoli, stirring to coat it with oil; continue cooking for 3 minutes. Add sea salt and chicken broth; bring to a boil. Reduce heat, cover, and simmer until broccoli is crisp-tender. Pour off all but 4 tablespoons of cooking liquid. To this, add butter, lemon juice, and jicama. Warm thoroughly and serve.

ๅ ๅ ๅ

LEMON BROCCOLI

1 pound broccoli

sea salt (optional)

freshly ground pepper

4 thin lemon slices

Prepare broccoli by removing the leaves, cutting away the tough stems, and peeling what is left of the stalk. Rinse it well and arrange it in a steamer basket. Sprinkle with sea salt and pepper; add lemon slices. Steam-cook over boiling water for 5 minutes or until broccoli is crisp-tender.

ๅ ๅ ๅ

LEMONED ONIONS

4 medium white onions

¼ cup oil

3 tablespoons fresh lemon juice

¼ teaspoon grated lemon rind

¼ teaspoon sea salt (optional)

Preheat oven to 325°.

Peel onions and steam-cook them whole until they are tender. Arrange them in a small baking dish. Whisk together the lemon juice, lemon rind, and sea salt and spoon the sauce over the onions. Warm them in the oven and serve.

ॐ ॐ ॐ

MARINATED CHARCOAL-BROILED VEGETABLES

MARINADE
¾ cup oil
¼ cup fresh lemon juice
1 garlic clove, pressed
2½ teaspoons Italian seasoning
½ teaspoon dry mustard

1 eggplant, peeled and cut in 2-inch cubes
3 carrots, cut in ½-inch rounds
2 cups zucchini, cut in 1-inch rounds
1 red bell pepper, cut in 1-inch squares
1 green bell pepper, cut in 1-inch squares
1 large white onion, cut in wedges
sea salt (optional)

Combine the marinade ingredients and whisk until blended (or shake them vigorously in a tightly lidded jar). Set this aside as you prepare the vegetables.

Soak eggplant cubes in lukewarm water for 20 minutes to draw out any bitterness; drain and steam-cook for 3 minutes. Steam-cook carrots for 6 minutes.

Put the vegetables and marinade in a sealable plastic bag or container; refrigerate for 4 to 24 hours. Drain off the marinade and save it for another use. Thread vegetables on skewers, alternating them in an attractive order. Place on a lightly oiled grill 5 inches above the hot coals; cook for 10 to 15 minutes. Turn kabobs so that they cook evenly. Sprinkle with sea salt and serve at once.

ॐ ॐ ॐ

MORE GREENS

broccoli florets and sliced stems
sliced zucchini

green onions, cut in ½-inch strips
collard greens (or other greens)

Steam-cook the vegetables, one kind at a time in the preceding order. Cook for 1 minute after each addition, continuing until they are crisp-tender.

ॐ ॐ ॐ

OPEN POTATO OMELETTE

2 large potatoes
2 tomatoes
2 eggs
1 tablespoon butter or oil

¼ cup chopped onion
½ teaspoon chopped fresh basil
freshly ground pepper

Wash, peel, and slice potatoes. Steam-cook them until tender; set aside. Drop tomatoes in boiling water for 15 seconds and retrieve them with a slotted spoon; peel them, seed them, and chop them up. Beat eggs with basil and add to tomatoes.

Preheat broiler.

Heat butter or oil in a skillet and sauté onion until softened. Arrange potatoes over onions and pour the egg mixture on top. Cover skillet and cook over low heat until the eggs are nearly set. Remove lid and stick the skillet under the broiler, watching carefully, until eggs are cooked. Wary of the hot skillet handle, slide the omelette onto a plate and serve with freshly ground pepper.

ॐ ॐ ॐ

POTATO "CHIPS"

potatoes or sweet potatoes   *sea salt (optional)*
oil

Preheat oven to 425°.

Cut potatoes or sweet potatoes in thin slices. Spray them lightly with oil and place them in a single layer on a baking sheet. Bake until they are browned. Season to taste and serve at once.

ఌ ఌ ఌ

POTATO DUMPLINGS

2 cups cooked potatoes, riced or mashed   *½ teaspoon paprika*
½ cup potato meal   *½ teaspoon sea salt (optional)*
½ cup butter   *a favorite tomato sauce or meat sauce*
½ teaspoon baking powder

Combine the ingredients in a bowl and beat them thoroughly. Roll the dough between your hands into logs 1½ inches in diameter; refrigerate until firm.

Preheat oven to 350°.

Cut the logs into ¼-inch slices and make a finger indentation on each. Arrange the dumplings in an oiled baking dish with the edges overlapping. Cover with a favorite sauce. Bake for 20 minutes or until heated through.

Variation

Add herbs from the mint family or a combination of rosemary and marjoram to the dumpling dough.

ఌ ఌ ఌ

POTATO PIE

2 tablespoons butter

¼ cup minced sweet onion

1 garlic clove, minced

a dash of freshly grated nutmeg

3 tablespoons fresh lemon juice

freshly ground pepper

2 pounds red potatoes, thinly sliced

2 bunches of spinach, coarsely chopped

2 cups "Chicken Stock"

butter dabs (optional)

Preheat oven to 375°.

Melt butter in a skillet and sauté onion and garlic for 2 to 3 minutes. Add nutmeg, lemon juice, and pepper; set aside.

In an oiled baking dish, arrange alternating layers of potatoes, spinach, and the onion mixture. Pour in enough chicken stock to just barely cover the ingredients. Dab with more butter if desired and bake for 50 minutes.

ॐ ॐ ॐ

SNOW PEAS AND TOMATOES

3 cups snow peas

1 tablespoon oil

¼ cup green onions, thinly sliced

1 garlic clove, minced

an 8-ounce can of sliced water chestnuts, drained

2 cups cherry tomatoes, halved

1 tablespoon Bragg Liquid Aminos

¼ teaspoon oregano leaves

Wash, trim, and cut snow peas in half diagonally.

Heat oil in a wok or skillet and stir-cook snow peas, green onions, garlic, and water chestnuts until crisp-tender. Add tomatoes, Bragg Liquid Aminos, and oregano; stir-cook for 2 minutes or until tomatoes are warmed.

Variation

Instead of fresh snow peas, use a 7-ounce package of frozen snow peas and add them with the tomatoes.

ॐ ॐ ॐ

SPICED STEWED TOMATOES

2 cups whole fresh tomatoes, peeled
2 tablespoons diced leeks
2 tablespoons diced green bell pepper
4 whole cloves
⅛ teaspoon red chili pepper
dashes of ground coriander, turmeric, ground cumin,
    and ground ginger
minced fresh parsley to garnish

Combine all of the ingredients in a saucepan and heat to piping hot. Garnish with parsley and serve.

ॐ ॐ ॐ

SPICY SPINACH

2 bunches of fresh spinach
2 tablespoons oil
2 medium onions, chopped
1 garlic clove, minced

1 small hot red pepper, seeded and minced
4 tablespoons chopped fresh parsley
½ teaspoon freshly ground pepper
¼ teaspoon snipped fresh dill

Rinse spinach thoroughly and steam-cook it for 2 minutes; set aside. Heat oil in a large skillet and sauté onions, garlic, and hot pepper over medium heat for 10 minutes. Add spinach, parsley, pepper, and dill and stir-cook until heated.

ॐ ॐ ॐ

STUFFED TOMATOES

12 ripe tomatoes
¼ cup oil
2 medium onions, chopped
4 garlic cloves, pressed or grated
¼ cup snipped fresh chives
2 cups cooked garbanzo beans (see "Cooking Tips" in Part 1)

½ teaspoon allspice
½ teaspoon ground cumin
a pinch of cayenne
½ teaspoon sea salt (optional)
½ teaspoon freshly ground pepper
2 tablespoons chilled butter

Preheat oven to 350°.

Cut the tops off of the tomatoes and scoop out the pulp with a spoon. Set aside the tomato shells and tops. In a bowl, combine the pulp with half of the sea salt and pepper; reserve.

Heat oil in a large skillet and stir-cook onions and garlic until softened. Add chives; stir-cook for 5 minutes. Remove skillet from heat and stir in garbanzo beans, spices, and the remaining sea salt and pepper. Spoon this mixture into the tomato shells and replace the tops. Place stuffed tomatoes in a baking dish, spooning the reserved pulp around them. Dab with butter and bake for 30 minutes or until tomatoes are cooked.

❧ ❧ ❧

STUFFED ZUCCHINI BOATS

6–8 zucchini
sea salt (optional)
1 cup chopped cooked spinach

¼ cup chopped water chestnuts
2 tablespoons almond oil
freshly ground pepper

Preheat oven to 350°.

Steam-cook whole zucchini for 7 to 8 minutes or until crisp-tender; cool. Then cut zucchini lengthwise and scoop out the seeds using a spoon. Arrange them, cut side down, on paper towels for 10 minutes to drain. Sprinkle zucchini boats with sea salt and stuff them with the combined spinach, water chestnuts, and chopped zucchini pulp. Arrange them in a shallow baking dish rubbed with almond oil, drizzling the remaining almond oil on top.

Bake them for 15 minutes and sprinkle with freshly ground pepper.

Note: Zucchini boats can be prepared ahead, refrigerated, and reheated at mealtime.

ॐ ॐ ॐ

SUMMER VEGETABLE MEDLEY

6 Roma tomatoes
5 small summer squash
3 petite eggplant (Japanese or other variety)
1 red onion

1 large garlic clove, peeled and thinly sliced
2 tablespoons crushed thyme leaves
½ lemon, thinly sliced
2–3 tablespoons oil

Preheat oven to 400°.

Rinse the vegetables and cut them diagonally into attractive 1-inch slices.

Oil a baking dish and sprinkle the bottom with half the garlic and 1 tablespoon thyme. Layer the vegetables in the dish (tomato slices on top of the eggplant). Tuck lemon slices and the remaining garlic and thyme among the vegetables. Drizzle with oil and cover dish with foil; bake for 15 minutes. Remove foil and baste vegetables with their own juices; bake uncovered for 10 minutes. Serve at room temperature.

ॐ ॐ ॐ

VEGGIES ITALIANO

½ green bell pepper, cut in ¼-inch slices
1 cup cauliflower florets
2 cups banana squash, peeled and sliced
3 green onions, chopped
2 celery stalks, sliced diagonally

2 tomatoes, cut in wedges
2 teaspoons Italian seasoning
1 garlic clove, pressed
3 tablespoons "Chicken Broth"
freshly ground pepper

Combine the vegetables, herbs, garlic, and chicken broth in a large skillet. Stir-cook over medium-high heat for 5 minutes or until vegetables are crisp-tender. Season with pepper to taste and serve.

ॐ ॐ ॐ

ZUCCHINI CASSEROLE

1 cup cooked brown rice (see "Grains")
2–3 cups zucchini, thinly sliced
½ cup chopped green onions
¼ cup chopped fresh parsley
¼ cup olive oil

2–3 eggs, beaten
½ teaspoon sea salt (optional)
¼ teaspoon garlic powder
½ teaspoon oregano

Preheat oven to 350°.

Combine the ingredients thoroughly in a mixing bowl. Transfer mixture to an oiled casserole dish and bake for 45 minutes to 1 hour or until eggs are set.

ॐ ॐ ॐ

Stir-Cook Dishes

Vary these recipes with different marinades, dressings, or sauces. And, of course, switch vegetables and other ingredients according to your preference.

ASPARAGUS STIR-COOK

1 pound asparagus, washed and trimmed
2 teaspoons arrowroot flour
1 tablespoon cold water
2 tablespoons oil

¼ cup green onion (white part only),
  thinly sliced
½ cup "Chicken Broth" or "Vegetable
  Stock"
1 tablespoon Bragg Liquid Aminos

Cut asparagus into 2-inch pieces. Mix arrowroot into cold water to make a smooth paste; set aside.

In a wok or skillet, heat oil and sauté asparagus and green onions over medium-high heat for 1 minute. Add chicken broth and simmer for 2 to 3 minutes. Making a well in the center of the asparagus mixture, add the arrowroot paste and Bragg Liquid Aminos. Stir-cook for 30 seconds longer or until the sauce is smooth and thickened. Serve immediately.

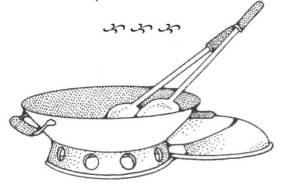

QUICK VEGGIE-MILLET-TURKEY STIR-COOK

oil
sliced okra (fresh or frozen)
frozen green peas
thin onion wedges
yellow squash cut in cubes

cooked millet (see "Grains")
cooked turkey meat (see "Poultry")
sea salt (optional)
freshly ground pepper

Heat oil in a large skillet. Add onions and, over medium-high heat, stir-cook for 1 minute. Add okra; stir-cook for 2 minutes. Add yellow squash and peas; stir-cook for 2 minutes. Add cooked millet and turkey; heat thoroughly. Season to taste with sea salt and pepper.

Variation

Substitute the millet with another cooked grain and/or the turkey with another meat or vegetable.

༄ ༄ ༄

MARINATED SCALLOP AND VEGETABLE STIR-COOK

½ cup scallops
2 tablespoons oil
1 tablespoon fresh lemon juice
⅛ teaspoon each of basil, savory, and tarragon
½ cup diced zucchini

½ cup shredded red cabbage
½ cup diced purple onion
½ cup green peas
½ cup mung bean sprouts

Rinse scallops in cold water and pat them dry with paper towels. Then whisk oil, lemon juice, and herbs together in a mixing bowl. Stir scallops into the marinade, cover, and chill for 1 hour.

In a heated wok or skillet, stir-cook scallops and vegetables until the vegetables are crisp-tender. (Do not overcook the scallops or they will be tough.) Serve with raw jicama sticks.

༄ ༄ ༄

Crab contains Vitamin A, Vitamin C, and Calcium. (See page 206)

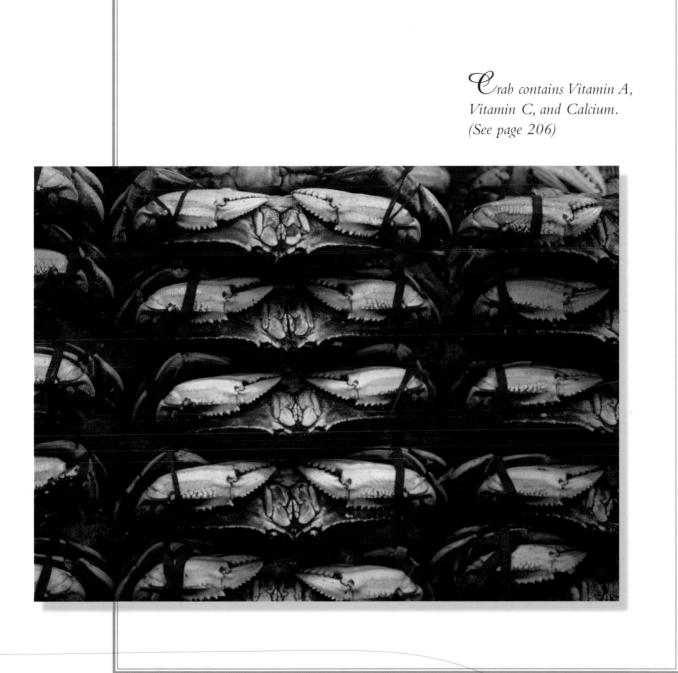

One serving of fish can contain up to 21% of your daily-recommended intake of calcium. (See page 200)

Using chicken in your fajitas turns your favorite meal into a healthy meal. (See page 210)

*U*se sweet potatoes to spice up your homemade chips. (See page 185)

Carrots are filled with beta-carotene, which defends your body against air pollution, cigarette smoke, and other carcinogens. (See page 176)

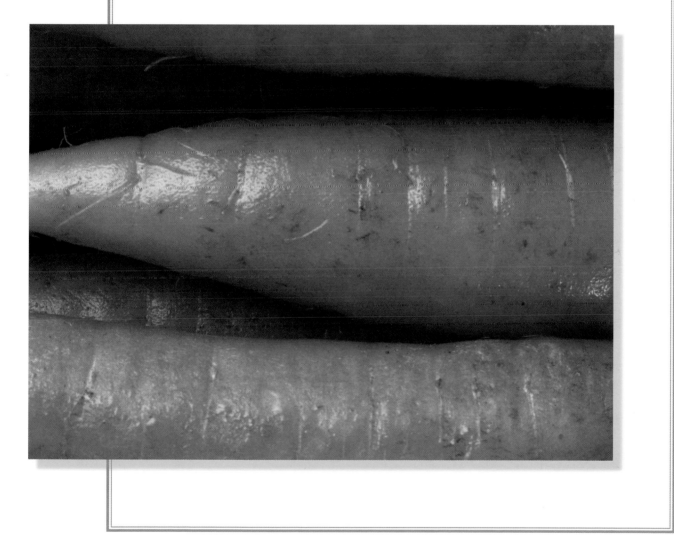

Lentils have been an important food staple since biblical times. (See page 160)

*Peas provide a great source
of protein for vegetarians.*
(See page 194)

A delicious garlic sauce can be served over just about anything.
(See page 114)

DR. JO'S FISH AND AVOCADO STIR-COOK

1 fish fillet

½ onion, sliced in thin wedges

2 celery stalks with leaves, sliced

¼ cup water

2–3 cups spinach leaves, firmly packed

½ ripe avocado

Rinse fish thoroughly under cold water, pat dry with paper towels, and cut into ¾-inch cubes; reserve.

Put onion and 2 tablespoons of water in a nonstick pan with a lid. Steam-cook this mixture until the water evaporates, remove the lid, and brown the onion a little. Add the remaining water with celery; steam until just crisp-tender. Stir in spinach leaves and fish, cooking until fish is flaky but not dry. Serve over chunks of avocado.

৵ ৵ ৵

TURKEY CHOW MEIN

SEASONINGS

3 tablespoons Bragg Liquid Aminos

¾ teaspoon freshly ground pepper

2 tablespoons oil

2 tablespoons sesame oil

½ pound ground turkey

3 green onions, sliced (white part only)

1 large yellow onion, chopped

2 thin slices gingerroot (or

¼ teaspoon ginger powder)

1 carrot, thinly sliced

½ medium-sized head of cabbage, chopped

3 celery stalks, thinly sliced

½ pound mung bean sprouts (or other variety)

green onion tops to garnish

Whisk together the seasoning ingredients; set aside. Prepare the vegetables.

In a heated wok or skillet, stir-cook the turkey until it turns white. Add the green and yellow onions and stir-cook for 1 minute. Add gingerroot, carrots, cabbage, and celery, stir-cooking a little after each addition. When vegetables are crisp-tender, add seasonings and bean sprouts; stir-cook for 1 minute. Garnish with chopped green onion tops and serve over brown rice.

৵ ৵ ৵

MASHED POTATO STIR-COOK

green onions, cut in 2-inch pieces (white
    parts only)
grated carrots
chopped Swiss chard

leftover cooked fish, poultry, or meat
sea salt (optional)
freshly ground pepper
hot mashed potatoes

In an oiled wok or skillet, stir-cook equal amounts of green onions, carrots, Swiss chard, and chosen leftovers. Drizzle a small amount of oil over the mixture, season to taste, and serve over mashed potatoes.

ॐ ॐ ॐ

GREENS, GREENS

broccoli or broccoflower florets
zucchini, cut in diagonal slices
green onions, cut in ½-inch pieces

collard greens (or other)
oil

Heat a few tablespoons of water in a wok or skillet. Steam-cook the vegetables quickly, beginning with broccoli and ending with collard greens. Drizzle with a little oil and serve.

ॐ ॐ ॐ

STIR-COOKED "SEVEN"

red cabbage, thinly sliced
rutabaga, cut in small strips
diced yellow crookneck squash
sliced celery

green beans, cut in ¼-inch pieces
green peas
sprouted garbanzo beans (or mung bean
    sprouts)

Using equal amounts of the ingredients, stir-cook cabbage and rutabaga in an oiled wok or skillet. Add crookneck squash, celery, green beans, and peas; cook until vegetables are crisp-tender. Stir in bean sprouts and serve over cooked brown rice or millet.

ॐ ॐ ॐ

EGGPLANT STIR-COOK WITH BROWN RICE AND KIDNEY BEANS

1 cup eggplant, cut in cubes
1 cup sliced zucchini
2–3 stalks bok choy, sliced
½ cup cooked brown rice (see "Grains")

¾ cup cooked kidney beans (see "Cooking
  Tips" in Part 1)
sea salt (optional)
freshly ground pepper
½ cup mung bean sprouts

In an oiled wok or skillet, stir-cook eggplant, zucchini, and bok choy until crisp-tender. Add brown rice and beans and heat through; season to taste with sea salt and pepper. Last, mix in mung bean sprouts and serve.

ॐ ॐ ॐ

CALIFORNIA SUMMER STIR-COOK

2-3 tablespoons olive oil
4-6 garlic cloves, minced
1 cup jicama, cut in small cubes
1 cup yellow crookneck squash, sliced
1 cup snow peas, trimmed
1 red bell pepper, cut in strips
4 green onions, cut in 2-inch pieces
½ cup shredded fresh basil leaves
  (or 2 tablespoons dried basil)

½ teaspoon sea salt (optional)
1 cup fresh spinach (washed, torn in pieces,
  and firmly packed)
2 cups cooked brown rice or millet
  (see "Grains")
ripe avocado to garnish
freshly ground pepper

Heat oil in a wok or skillet. Stir-cook garlic, jicama, crookneck squash, snow peas, red bell pepper, and green onions until crisp-tender. Add basil and salt; stir-cook for 2 minutes. Add spinach and cook only until it wilts. Serve immediately over cooked millet or brown rice. Garnish with cubes of avocado and freshly ground pepper.

ॐ ॐ ॐ

NURSIE'S STIR-COOKED CHICKEN

2 boneless chicken breasts, cut in ½-inch slices
4 slices of gingerroot
2 garlic cloves, peeled and sliced
Bragg Liquid Aminos to taste

1 cup chopped green onions, white part only
2 cups snow peas
1 can sliced water chestnuts, drained
2 cups mung bean sprouts

Combine chicken slices with gingerroot, garlic, and Bragg Liquid Aminos; marinate for 1 hour.

In an oiled wok or skillet, stir-cook chicken and marinade until chicken is nearly done. Add green onions; cook for 1 minute. Add snow peas, water chestnuts, and mung bean sprouts; continue cooking until just heated through. Serve with brown rice or another cooked grain.

ॐ ॐ ॐ

STIR-COOKED PRAWNS WITH VEGETABLES

1 tablespoon arrowroot flour
2 tablespoons cold water
16 prawns or large shrimp (about 1½ pounds)
3 tablespoons oil
1 garlic clove, pressed
1 tablespoon freshly grated gingerroot
1 cup celery, thinly sliced

1 onion, cut into thin wedges
3 stalks of Swiss or Chinese chard, sliced
    diagonally
2 cups snow peas
    (or 1 cup frozen petite peas)
1 teaspoon fresh lemon juice

Dissolve arrowroot in cold water; set aside. Remove shells from prawns, devein them, wash them thoroughly in cold water, and blot dry with paper towels.

In a wok or skillet, gradually heat oil. Add prawns and stir vigorously for a few seconds. Add garlic and stir-cook until prawns turn pink. Remove prawns and set them aside. Stir-cook gingerroot, celery, onion, chard, and snow peas for 3 minutes. Add prawns, lemon juice, and arrowroot mixture and stir for 2 minutes or until sauce thickens. (Note: Take care not to overcook the prawns or they will become tough.)

ॐ ॐ ॐ

STIR-COOKED CHICKEN WITH LEEKS

4 whole chicken breasts

6 tablespoons butter or oil

4 cups chopped leeks

2 large celery stalks, chopped

sea salt (optional)

freshly ground pepper

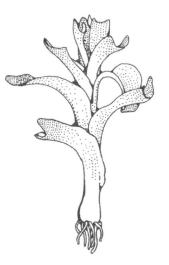

Bone chicken breasts, making sure to remove tendons; set aside. In a wok or skillet, stir-cook leeks and celery in butter or oil until crisp-tender. Lay chicken breasts over vegetables. Cover and cook over low heat for 8 to 10 minutes or until chicken is done. Season with sea salt and pepper and serve.

Note: Chicken legs and thighs are equally good but take longer to cook (25 to 30 minutes). if you use them, add the vegetables for the last 8 to 10 minutes of cooking time.

و‍‍‍‍ح وح وح

HAMBURGER STIR-COOK

1 pound ground beef (or ground turkey)

1 large onion, chopped

1 cup cooked brown rice (see "Grains")

½ cup cooked baby lima beans (see "Cooking Tips" in Part 1)

¾ cup green peas or chopped celery

a dash of garlic powder

sea salt to taste (optional)

mung bean sprouts to garnish

In a heated wok or deep skillet, brown ground beef. Add onion and cook until golden. Stir in brown rice, lima beans, and peas or celery. Heat through and add seasoning to taste. Before serving, toss in a handful of mung bean sprouts.

Serve with a raw vegetable salad.

وح وح وح

Fish and Seafood

COOL HALIBUT SALAD

1 pound halibut, poached
3½ cups brown rice, cooked and cooled
   (see "Grains")
1 cup celery, sliced diagonally
½ cup green onions, sliced diagonally
1 red bell pepper, seeded and cut into
   ½-inch squares
½ teaspoon dried dill

¼ cup "Chicken Broth" (see recipe)
¾ cup "Blender Mayonnaise" or "Eggless
   Mayonnaise" (see recipes)
sea salt (optional)
freshly ground pepper
2 cooked artichoke hearts, sliced
lettuce leaves for garnish

To poach halibut: In a deep skillet, put water to a depth of 1 inch and sprinkle with salt (optional); bring to boil. Add halibut that has been thawed, boned, skinned, and sliced diagonally. When contents return to a boil, reduce heat, cover, and simmer for 10 minutes for each inch of thickness of halibut—or until halibut flakes easily with a fork. Remove fish carefully with a slotted spoon. Chill.

To prepare salad: Combine brown rice, celery, onions, and red bell pepper in a large bowl; set aside. In a small saucepan, bring chicken broth and dill to a boil and remove from heat. Transfer to a bowl, cool, and then gradually add mayonnaise. Pour over rice mixture and mix lightly but thoroughly. Season with salt and pepper; chill.

To serve, arrange poached halibut, artichoke hearts, and rice on individual lettuce-lined plates.

ᗰ ᗰ ᗰ

POACHED HALIBUT

1 pound of halibut
boiling water to cover
sea salt (optional)
2 tablespoons fresh lemon juice

¼ cup diced onion
a sprig of parsley
6 peppercorns
3 whole cloves

Remove skin and bones from halibut; cut fish into chunks. Place halibut in a deep skillet with boiling salted water to barely cover. Season with lemon, onion, parsley, and spices. Cover and simmer for 6 to 8 minutes or until halibut flakes easily with a fork. Remove halibut from liquid and cool. Makes about 2½ cups.

ॐ ॐ ॐ

DR. JO'S SPICY FISH ROLLS

2 large leaves of Swiss chard
1 tablespoon dry mustard
2 teaspoons fresh lemon juice
2 fillets of Dover sole (or other whitefish)
¼ cup diced celery

¼ cup diced red onion
sea salt (optional)
cayenne
lemon wedges
¼ cup grated jicama

Wilt Swiss chard by holding leaves by end of stems and dipping them in boiling water until just limp. Run immediately under cool water, trim out stem, and set aside. Mix mustard and lemon juice together; reserve.

Lay a fish fillet on each wilted Swiss chard leaf. Spread half of the lemon-mustard sauce over each and then the celery and red onion. Sprinkle with sea salt, cayenne, and a squeeze of lemon. Carefully roll up Swiss chard and fish and fasten with toothpicks. (If fish is too thick to roll, fold it in half and fasten.) Steam-cook the fish rolls on a flat surface until the fish flakes easily. Transfer to a serving platter, top with freshly grated jicama, and serve.

ॐ ॐ ॐ

FISH 'N' POTATO HASH

1 tablespoon oil
½ cup diced green onion
3 cups potatoes (peeled, diced, and
    steam-cooked)
2 cups cooked whitefish, salmon, or tuna

¼ teaspoon cayenne
1 teaspoon sea salt (optional)
1 teaspoon freshly ground pepper
2 tablespoons minced cilantro

Heat oil in a saucepan and sauté onion over medium heat until limp. Lower heat; add potatoes and stir-cook for 4 to 5 minutes. Flake fish with a fork and combine with potatoes. Add cayenne, salt, and pepper. Transfer hash to a serving dish, sprinkle with cilantro, and serve.

ૐ ૐ ૐ

FISH AND SPINACH TARRAGON

1 bunch fresh spinach (washed, stemmed
    and dried)
2 pieces whitefish (halibut, sole, orange
    roughy, etc.)
2 sprigs of fresh tarragon
    (or ½–1 teaspoon dried tarragon)

sea salt (optional)
freshly ground pepper
4 lemon slices, paper thin
2 teaspoons fresh lemon juice
½ teaspoon butter or oil

Fill the base of a steamer pot with an inch of water. In a round cake or pie plate smaller in diameter than the steamer pot, place spinach. Over spinach, lay the fish pieces and then, after crushing it slightly between your palms, the tarragon. Season with sea salt and pepper and arrange 2 lemon slices on each piece of fish. Put the plate on the steamer rack. Cover the pot, bring to a boil, and steam for 8 to 10 minutes or until fish is opaque. Carefully remove the plate and drain juices into a small saucepan. Add lemon juice and cook over high heat until sauce reduces to 2 tablespoons; stir in butter or oil. Transfer fish and spinach to a serving platter and dress it with the sauce.

ૐ ૐ ૐ

HALIBUT AND SHRIMP SALAD WITH TARRAGON DRESSING

DRESSING
¾ cup "Blender Mayonnaise" or "Eggless Mayonnaise"
¼ teaspoon crushed tarragon

1 cup poached halibut (see "Poached Halibut" recipe)
¼ cup cooked shrimp (or crabmeat)
1 cup petite green peas
¼ cup green onion, diagonally sliced
sea salt to taste (optional)
lettuce leaves to garnish plates
freshly ground pepper

Combine mayonnaise with tarragon; set aside.

Prepare poached halibut and cook shrimp; cool. If peas are frozen, run them under hot water to thaw. In a bowl, combine the fish with shrimp, peas, green onion, and salt. Gently stir in dressing. Arrange on a chilled platter lined with lettuce leaves. Sprinkle with fresh pepper.

☙ ☙ ☙

BAKED HALIBUT WITH VEGETABLES

a 12-ounce halibut steak
2 tablespoons fresh lemon juice
½ teaspoon sea salt (optional)
1 small tomato (scalded, peeled, and chopped)

1 medium carrot, shredded
2 tablespoons sliced green onion
2 tablespoons chopped fresh parsley
lemon wedges

Preheat oven to 350°.

Rinse halibut under cool water and, with a paper towel, pat it dry. Put fish in a small oiled baking dish; sprinkle with lemon juice and salt. Mix tomato, carrot, green onion, and parsley together and spread it over fish. Cover the dish and bake for 25 to 30 minutes or until fish flakes easily. Transfer the fish and vegetables with a slotted spatula to a serving platter. Serve garnished with lemon wedges.

☙ ☙ ☙

BAKED SALMON WITH BROCCOLI AND HERBS

2 salmon steaks (6 or 8 ounces each)
1½ cups broccoli florets

⅛ teaspoon each of dried oregano and thyme
   (or a crushed sprig of the fresh herbs)
1 tablespoon minced fresh parsley

Preheat oven to 450°.

   Rinse salmon under cool water, pat dry, and place in an oiled shallow baking dish. Arrange broccoli on and around fish; sprinkle with oregano and thyme. Cover dish and bake. Allow 10 minutes cooking time per inch of fish thickness (measured at its thickest part) or until salmon flakes easily with a fork. Sprinkle with parsley and serve.

ॐ ॐ ॐ

OVEN SWORDFISH KABOBS

FOR MARINADE
1½ tablespoons fresh lemon juice
1 tablespoon olive oil
½ teaspoon sea salt (optional)
½ teaspoon oregano
1 garlic clove, minced
1 chopped green onion

1 pound swordfish or halibut, cut in 1 ¼-inch
   cubes
12 fresh bay leaves (optional)
12 zucchini rounds
12 cherry tomatoes
12 carrot rounds, slightly steamed
1 lemon cut in wedges (garnish)

In a large bowl, prepare a marinade by combining lemon juice, oil, salt, oregano, garlic, and onion. Add fish cubes and coat well with marinade. Cover and refrigerate for 1 hour, stirring every 15 minutes.

   Preheat oven to 350°. On skewers, alternate the fish, vegetables, and fresh bay leaves if available. (Warning: Dried bay leaves will burn!) Place the kabobs on a broiler pan in the oven and broil for 10 minutes, turning every 2 to 3 minutes and basting with marinade. Serve with lemon wedges.

Variation

Marinate vegetables separately from fish.

৵ ৵ ৵

POACHED RED SNAPPER

4 6-ounce portions of red snapper, boned and
   skinned
1 lemon, sliced
1 small onion, sliced
3 whole peppercorns

2 sprigs of parsley
1 bay leaf
2 cups water
freshly ground pepper

In a deep skillet, arrange the fish, lemon, onion slices, and seasonings. Add water. Cover skillet, bring to a boil, and simmer for 5 to 8 minutes or until fish flakes easily with a fork. Serve with some freshly ground pepper.

৵ ৵ ৵

SCALLOP KABOBS

½ pound sea scallops
¼ cup Bragg Liquid Aminos
2 tablespoons grated gingerroot

8–10 large, firm cherry tomatoes
8–10 small mushrooms (optional)
1 large red bell pepper, cut in 1-inch squares

Wash scallops thoroughly in cool water, pat them dry with paper towels, and set them aside in a bowl. Combine Bragg Liquid Aminos with gingerroot and pour over scallops; refrigerate. While scallops marinate, prepare the vegetables. Then:

Starting with a mushroom, thread scallops and vegetables onto skewers. In a preheated 350° oven, broil the kabobs on a broiler pan for about 5 minutes or until the top side is done. Turn them carefully, baste with marinade, and broil the other side.

Note: Omit mushrooms if you have candida or yeast/mold sensitivities.

৵ ৵ ৵

SHRIMP ON A STICK

MARINADE

3 tablespoons fresh lemon juice

3 tablespoons olive oil

2 garlic cloves, peeled and crushed

1 tablespoon chopped fresh parsley

1 minced green onion

teaspoon oregano

1 teaspoon sea salt (optional)

¼ teaspoon freshly ground pepper

1½ pounds large raw shrimp (or a mix of
   shrimp and scallops)

2 large onions, peeled and cut in big wedges

3 zucchini, cut in 1-inch rounds

Prepare a marinade by combining lemon juice, olive oil, garlic, parsley, onion, oregano, salt, and pepper; set aside in a large bowl. Clean shrimp, leaving tail shells intact. With a sharp knife, split shrimp meat halfway to the tail and wash out the exposed vein. Marinate in the refrigerator for 30 minutes, stirring occasionally.

    Thread skewers alternately with onions, shrimp, and zucchini. Barbecue kabobs over a medium-hot grill for 4 to 5 minutes or until shrimp turn pink and curl up. (You also can broil them in the oven, as described in the "Scallop Kabobs" recipe.)

చా చా చా

SHRIMP WITH JERUSALEM ARTICHOKES AND BRUSSELS SPROUTS

¾ pound small brussels sprouts

1 pound raw shrimp

4 tablespoons butter

1 tablespoon oil

juice of half a lemon

2 tablespoons minced shallots (or green onion)

½ cup sliced Jerusalem artichokes (or water
   chestnuts)

sea salt (optional)

freshly ground pepper

Wash, trim, and steam-cook brussels sprouts until they are crisp-tender; run them quickly under cool water to stop the cooking process; set aside. Wash shrimp in cold water, pat them dry, peel and devein them; set aside.

    In a large skillet, sauté shallots in butter and oil for 1 minute. Stir in shrimp and cook for 3 to 4 minutes or until they turn pink. Add brussels sprouts and Jerusalem artichokes; sprinkle with lemon juice, salt, and pepper. Stir until heated and serve at once.

ॐ ॐ ॐ

PAELLA

¼ cup olive oil

2 pounds of fryer chicken

½ teaspoon sea salt (optional)

½ teaspoon freshly ground pepper

¼ cup olive oil

1 small onion, minced

2 garlic cloves, peeled and crushed

1 red bell pepper, cut into ¼-inch strips

2 cups brown rice, rinsed and drained

1 cup chopped tomatoes

6 cups "Chicken Stock" or water

1 dried bay leaf

½ teaspoon crushed saffron

12 medium clams, washed and scrubbed

8 large unshelled raw shrimp

1 cup frozen peas (or green beans or asparagus)

1 teaspoon cayenne

1 lemon, cut in wedges

Preheat oven to 350°.

After washing the chicken in cool water, dry it with paper towels, cut it into pieces, and remove the skin. In a large ovenproof skillet, heat ¼ cup olive oil. Add chicken seasoned with salt and pepper and cook until golden brown; transfer to paper towels and reserve.

Add another ¼ cup olive oil to the pan and sauté onion, garlic, bay leaf, cayenne, and red bell pepper strips over medium heat for 3 minutes. Add brown rice and stir-cook until well coated with oil. Add tomatoes and, stirring frequently, cook until liquid evaporates.

In a separate pot, bring chicken stock to a boil; lower heat. Remove 1 cup of stock and, in it, dissolve saffron; add to the rice mixture and stir until blended. Pour 1 cup of hot stock over rice. Over medium-high heat, stir gently and continuously until liquid is absorbed. Add 2 more cups of stock to rice and follow same procedure. (Take care not to burn the skillet bottom.) Remove skillet from the heat.

Distribute clams, shrimp, and peas throughout the rice. Arrange chicken pieces over all and add the remaining 2 cups of stock. Place skillet in the oven; bake for 20 minutes or until liquid is absorbed, rice is done, clams open, and shrimp turn pink. Garnish with lemon wedges and serve.

ॐ ॐ ॐ

DUNGENESS CRAB WITH TOMATO SALSA

1 cooked Dungeness crab, 2½–3 pounds
2 medium tomatoes (scalded, peeled, and finely
    chopped)
¼ cup chopped green chilies
2 tablespoons minced onion

1 tablespoon minced fresh parsley or cilantro
1 tablespoon fresh lime or lemon juice
2 teaspoons oil
sea salt to taste (optional)
lime and/or lemon wedges

Lift off the crab's shell; remove and discard viscera and gills. Rinse crab thoroughly under cool running water. Break off the legs and crack along the edges. Break body section in half and each half into several pieces. Cover crab and refrigerate.

In a bowl, combine the remaining ingredients to make a salsa. Chill for 30 minutes. Arrange the chilled crab on a platter, garnish with wedges of lime and/or lemon and serve with the tomato salsa.

Variation

Steam crab over boiling water for 5 minutes or until heated. Serve with warmed tomato salsa.

ॐ ॐ ॐ

BAKED SALMON WITH DILL

1 fresh salmon (or half a salmon)
butter, chilled and cut in pieces
1–2 lemons, sliced thin
1 medium onion, thinly sliced

sea salt to taste (optional)
freshly ground pepper
sprigs of fresh dill (or dried dill)

Preheat oven to 350°.

Slice the salmon lengthwise down the backbone to "butterfly"; remove bones. Arrange dabs of chilled butter, lemon slices, and onion slices over the fish. Season with sea salt, pepper, and dill. Fold salmon halves together and wrap in aluminum foil (dull side out, seam side up). Bake on a baking sheet for 1 hour or until juices barely begin to drain from salmon.

ॐ ॐ ॐ

SPICY SALMON STEW

1 tablespoon olive oil
1 cup diced onion
1 cup diced green bell pepper
2 garlic cloves, peeled and crushed
2 cups chopped tomatoes
1½ cups "Poultry Stock" (see recipe) or water

½ teaspoon thyme
½ teaspoon chili powder
½ teaspoon sea salt (optional)
1 cup uncooked brown rice
1½ cups fresh salmon, cut in chunks
freshly ground pepper

In a soup pot, heat olive oil and sauté onion, celery, green bell pepper, and garlic until onion is softened. Transfer mixture to a bowl and set aside. Combine tomatoes, stock, and seasonings in the pot and bring to a boil. Add rinsed brown rice. Reduce heat, cover, and simmer for 40 minutes, stirring occasionally. Add sautéed vegetables and simmer for 5 minutes more. Add salmon and cook for 5 minutes or until salmon flakes easily. Serve with freshly ground pepper.

Variation

Instead of brown rice, use 2 cups of cubed potatoes.

BAKED WHITEFISH WITH ZUCCHINI

1 pound of cod, pollock, or rockfish fillets

an 8-ounce can of sugar-free tomato sauce

½ cup sliced mushrooms (optional)

¼ teaspoon dried basil

a pinch of freshly ground pepper

sea salt (optional)

½ cup water

2 teaspoons oil

2 tablespoons chopped onion

2 cups zucchini, sliced in julienne strips

Preheat oven to 350°.

Rinse fish in cool water, dry, and cut into thin serving-size pieces; set aside. Combine tomato sauce, mushrooms, seasonings, and water in a small bowl and mix well; reserve.

Heat oil in a skillet and sauté onion until softened. Add zucchini and cook until crisp-tender. Place some zucchini mixture on each fish fillet, roll them carefully, and secure with toothpicks. Place the fish rolls in a shallow baking dish and spoon on the tomato mixture. Cover and bake for 20 minutes or until fish flakes easily with a fork.

అ అ అ

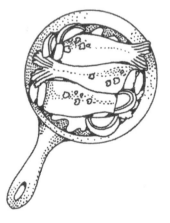

Poultry

SAVORY BARBECUE CHICKEN

1 garlic clove, peeled and crushed
½ teaspoon sea salt (optional)
½ cup fresh lemon juice
¼ cup salad oil
2 tablespoons grated onion

1 tablespoon chopped fresh parsley
½ teaspoon seasoned pepper
½ teaspoon dried thyme
1 2- or 3-pound fryer chicken

With a mortar and pestle (or on a cutting board with the flat side of a knife), mash garlic into the salt. Add to the lemon juice, oil, onion, and herbs; mix well. Chill for 24 hours. (This recipe makes about ¾ cup of sauce so make adjustments depending on the amount of chicken you intend to cook.)

Wash chicken thoroughly and cut it into pieces. Break the hip, knee, and wing joints to keep the chicken flat on the grill. Marinate it in the barbecue sauce.

Prepare grill. When the coals are glowing, arrange chicken on the grill and cook slowly for 20 to 30 minutes or until cooked. Baste often with remaining sauce.

ぷ ぷ ぷ

CHICKEN AND BEAN STEW

1 fryer chicken

4 quarts water

½ cup navy beans, washed and pre-soaked
   (see "Cooking Tips" in Part 1)

1 cup kidney or pinto beans, washed and
   pre-soaked

2 onions, chopped

2–3 tomatoes, chopped

½ teaspoon basil

½ teaspoon thyme

1 cup chopped carrots

1 cup chopped celery

1 cup cooked brown rice

sea salt (optional)

freshly ground pepper

Wash chicken thoroughly, cut into pieces, and remove the skin by holding it under running water. In a large pot, bring chicken, water, and navy beans to a boil; reduce heat, cover, and simmer for 30 minutes. Add kidney or pinto beans, onions, tomatoes, and seasonings; simmer covered for 1 hour. Add carrots and celery, cooking until carrots are crisp-tender. Remove chicken pieces, bone them, chop the meat, and return meat to the stew. Add brown rice and cook for 2 minutes until heated through. Season with sea salt and freshly ground pepper to taste.

ॐ ॐ ॐ

BECKY'S FAJITAS

MARINADE

2 tablespoons oil

2 tablespoons fresh lemon juice

1 garlic clove, minced

¼ teaspoon sea salt (optional)

¼ teaspoon chili powder

¼ teaspoon crushed cayenne pepper

freshly ground pepper

1½ pounds boned chicken

¾ tablespoon oil

½ cup sliced onion

½ cup chopped green onion

1 cup zucchini, cut in julienne strips

1 cup sliced red bell pepper

2 ripe avocados, peeled and cut in chunks

shredded lettuce

cooked brown rice

"Juana's Salsa" or "Salsa in the Fast Lane"
   (see recipes)

Whisk marinade ingredients together in a bowl. Slice chicken into strips. (Hint: Freezing chicken slightly makes it easier to slice.) Combine with marinade and refrigerate for 2 hours, stirring occasionally.

In a hot skillet, heat oil and sauté onions, green onions, zucchini, and red bell pepper until crisp-tender; transfer to a bowl and reserve. Sauté marinated chicken for 4 minutes or until cooked—but not overcooked. Combine chicken strips with sautéed vegetables. Arrange on a serving platter and garnish with shredded lettuce and avocado chunks. Serve with brown rice and a bowl of fresh salsa!

შ შ შ

CHICKEN BAKED IN PARCHMENT PAPER

2 large chicken breasts, skinned and boneless
parchment paper (available at cooking supply
　　stores)
2 medium carrots
2 medium zucchini
1 medium leek (or 3 green onions)

1 tablespoon minced fresh parsley
1½ teaspoons grated lemon peel
½ teaspoon sea salt (optional)
⅛ teaspoon freshly ground pepper
4 tablespoons chilled butter

Preheat oven to 375°. Cut four 12-inch squares of parchment paper. Cut chicken into ½-inch slices. Slice carrots, zucchini, and leek into ¼-inch sticks, 3 inches long. In a large bowl, combine chicken, vegetables, parsley, lemon peel, and seasonings. Mix well.

Place a fourth of the chicken mixture on one-half of each parchment square and dot mixture with dabs of butter. To seal the packets, fold the other half over and crimp the edges all the way around. Place packets on a baking sheet and bake for 20 minutes or until paper is puffed and browned and chicken is tender. Place a packet on each of four plates, slash open, and serve with steamed new potatoes or a cooked grain.

შ შ შ

SEASIDE CHICKEN DINNER

1 fryer chicken, washed and cut in pieces
3 cups water
1 cup dried sea vegetables (alaria, wakame,
  or kombu)

¼ cup chopped onion
cooked brown rice

Brown chicken in a heavy oiled pot. Add water, sea vegetables, and onion. Let stand for 20 minutes to allow sea vegetables to soak up the water. If all the water is absorbed, add another cup. Bring to a boil, cover, and simmer for 20 minutes. Serve over brown rice with Bragg Liquid Aminos.

න් න් න්

CHICKEN EXCELLENCE

1½ cups uncooked brown rice
1½ cups "Chicken Broth" or water
1 10" × 16" oven-cooking bag
1½ tablespoons rice flour
1½ tablespoons butter
1½ cups sliced carrots
1 cup chopped celery
1 cup chopped onion

¾ cup "Chicken Broth" or water
1 tablespoon chopped fresh parsley
¾ teaspoon dried basil
¼ teaspoon garlic powder
3–3½ pound whole fryer chicken
4 tablespoons oil
sea salt (optional)
fresh ground black pepper, paprika

Preheat oven to 350°.

In a saucepan, bring rinsed brown rice and chicken broth or water to a boil. Reduce heat, cover, and simmer for 20 minutes; set aside.

Put rice flour in the cooking bag, shake well, and place in a 13" × 9" baking pan. In a bowl, combine the partially cooked brown rice, butter, carrots, celery, onion, chicken broth or water, parsley, basil, and garlic. Spoon mixture into the bottom of the cooking bag.

Wash chicken thoroughly, dry with paper towels, and secure legs with cooking string, Brush chicken with oil and sprinkle with sea salt, pepper, and paprika. Put on top of the rice mixture in the cooking bag. Tie bag shut and make 6 small slits in the top. Bake for 1 ¼ hours or until the thigh joint moves easily.

ॐ ॐ ॐ

CHICKEN IN A CROCK-POT

1 whole fryer chicken (about 3¼ pounds)

2 parsnips, cut in strips

2 carrots, sliced

2 celery stalks, sliced

4 new potatoes, whole (optional)

1 large onion, quartered

2 garlic cloves, peeled and crushed

½ cup minced fresh parsley

2 cups "Chicken Broth" or water

½ teaspoon oregano or 1 teaspoon basil

6 peppercorns

½ teaspoon sea salt (optional)

Rinse chicken thoroughly in cool water and dry it with paper towels. In a large oiled skillet, brown chicken and transfer it to the Crock-Pot. Arrange the vegetables around it and add the seasonings and stock. Cook on the "low" setting for 8 hours.

ॐ ॐ ॐ

CHICKEN TACOS

hot mashed pinto beans

slices of "Roasted Tarragon Chicken"
  (see recipe)

avocado slices

garlic powder and onion salt to taste

black olives

chopped lettuce

alfalfa sprouts

corn tortillas

Layer the ingredients over warmed corn tortillas, arrange on a serving platter, and serve with salsa on the side.

ॐ ॐ ॐ

GARLIC ROASTED CHICKEN

1 whole fryer chicken
20 garlic cloves
2 tablespoons butter
½ teaspoon grated lemon peel
¼ teaspoon thyme

⅛ teaspoon rosemary
2 thin slices of lemon
sea salt (optional)
freshly ground pepper

Preheat oven to 375°.

Wash the chicken thoroughly. Prepare a space between the skin and the meat, starting at the breast bone. Carefully work your fingers under the fowl's skin and around the breast and legs. (Holding the chicken under warm running water makes this procedure easier.)

Peel and press 10 garlic cloves; combine with softened butter, lemon peel, thyme, and rosemary. Spread garlic butter under the skin using your hands. Place remaining unpeeled garlic cloves and lemon slices into the body cavity. Season the chicken lightly with sea salt and pepper. Roast for 75 to 90 minutes. Remove garlic cloves from the cavity, peel them, and serve them with the roasted chicken.

಄ ಄ ಄

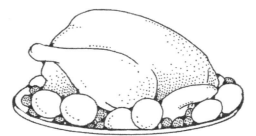

GREEN CHILI CHICKEN

1 whole fryer chicken
2 teaspoons chili powder
¼-½ teaspoon cayenne
1 teaspoon ground cumin (optional)
1 teaspoon sea salt (optional)
1 tablespoon oil
2 cloves garlic, pressed

½ cup minced onion
a 4-ounce can of diced green chilies (or fresh chilies to taste)
¾ cup "Chicken Broth"
2 tablespoons arrowroot flour
2 tablespoons cold water

Wash the chicken thoroughly, dry it with paper towels, and rub the outside with the combined chili powder, cayenne, cumin, and salt. Heat oil in a deep pot and brown the chicken on all sides. Add garlic, onion, chilies, and chicken broth. Cover and simmer for 35 to 45 minutes (or cook in a Crock-Pot on the "low" setting for 3 hours). Transfer the chicken to a serving platter, returning any cooking juices to the pot. Skim off any fat from the stock. Mix arrowroot flour with cold water until smooth and add to the sauce. Stir until thickened, pour over chicken, and serve.

ॐ ॐ ॐ

CALIFORNIA CHICKEN BREASTS

3 or 4 chicken breasts, skinned and boned
1 ripe avocado, mashed
½ tomato, diced
fresh lemon juice

a small can of whole green chilies (or mild fresh chili peppers)
sea salt (optional)
freshly ground pepper to taste

Broil chicken breasts until cooked. Combine avocado, diced tomatoes, and fresh lemon juice to taste; set aside. Split the green chilies lengthwise and place a half on each chicken breast. Season with sea salt and pepper to taste, garnish with a dollop of the chunky guacamole, and serve.

ॐ ॐ ॐ

MARINATED CHICKEN BREASTS

4 chicken breasts (rinsed, skinned, and
   trimmed of fat)
½ cup fresh lemon juice
2 cloves garlic, peeled and crushed
2 teaspoons oil

½ teaspoon freshly ground pepper
1 teaspoon tarragon
½ teaspoon thyme
¾ teaspoon sea salt (optional)

Place chicken breasts in a large bowl. Combine the remaining ingredients to make a marinade and pour over the chicken. Refrigerate for 1 hour, stirring occasionally.

Preheat oven broiler. Place the chicken breasts top side down in an ovenproof baking dish. Place the dish 3 to 4 inches below the broiler. Broil for 15 to 18 minutes on each side, basting occasionally with the marinade.

Variation

Cut chicken breasts into chunks, marinate them, string on skewers with vegetables of your choice, and grill or broil.

ﺣ ﺣ ﺣ

MOORISH CHICKEN

2 pounds chicken breasts (skinned, boned, and
   cut in 1-inch cubes)
2 tablespoons olive oil
1 garlic clove, peeled and crushed
1 teaspoon tarragon

½ teaspoon sea salt (optional)
½ teaspoon freshly ground pepper
½ teaspoon thyme
⅛ teaspoon cayenne
1 cup water

Preheat oven to 350°.

In a heated skillet, sauté chicken cubes in olive oil over medium heat for 3 minutes. Add garlic and stir-cook for 5 minutes; transfer to a baking dish. In a small bowl, whisk the remaining ingredients and pour over the chicken. Cover the dish and bake for 20 minutes.

Remove the lid and bake for another 15 minutes or until chicken is tender. Serve with steamed vegetables and a cooked grain.

৯৯ ৯৯ ৯৯

LIME-ROASTED CHICKEN WITH VEGETABLES

1 whole roaster chicken

¼ cup fresh lime juice

¼ cup oil

½ teaspoon sea salt (optional)

⅛ teaspoon freshly ground pepper

1 tablespoon chopped fresh parsley

2 carrots, thinly sliced

2 leeks, cut in ¼-inch slices

3 potatoes, cut in ¼-inch slices

2 cups cubed zucchini

lime slices to garnish

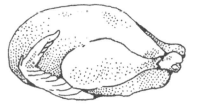

Preheat oven to 350°.

Place chicken in a large bowl. Combine lime juice with oil, sea salt, pepper, and parsley; pour mixture over the chicken and into the cavity. Refrigerate for 1 hour, turning frequently. Transfer chicken to a roasting pan and bake it for 1 hour, basting and turning it every 20 minutes.

As chicken roasts, steam vegetables for 5 minutes. When chicken has about 20 minutes of roasting time remaining, arrange the steamed vegetables around it. Baste with marinade and continue cooking until chicken is cooked to the bone. Serve garnished with lime slices and drizzled with cooking juices.

Alternate method: Marinate steamed vegetables before roasting.

৯৯ ৯৯ ৯৯

ROASTED CHICKEN WITH JAMBALAYA RICE

1 cup "Chicken Broth"
¼ cup chopped onion
¼ cup chopped green bell pepper
¼ cup chopped red bell pepper
⅛ teaspoon garlic salt
3 dashes hot pepper sauce
a pinch of thyme

1 cup partially cooked brown rice
  (see "Cooking Tips" in Part 1)
1 cup chopped tomatoes
2 chicken breasts, halved and skinned
freshly ground pepper
butter

Preheat oven to 350°.

Combine chicken broth, onion, bell peppers, garlic salt, hot pepper sauce, and thyme in a saucepan. Bring to a full boil and add partially cooked brown rice. Cover and remove from heat; let stand for 5 minutes.

Stir tomatoes into the rice mixture and spoon into four individual baking dishes or one large baking dish. Season chicken lightly with pepper and place a half breast on top of rice in each dish. Dot with butter and bake for 20 to 30 minutes or until chicken is golden brown.

ॐ ॐ ॐ

ROASTED TARRAGON CHICKEN

1 whole chicken
2 tablespoons fresh lemon juice
½ teaspoon sea salt

2 tablespoons butter
1½ teaspoons dried tarragon, crushed

Preheat oven to 375°.

Brush chicken with fresh lemon juice inside and out and rub with ½ teaspoon sea salt. Skewer neck skin to the back and tie the legs to the tail; twist the wings under the back. Place, breast up, on the rack in a roasting pan. Melt butter, stir in tarragon, and brush over the chicken. Roast uncovered, basting occasionally, for 75 to 90 minutes or until cooked.

ॐ ॐ ॐ

TARRAGON CHICKEN WITH VEGETABLE STUFFING

1 whole fryer chicken
1 large onion, thinly sliced
2 cups shredded zucchini
½ cup shredded carrots
2 garlic cloves
3 tablespoons butter (or oil)

1½ teaspoons dried tarragon
2 tablespoons plus 2 teaspoons fresh
   lemon juice
½ teaspoon grated lemon peel
sea salt (optional)
freshly ground pepper

Preheat oven to 375°. Rinse and dry chicken; set aside.

Melt 1 tablespoon of butter in a deep skillet. Sauté onions, zucchini, carrots, and 1 pressed garlic clove until vegetables are softened but not browned. Stir in ½ teaspoon tarragon, 2 teaspoons lemon juice, and lemon peel. Add sea salt and pepper to taste; set aside to cool.

In a small skillet, prepare tarragon butter. Melt remaining 2 tablespoons butter; add 1 pressed garlic clove, 1 teaspoon tarragon, and 2 tablespoons lemon juice.

Stuff chicken cavity with cooled vegetable mixture and roast the chicken for 75 to 90 minutes. Baste frequently with tarragon butter. Cover loosely with foil if the skin browns too quickly.

Note: For outdoor cooking, roast chicken in a covered grill over indirect medium heat (for about 90 minutes) or on a rotisserie (for 90 minutes to 2 hours).

Variation

Stir-cook the vegetables by themselves and serve on the side.

ॐ ॐ ॐ

SPICY MEXICAN STEW

CHICKEN AND STOCK
1 whole chicken
1 onion, coarsely chopped
2 celery stalks, coarsely chopped
1 carrot, cut in large chunks
2 teaspoons sea salt (optional)
4 peppercorns
water to cover

STEW
2 large onions, chopped
1–2 celery stalks
2 bell peppers
reserved chicken stock
water
4–5 cups sugar-free tomato sauce
4–6 garlic cloves

2 teaspoons thyme
1–2 tablespoons chili powder
2 tablespoons ground cumin
2 teaspoons basil
3 potatoes, cut in cubes
6 carrots, sliced
4 zucchini, cut in rounds
1 bunch broccoli (cut in florets and stems sliced)
6 tomatoes (or 5 cups of canned whole tomatoes, drained)
1 16-ounce package of frozen corn (or kernels from 6 ears of uncooked fresh corn)
1 16-ounce package of frozen peas
sea salt (optional)
freshly ground pepper to taste
chopped green onions to garnish

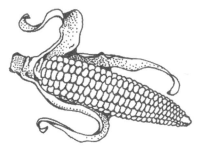

Place chicken and other ingredients in a stockpot. Add water to cover plus 4 more inches. Bring to a boil, lower heat, and simmer for 50 minutes. Remove chicken, bone it, and cut the meat into cubes; set aside. Strain the stock through a sieve; reserve.

Rinse, dry, and oil the stockpot. In it, sauté onions, celery, and bell peppers until softened. Add chicken stock (plus water if necessary), tomato sauce, seasonings, potatoes, carrots, zucchini, broccoli, and tomatoes. Bring to a boil, lower heat, and simmer until vegetables are crisp-tender. Add chicken meat, corn, and peas. Adjust seasoning to taste and garnish with chopped green onions.

Note: To make the recipe spicier, use more garlic and cumin.

శ్రీ శ్రీ శ్రీ

VEGETABLE-STUFFED CHICKEN BREASTS

3 chicken breasts, skinned and boned
a dash of sea salt (optional)
freshly ground pepper
1 teaspoon olive oil
½ cup chopped fresh spinach, firmly packed
¼ cup diced celery

¼ garlic clove mashed with ¼ teaspoon
  sea salt (optional)
3 medium carrots, peeled
iceberg lettuce leaves
¾ cup diced zucchini
½ teaspoon chopped fresh parsley

Preheat oven to 350°.

Pound chicken breasts between 2 sheets of wax paper until slightly flattened. Season both sides with sea salt and pepper; set aside.

Heat oil in small skillet. Sauté spinach, celery, and mashed garlic over medium heat for 1 minute. Spread a third of the spinach mixture over the boned side of each chicken breast. Top the spinach with a carrot placed diagonally about 1 inch from the edge of the chicken breast. Fold the breast over the carrot; roll tightly and secure with toothpicks.

Cover the bottom of an 8-inch baking pan with lettuce leaves and arrange the rolled chicken breasts on top. (The lettuce keeps the chicken moist as it bakes.) Sprinkle zucchini over chicken. Cover pan and bake for 50 minutes or until chicken breasts are cooked. Discard lettuce and serve garnished with parsley.

శ్రీ శ్రీ శ్రీ

CINNAMON-ROASTED CORNISH HENS

2 Cornish hens (about 1½ pounds each)

MARINADE
1 lime, juice and pulp
3 cloves garlic, peeled and mashed
1 teaspoon grated gingerroot
½ teaspoon dried summer savory

½ teaspoon dried dill
½ teaspoon ground cinnamon
¼ teaspoon curry powder
¼ teaspoon saffron threads, crushed
2 crushed allspice berries (or
¼ teaspoon dried allspice)

Wash and dry the Cornish hens; reserve. Combine lime juice, chopped lime pulp, and the other marinade ingredients in a large ovenproof dish. Rub Cornish hens with marinade, leave in the dish, cover, and refrigerate overnight.

Preheat oven to 375°. Place Cornish hens skin side up on an oiled roasting rack. Bake for 30 to 35 minutes or until browned and cooked through. (Juices should run clear when bird is punctured with a knife.)

Note: This marinade has no fat, no salt, and is excellent with turkey and other fowl.

৯ ৯ ৯

BAKED STUFFED CORNISH HEN FOR ONE

1 Cornish hen
½ cup cooked brown rice
1 tablespoon sautéed onions
sea salt (optional)

freshly ground pepper
1 small garlic clove, minced
1–2 tablespoons "Chicken Broth"
1 cup each broccoli and cauliflower florets

Preheat oven to 350°.

Stuff bird with cooked brown rice to which onions, sea salt (optional), black pepper, garlic, and chicken broth have been added. Lightly salt and pepper the outside of the hen. Seal in an oven cooking bag with broccoli and cauliflower and bake for about 1 hour.

৯ ৯ ৯

TURKEY POT ROAST

a quarter of a turkey
2 teaspoons sea salt (optional)
¼ teaspoon freshly ground pepper
4 large carrots, cut in pieces

4 celery stalks, sliced
6 medium potatoes, scrubbed and whole
6 medium onions, peeled and whole
1 cup water

Preheat oven to 325°.

    Season turkey to taste and place in large roasting pan. Arrange vegetables around it, add water, and cover tightly. Roast for 2½ hours or until turkey is golden brown and tender.

    Alternate method: Roast turkey uncovered for 30 minutes per pound.

ぷ ぷ ぷ

TURKEY BREAKFAST SAUSAGE

½ teaspoon each of basil,
   thyme, and sage
¼ teaspoon each of
   ground cumin,
   marjoram, freshly

ground pepper, oregano, and cayenne
⅛ teaspoon each of garlic powder, nutmeg,
   and ginger
2 tablespoons brown rice flour or oat bran
1 pound turkey breast, freshly ground

Mix the spices first with the rice flour and then into the ground turkey. Refrigerate for 3 hours. Form mixture into patties, place on a nonstick baking sheet, and bake them in a preheated 400° oven for about 10 minutes or until cooked through and browned.

ぷ ぷ ぷ

CHINESE MEATBALLS WITH SNOW PEAS

½ pound turkey, freshly ground

½ cup cooked brown rice

¼ cup chopped onion

¾ teaspoon dry mustard

1 teaspoon grated gingerroot

1 small garlic clove, minced

sea salt (optional)

freshly ground pepper

2 cups "Chicken Broth"

1 tablespoon Bragg Liquid Aminos

1 tablespoon arrowroot flour

1½ cups snow peas, washed and trimmed

In a food processor, mix ground turkey, cooked brown rice, onion, mustard, gingerroot, garlic, salt, and black pepper until thoroughly combined. Shape into a dozen meatballs the size of walnuts. In a lightly oiled skillet, sauté them over medium-low heat. Turn them frequently to brown on all sides. Add 1½ cups of chicken stock; bring to a boil, lower heat, and simmer for 10 minutes.

Whisk Bragg Liquid Aminos and arrowroot flour into the remaining ½ cup of broth; set aside. When meatballs are nearly done, add the snow peas and simmer until they are crisp-tender. Pour arrowroot mixture into the pan, stirring constantly until thickened and transparent. Serve over steamed rice.

ॐ ॐ ॐ

ROASTED TURKEY

9–12 pound turkey

1 onion

1 celery stalk with leaves

1–2 sprigs of fresh parsley and sage

sea salt (optional)

Preheat oven to 325°.

Remove giblets and neck from turkey; discard or reserve for another purpose. Wash turkey with cold water inside and out. Dry with paper towels. Sprinkle cavity with sea salt and put celery, onion, and fresh herbs inside.

Place turkey on an oiled rack in a large roasting pan. Bake for 4½ hours or until the meat is tender and the juices run clear when pricked with a knife. Save the drippings for gravy. (**Note:** Let the turkey cool slightly before carving it.)

ॐ ॐ ॐ

SLOW ROASTED TURKEY

Preheat oven to 325°.

Prepare fowl as in "Roasted Turkey" recipe, seasoning it to taste with favorite herbs and spices. Breast side up, place turkey on an oiled rack in a roasting pan. Cook for 30 minutes to kill any germs. Reduce heat to 180–200° and roast overnight. It will take 12 to 18 hours depending on the turkey's size.

Turkey meat is very tender and moist when cooked slowly. It is usually done when the juices barely start to run out of the bird. If the skin browns too quickly, cover it with cheesecloth dipped in oil or melted butter. Remove the cloth during the last 15 minutes of roasting.

To roast a single turkey breast: Season turkey breast and place it skin side up on an oiled rack in a roasting pan. Bake in a preheated 325° oven for 30 minutes. Reduce the heat to 180-200° and cook it for 2½ hours or until done.

જ્જ જ્જ જ્જ

TURKEY PAN GRAVY

*3 tablespoons (approximately) pan drippings
  from roasted turkey*
3–4 tablespoons arrowroot flour

3–4 cups boiling "Turkey Stock"
sea salt (optional) to taste

Remove the cooked turkey from the roasting pan and pour off excess fat until about 3 tablespoons remain in the pan. Place the pan over low heat. Stirring constantly, add arrowroot flour a tablespoon at a time until all of the fat is absorbed. Slowly stir in the boiling turkey stock and cook until thickened. (Add more arrowroot flour or decrease stock as needed.) Add sea salt to taste.

જ્જ જ્જ જ્જ

LOW-FAT TURKEY GRAVY

9–12 pound turkey
1 onion
1 celery stalk with leaves

1–2 sprigs of fresh parsley and sage
sea salt (optional)

Bring turkey stock to a boil. Season to taste. Whisk arrowroot into cold water and add to the stock, stirring constantly until it thickens.

అ అ అ

TURKISH EGGPLANT WITH TURKEY

2 cups "Chicken Broth"
1 cup uncooked brown rice
½ pound turkey, freshly ground
1 medium eggplant
1 teaspoon oil
½ cup diced celery
⅓ cup chopped onion

⅓ cup chopped green bell pepper
2 cups "Spiced Stewed Tomatoes" (see recipe)
1 large garlic clove, minced
1 teaspoon dried basil
sea salt (optional)
freshly ground pepper
1 cup chopped fresh parsley

In a saucepan, bring chicken broth to a boil and add the rinsed uncooked brown rice. Lower heat, cover, and simmer for 40 minutes; reserve.

Spread ground turkey on a baking sheet and broil 6 inches from the heat until the meat is lightly browned; set aside. Cut eggplant in half, remove pulp, and chop it to make 2½ cups. In a large oiled skillet, sauté eggplant, celery, onion, and, green bell pepper until crisp-tender. Add cooked turkey, stewed tomatoes, garlic, and seasonings; heat thoroughly. Mix parsley into the cooked brown rice and serve with the eggplant dish.

అ అ అ

Beef

SUKIYAKI

3 tablespoons salad oil
3 medium onions, thinly sliced
¾ pound round steak, sliced across the
 grain as thin as possible
1 bunch green onions, cut into 2-inch
 pieces

6 celery stalks, cut in 1-inch lengths
½ pound sliced fresh mushrooms (optional)
½ pound fresh spinach, coarsely chopped
an 8-ounce can of sliced bamboo shoots
½ cup "Beef Stock"
¼ cup Bragg Liquid Aminos

In a wok or heavy skillet, heat oil and sauté onions until soft. Add round steak and brown it well on both sides. In separate layers over the meat, spread green onions, celery, mushrooms, spinach, and bamboo shoots. Combine beef stock with Bragg Liquid Aminos and pour them over the meat and vegetables. Stirring carefully, cook the sukiyaki uncovered until the vegetables are crisp-tender.

Serve with hot brown rice or another grain.

ૐ ૐ ૐ

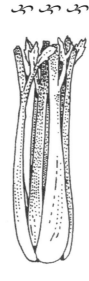

BEEF CHOP SUEY

4 tablespoons olive oil
1 garlic clove, pressed
½ pound lean beef
¾ cup sliced leeks
2 cups broccoli florets and sliced stems
1½ cups bok choy (Chinese cabbage)

SAUCE

1½ tablespoons arrowroot flour
2 tablespoons cold water
3 tablespoons Bragg Liquid Aminos
a pinch of ground ginger
freshly ground pepper to taste

Slice beef across the grain into thin strips. Press garlic. Slice leeks. Trim broccoli into florets and, after peeling, thinly slice the stems. Cut the white stalks of bok choy into squarish pieces. Set everything aside while you prepare the sauce.

In a small bowl, whisk arrowroot flour into cold water and Bragg Liquid Aminos. When smooth, add spices; set aside.

In a wok or heavy skillet, heat 3 tablespoons of olive oil and stir-cook garlic and leeks for 1 minute. Add beef and stir-cook for 3 to 4 minutes, browning on both sides. Transfer mixture to a bowl and reserve. In the pan, heat the remaining tablespoon of olive oil and stir-cook broccoli and bok choy over relatively high heat for 3 minutes. Add the beef mixture and sauce ingredients, stirring evenly for 1 to 2 minutes or until sauce thickens.

Serve with brown rice or another grain.

ॐ ॐ ॐ

CHILI

1 cup freshly ground beef (or ground turkey)
3 medium onions, chopped
2 celery stalks, thinly sliced
1 cup grated carrot
1 cup diced potatoes
3 garlic cloves, pressed
2 cups chopped green bell pepper

10 large tomatoes, chopped
2 tablespoons chili powder
1 tablespoon ground cumin
¾ teaspoon sea salt (optional)
3 cups cooked kidney beans (see "Cooking Tips" in Part 1)

In a large pot, sauté ground meat, onions, celery, carrots, potatoes, and garlic over medium heat until onions are soft. Add peppers, tomatoes, spices; bring to a slow boil. Add kidney beans and simmer until mixture thickens. Adjust seasoning.

Serve with a raw vegetable salad.

ঙ ঙ ঙ

QUICK BEEFY CHILI

1¼ pounds lean ground beef
1 large onion, chopped
4 cups cooked kidney beans (see "Cooking Tips")

1 cup water
2 tablespoons chili powder
½ teaspoon garlic powder
¾ teaspoon sea salt (optional)

In a soup pot, brown ground beef. Add onion and sauté until transparent. Drain off any fat (or absorb it with a folded paper towel). Add kidney beans, water, and spices; simmer for 5 to 10 minutes.

Serve with a raw vegetable salad.

ঙ ঙ ঙ

RICE AND BEEF MEAT LOAF

1 pound lean ground beef
1 cup cooked brown rice (see "Grains")
3 medium carrots, shredded
1 small onion, chopped
1 egg white

½ teaspoon basil
½ teaspoon sea salt (optional)
¼ teaspoon freshly ground pepper

Combine the ingredients in a bowl and mix well. Mold into a loaf shape and place in an ungreased shallow baking dish. Bake at 350° for 45 to 50 minutes.

Serve with "Sugar-free Catsup" (see recipe) and a raw vegetable salad.

ঙ ঙ ঙ

BEEF STEW WITH VEGETABLES

2 pounds boneless beef chuck
½ cup arrowroot flour
¾ teaspoon sea salt (optional)
¼ teaspoon freshly ground pepper
1 chopped onion
1 garlic clove, minced
3 tablespoons oil
2 cups "Beef Stock" or water

½ teaspoon thyme
½ teaspoon oregano
2 bay leaves
3 potatoes, peeled and cut in cubes
3 carrots, cut diagonally into rounds
1 medium zucchini, sliced
¼ cup cold water
3 tomatoes, cut in wedges for garnish

Cut beef into ½-inch cubes and, in a pie pan, dredge in arrowroot flour seasoned with salt and pepper. Reserve unused arrowroot.

Sauté onion and garlic in oil until soft. Add beef and brown on all sides. Add beef stock or water, thyme, oregano, and bay leaves. Bring mixture to a boil, lower heat, cover, and simmer over low heat for 30 minutes. Remove bay leaves.

Meanwhile, steam-cook the vegetables in a steamer basket in a covered saucepan with 1 inch of boiling water. First, steam carrots and potatoes for 3 minutes. Then add zucchini and steam for 2 more minutes. Add the steamed vegetables to the meat mixture and cook for 2 more minutes; vegetables should be crisp-tender. Whisk reserved arrowroot flour into cold water until smooth, add to stew, and stir constantly until sauce thickens.

Garnish with tomato wedges and serve with a raw vegetable salad.

◈ ◈ ◈

HAMBURGER VEGETABLE SOUP

2 pounds lean ground beef

1 medium onion, chopped

6 cups water

6 tomatoes, chopped

1 cup tomato juice

1½ teaspoons each of basil and dill

1 teaspoon garlic powder

¾ teaspoon thyme leaves

¼ teaspoon freshly ground pepper

1 bay leaf

1 cup diced potatoes

1 cup chopped cabbage

1 cup diced green bell pepper

½ cup carrots, thinly sliced

1½ cups frozen corn

1 cup cut green beans (fresh or frozen)

In a large pot, brown beef and onions. Drain off drippings (or absorb with a folded paper towel). Add water, tomatoes, tomato juice, and seasonings; bring to boil. Cover pot, reduce heat, and simmer for 30 minutes. Add potatoes and cabbage; cook for 10 minutes. Add green peppers, carrots, corn, and green beans. Cover and simmer for 5 minutes or until vegetables are crisp-tender. Remove bay leaf and serve.

ॐ ॐ ॐ

CROCK-POT SWISS STEAK

2–3 pounds round steak, tenderized and cut
   into serving pieces

2 tablespoons oil

1 medium onion, chopped

1 cup chopped celery

1 cup tomatoes (scalded, peeled, and chopped)

1 cup carrots, thinly sliced

¼ cup chopped green bell pepper

2 bay leaves

2 cups water

In a heated skillet, brown round steak in oil and transfer to a Crock-Pot. Add the vegetables, water, and bay leaves. Cover and cook on the "low" setting for 3 or 4 hours or on the "high" setting for 2 hours.

ॐ ॐ ॐ

ITALIAN MEAT SAUCE

3 tablespoons oil

2 pounds lean ground beef (or ground turkey)

1 garlic clove, pressed

1 medium onion, diced

2 stalks celery, diced

½ cup diced green bell pepper

1 cup grated carrots (for sweetness)

½ cup grated zucchini (optional)

½ cup grated eggplant (optional)

6–8 fresh tomatoes (chopped, pressed, and drained in a colander)

1–2 tablespoons mixed Italian spices (basil, rosemary, thyme, etc.)

2 teaspoons oregano

sea salt to taste (optional)

a dash of cayenne

In a large pot, heat oil. Sauté ground beef, garlic, onion, celery, and green bell pepper until the meat is nearly done. Add carrots, zucchini, eggplant, tomatoes, and seasonings. Simmer until vegetables are crisp-tender and sauce thickens. If more liquid is needed, add a little tomato juice or vegetable broth.

Serve over spaghetti squash (see "Cooking Tips" in Part 1), steamed potatoes, brown rice, or millet. Serve with a raw vegetable salad.

ॐ ॐ ॐ

BEEF STEW WITH SEA VEGETABLES

2 pounds beef stew meat

arrowroot flour for dredging

1 chopped onion

water to cover

1 cup crumbled dried seaweed (alaria, wakame, or kombu), 4 cups if fresh

4 sliced carrots

1 cup uncooked brown rice

Trim fat from the meat. Dredge meat in arrowroot flour and brown in a heated and oiled cast-iron pot. Add onion, cover with water, and simmer until beef is tender. With a slotted spoon, transfer the meat-onion mixture to a bowl; reserve.

If there are not 3 cups of beef stock in the pot, add water to make 3 cups. Add the sea vegetable and let stand for 20 minutes. If all of the stock is absorbed, add 1 cup of water. Add rinsed brown rice, bring to a boil, and simmer covered for 30 minutes. Add carrots and continue cooking until rice is done and vegetables are crisp-tender (about 40 minutes total). Stir in the reserved beef and onions and serve with a raw vegetable salad.

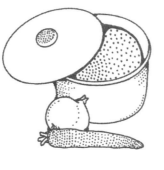

ৡ ৡ ৡ

BEEF AND BROWN RICE CASSEROLE

1 pound lean ground beef	2 cups sliced celery
2 teaspoons garlic salt	1 cup chopped green bell peppers
¼ teaspoon hot pepper sauce	1 cup diced onions
1 tablespoon fresh lemon juice	3 tomatoes, cut into wedges
1 cup "Blender Mayonnaise" or "Eggless Mayonnaise"	1 cup corn (fresh or frozen)
	sea salt to taste (optional)
3 cups cooked brown rice (see "Grains")	freshly ground pepper

Preheat oven to 375°.

In a heated skillet, stir-cook meat lightly; transfer to a large mixing bowl. Whisk garlic salt, hot pepper sauce, and lemon juice into mayonnaise; stir into the beef. Add brown rice and vegetables, season to taste, and mix well. Place mixture in a buttered 2-quart casserole dish and bake for 15 to 20 minutes.

Variation

Substitute cooked wild rice or another grain for the brown rice.

ৡ ৡ ৡ

About the Author

Bessie Jo Tillman, M.D., is a vigorous supporter of preventive medicine and renewed health. A 1970 graduate of the University of California Medical School San Francisco, she is active in her field as both proponent and practitioner. The philosophy behind her "wellness" medical practice is presented in her own words:

> Healthy habits allow the body chemistry to balance and the body to heal or stay well. Unhealthy habits upset the body chemistry and lead to degenerative diseases. My goal is to evaluate the present body conditions, educate about lifestyle changes that will serve the body well, and encourage people to live a healthy lifestyle.

Her clinic practice includes nutritional evaluation and counseling, exercise counseling, allergy care including testing and desensitization, chelation therapy, and detoxification modalities.

Dr. Tillman previously served on the Board of Directors of the Price-Pottenger Nutrition Foundation, including a four-year term as president. Membership affiliations include the American Preventive Medical Association, the American College for Advancement in Medicine, and the American Academy of Environmental Medicine. Dr. Tillman is a diplomate of the American Board of Chelation Therapy.

Her clinic is in Redding, California, where she is also active in community, school, and church affairs. She is a popular and enthusiastic speaker on health matters and is happily married with two beautiful daughters married to two wonderful sons-in-law, and one delightful grandson. She participates in short triathlons and loves cross-country skiing.

From the Executive Director
of the Price-Pottenger Nutrition Foundation

I have had the pleasure of knowing Dr. Bessie Jo Tillman for over a decade through her association with the Price-Pottenger Nutrition Foundation. She has been an incredible asset in disseminating the message of optimal health.

Dr. Jo truly recognizes the radical transformation of foods available and the changes in eating patterns and lifestyles that have occurred in the past 100 years. She sees renovated, devalued, and synthetic foodstuffs replacing traditional foods and how they relate to imbalances in the body chemistry of her patients. Without our awareness—or our permission—we have become part of the largest unplanned biological experiment ever foisted upon an unsuspecting populace!

In her practice, Dr. Jo leads her patients through the changes in lifestyle, eating patterns, thought processes, and living patterns necessary to restore optimal health and function to their lives. In *The New Natural Healing Cookbook*, she leads the reader away from foods that disrupt the balances of body chemistry by suggesting foods and food combinations that serve the body well. Thousands of blood tests have shown the efficacy of these wise food choices—but only we can choose this inspiring wellness program.

I have often said that I wish Dr. Jo could be "cloned" so that my community and others could have the advantage of her medical guidance. Now she has given us the next best thing by putting her patient information into a book to share with those privileged to come into contact with it.

—Marion Patricia Connoly

About the
Price-Pottenger Nutrition Foundation

For 30 years, the nonprofit Price-Pottenger Nutrition Foundation (PPNF) has collected and disseminated information on practical ways to create a safer, healthier world. Its educational outreach to health care professionals, researchers, and laypeople incorporates one of the most unique alternative health resource/research collections in the country, housing over 8,000 books, tapes, and reprints. It includes the work of 250 years of collective research conducted by pioneers in the fields of medicine and dentistry. PPNF is the conservator of many of these original manuscripts, photos, and research memorabilia.

PPNF's goal is to make the message of optimal health available to everyone. Its philosophy is that health starts from the ground up in the belief that there is a link between healthy soil and healthy people, animals, and plants. Members receive quarterly journals and have access to referral listings of health care professionals as well as to information on topics such as air/water filtration, chronic fatigue, ecological pest control, electromagnetic pollution, healthy foods and their preparation, healthy gardening, nontoxic dentistry, natural pet care, learning disabilities, and women's health issues. Membership is open to the public.

Price-Pottenger Nutrition Foundation
P.O. Box 2614
La Mesa, California 91943-2614
Phone (619) 574-7753

Index